HEAVY METAL

ALSO BY RON MARTZ

*Disposable Patriot: Revelations of a Soldier in
America's Secret Wars* (with Jack Terrell)

Solitary Survivor: The First POW in Southeast Asia
(with Col. Lawrence R. Bailey, Jr., USA [Ret.])

White Tigers: My Secret War in Korea
(with Col. Ben S. Malcom USA, [Ret.])

An AUSA Book

HEAVY METAL

A Tank Company's Battle to Baghdad

JASON CONROY
with Ron Martz

Potomac Books, Inc.
Washington, D.C.

Library of Congress Cataloging-in-Publication Data

Conroy, Jason, 1972–
   Heavy metal : a tank company's battle to Baghdad / Jason Conroy with Ron Martz.—1st ed.
      p.   cm.
   Includes bibliographical references and index.
   ISBN 1-57488-856-0 (hardcover : alk. paper)
   1. Iraq War, 2003—Campaigns—United States.   2. Iraq War, 2003—Personal narratives, American.   3. United States. Army—History—21st century.   I. Martz, Ron, 1947–   II. Title.
   DS79.764.U6C66   2005
   956.7044′342—dc22   2004021630

Hardcover 1-57488-856-0
Paperback 1-57488-857-9

Printed in Canada on acid-free paper that meets the American National Standards Institute Z39-48 Standard.

Potomac Books, Inc.
22841 Quicksilver Drive
Dulles, Virginia 20166

First Edition

10   9   8   7   6   5   4   3   2   1

For the soldiers of Charlie Company,
who battled to Baghdad and beyond
with courage, skill, and professionalism;
and to their families,
who were with them
every step of the way

Contents

Illustrations

Foreword

EVERY army has its "immortals." Once the subject of ballads and storytellers, modernity has reshaped their public image. For most of the twentieth century, historians or Hollywood have picked them for us: Alvin York relentlessly hunting machine gunners in the Argonne, Joshua Chamberlain holding the line at Gettysburg with his Maine volunteers, Audie Murphy standing on a burning tank destroyer fighting off a full enemy company. These images and others, from books or movies, have stuck in the American psyche as American soldiers at war. Vietnam brought war into the living room, and CNN has made war to be seemingly a spectator event, complete with "talking heads" and instant "analysis" by a variety of people with varied credentials. But for those of us who have felt the fire of battle, we each carry our own "immortals" close to our hearts—comrades we knew, whose lives and spirit will only die when the last of those who knew them go to their final resting place.

Heavy Metal will add a new group to the public list. Charlie Company, Task Force 1-64 Armor, 3rd Infantry Division, has its own immortals, and the young commander of that company, and the journalist "embedded" with that unit, have told their story as they saw it. It is a story from the commander's perspective, how he prepared his company, what the company expected, how they fought, and what he thinks his unit accomplished. But more than a military report, it is a story of the humanity and endeavor of men fighting for a cause in which they believe. It is also a tale of young soldiers in battle and the proud story of a famous division once again on the leading edge of our national policy.

As a young officer, I was raised on the reading fare of the pre-Vietnam generation. The most frequently read book then by young officers was *Company Commander* by Charles MacDonald. For us, the World War II experience was what we all believed we would experience if war ever came to us. Vietnam proved to be far different, though some of MacDonald's words rang true. And while the World War II type of fighting is gone forever, some lessons transcend time. *Heavy Metal* is the new gold standard for the junior leader's book. In it, you will find timeless principles and a realistic look at the future. Jason Conroy's words have special merit today, not only because his experience is recent but because the type of challenge our new breed of warrior-captains faces is far more multidimensional than was the norm in World War II. Jason summarizes it aptly: "We learned that real life does not follow the training script. The reality of it was we did not know what was coming up next."

Given his missions, the old army would have balked at any discussion of whether a tank company could handle the whole gamut of mounted high-intensity combat with other tanks to the relatively people-intensive, and more police-oriented, missions of urban stability and security. Moreover, Charlie Company participated in the now legendary "Thunder Run" of 3rd Infantry Division's heavy units into Baghdad, first as a show of force, then to occupy the town. With new high-tech communication and sighting systems, the new breed of tanker had changed the entire face of mounted armored warfare.

Conroy is clear on the changes he saw: "The war we set out to fight in Iraq was not the war we fought. The enemy we war-gamed to fight was not the enemy we fought. . . . The war forced us to be adaptive and innovative about how we used our tanks and ourselves. We were forced to learn on the fly. . . . The grand schemes of tacticians and planners often gave way to snap judgments on the battlefield by young soldiers and young commanders facing enemy fire for the first time." Learning this lesson is important; sharing it with those who have not experienced combat is vital to the long-term growth of our Army.

The men of Charlie Company were typical of most of the Army's new immortals. Since Vietnam, and indeed since the first Iraq War of 1991, the Army has continued to upgrade equipment, to develop more highly innovative training programs, and to hone warriors to a greater degree than it has ever done in its history. The new systems and training programs encourage new-breed warriors to master any fighting environment, and the successful campaign of the 3rd Division was proof of how effective units had become in performing on a highly changing and more varied battlefield. The story of C Company, 1st Battalion, 64th Armor, is a proud story well told of courageous troops and adaptive and caring leaders, but more important it is a window into the adaptiveness, flexibility, and courage of all our troops and the power of our equipment.

Charlie Company, 1-64 Armor, and its wartime commander are proof of the dedication and valor of our soldiers. Their story is a story of which every American can be proud.

Gen. Gordon R. Sullivan, USA (Ret.)
Chief of Staff, 1991–1995

Preface

THE ranks of all Charlie Company soldiers mentioned and listed in the book are the ranks they obtained by the time the company departed Iraq in July 2003. Some incidents in the book will mention soldiers at a higher rank than they were when the incidents actually occurred. But since some soldiers were promoted during the war, and some shortly after it, the authors have decided to list the higher ranks from the beginning of the book for the sake of uniformity and clarity and to avoid confusing the reader. (A roster of Charlie Company personnel and their assignments appears in the appendix.)

Although we have included no footnotes or endnotes, we have drawn on a wide variety of sources in the writing of this book.

Many of the conversations reproduced here were heard first-hand by one or both of the authors. Where we were not privy to those conversations, we tried to verify exact quotes from several sources who overheard them. Most of the events were witnessed by both authors as they happened.

The diaries of Sgt. 1st Class Brett Waterhouse provided needed details for the foundation of the book. Operations orders given during the war helped fill in many details, and extensive postwar interviews with Charlie Company soldiers and other task force and division officials fleshed out the story and gave it needed substance and balance.

The conversation between Maj. Gen. Buford Blount and Lt. Gen. William Wallace on 7 April 2003 about whether the 2nd Brigade could stay in Baghdad originally appeared in an 18 April 2003 *USA Today* story by Steve Komarow, David Lynch, and John Diamond.

The quotes from "Baghdad Bob," the Iraqi Minister of Information, were culled from several websites, including CNN, The Associated Press, and military-quotes.com.

Some of the information in chapter 16 on the Iraq National Museum was compiled from various sources. Particularly helpful were the summer 2003 article in *Artnews* by Roger Atwood, titled "Inside Iraq's National Museum"; the 6 May 2003 CBS News online report, titled "Many Baghdad Treasures Intact"; David Aaronovitch's 10 June 2003 piece in *The Guardian*, titled "Lost from the Baghdad museum: Truth"; and the June 2003 and October 2003 issues of *National Geographic* magazine.

A glossary of military terms and abbreviations appears on page 277.

The opinions expressed in this book are solely those of the authors and do not reflect the official positions of the United States Government, the Department of Defense, or the United States Army.

The road to Baghdad

Courtesy of Dale Dodson

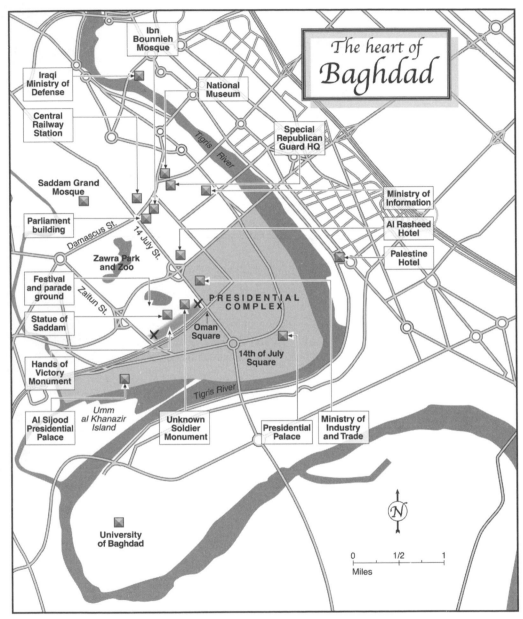

The heart of Baghdad

Courtesy of Dale Dodson

Acknowledgments

AS with any project of this magnitude, it is impossible to thank all those who contributed. But a few deserve special mention.

First and foremost are the soldiers of Charlie Company, without whom none of this would have been possible. Their dedication to duty, professionalism as soldiers representing the United States, and combat skills and ability to adapt and improvise under fire made it possible for the entire company to complete the mission of getting to Baghdad, getting rid of Saddam Hussein, and returning home alive. 1st Sgt. Jose Mercado was the company's conscience and heart. He was also my right-hand man during the formation of Charlie Company at Fort Stewart, Georgia, during training in Kuwait, and through the war in Iraq. Without his experience and expertise the war would have been far more difficult than it was. He always had the best interests of the soldiers at heart and was the epitome of what a first sergeant should be.

The platoon leaders—1st Lt. Roger Gruneisen, 1st Lt. Jeremy England, and 2nd Lt. Erik Balascik—and their platoon sergeants were the keys to the success of Charlie Company during the war.

1st Lt. Shane Williams, Charlie Company's executive officer, handled many duties that were neither pleasant nor easy and was often the tail-end Charlie to make sure everyone got to where they were supposed to go.

The families of Charlie Company soldiers also were instrumental in our success during and after the major combat phase of the war for the manner in which they conducted themselves on the home front. A special thanks goes to my wife, Susan Conroy, who headed the company Family Readiness Group and answered frantic phone calls and e-mails at all hours of the day and night from wives, mothers, and members of the media. And a special thank-you goes to Ashlie and Amanda Conroy, for their help and their love.

Col. David Perkins of the 2nd Brigade Combat Team Spartans was daring and insightful as a combat commander. He also saw the value of having embedded media with the brigade, which made the telling of this story possible.

Lt. Col. Rick Schwartz, Maj. Rick Nussio, Maj. Mike Donovan, Capt. Joe Linn, and the command staff of Task Force 1-64, the Desert Rogues, provided the leadership necessary for soldiers to conduct successful combat operations in Iraq. They also opened up their tactical operations center so the media could get a full and uncompromising view of American soldiers at war on the 21st century battlefield.

Col. Rick Thomas and the public affairs staff at the Combined Forces Land Component Command helped pave the way for embedded media within the 3rd Infantry Division and throughout the theater—without them this story could not have been told.

Lt. Col. Mike Birmingham and M. Sgt. Emma Krouser of the 3rd Infantry Division's public affairs staff helped make the embed system work during the war and in the sometimes chaotic aftermath.

Lt. Col. Peter Bayer, the division G-3, provided valuable insights about the planning process before and during the war, as well as an overview of events as they unfolded outside of the very narrow scope of Charlie Company operations. He also read portions of the manuscript and provided comments and suggestions to help ensure historical and technical accuracy.

Sgt. 1st Class Brett Waterhouse made his detailed diaries available and they proved to be valuable in making sense of occasional confusing timing of key events. His no-nonsense leadership and sense of rightness also was a valuable resource for Charlie Company's first platoon.

S.Sgt. Jabari Williams, Charlie Company's master gunner, was a font of knowledge about the characteristics of 120mm rounds and the maneuver schemes and formations in tank warfare.

John Glenn, photo editor of the *Atlanta Journal-Constitution*, was instrumental in securing most of the photographs taken by Brant Sanderlin that are an important part of this book. Those photos chronicled Charlie Company's successes and heartaches and will help the reader better understand just what the soldiers endured.

On relatively short notice, Dale Dodson drew the maps and graphics that give the necessary detail to explain Charlie Company's movement into Iraq and later into downtown Baghdad as part of Task Force 1-64 and the 2nd Brigade Combat Team.

Julia Wallace and Hank Klibanoff opened up the photo and news archives of the *Atlanta Journal-Constitution* and were of great assistance in getting this project completed. They also were an invaluable source of moral support during and after the war.

Don McKeon at Brassey's, Inc., saw the merit in a book about a single tank company even while Charlie Company was still in Iraq, provided encouragement when needed, and a kick in the pants when needed.

Lloyd M. Burchette, Jr., supplied key research throughout the project, often responding on just a few moments' notice to requests for detailed technical information about various weapons systems and events that occurred far from Charlie Company's area of operations. This book never could have been written without his assistance, wise counsel, and insightful knowledge of military affairs, which he freely dispensed during the research and writing of this book.

I would be remiss without making special mention of Brant Sanderlin, the photographer from the *Atlanta Journal-Constitution*, who accompanied Charlie Company during the war. Often at the risk of his own life, he took photos that provided a gripping portrait of one tank company's battle to Baghdad. His work appeared in publications all over the world and gave many people a true picture of what combat is really like for soldiers on the front lines. He also was a much-needed link between soldiers and families not only with his photos, but with his satellite telephone, which helped soldiers communicate with their families.

If there are errors in this work, they are unintentional. In the end, though, credit for all that is right in this book goes to the soldiers of Charlie Company.

POINT BLANK:
THE BATTLE FOR MAHMUDIYAH

SGT. Scott Stewart saw the tanks first.

They were partially hidden in the late afternoon shadows that stretched across the narrow street lined with three-story buildings. The Iraqi T-72 tanks sat nearly side-by-side, the one on the right with its gun tube pointing north, the other close to the curb with its gun tube pointing south, directly at the lead tank in which Stewart was riding.

Stewart, only a few months into his job as trigger puller on an M1A1 Abrams, stared into the gunner's primary sight as his 70-ton tank rounded a corner and slowly moved north through a dingy, dun-colored southern suburb of Baghdad called Mahmudiyah.

"Tanks!" Stewart radioed to his tank commander, S.Sgt. Randy Pinkston.

Pinkston, a tall, lanky Texan, was buttoned up inside, peering through the small vision blocks in the commander's hatch. He could not quite make out the shapes of the two objects in the middle of the street about 500 meters ahead. Pinkston looked down the sights of his .50-caliber machine gun and thought the two indistinct blobs looked more like BMPs, Soviet-made amphibious troop carriers, than T-72 tanks.

Whatever they were, they were certainly not friendly. Nothing about this entire city about fifteen miles south of Baghdad was friendly. It was home to a portion of the Medina Division, one of Saddam Hussein's vaunted Republican Guard units, and the whole city seemed to be dripping with ill-disguised contempt for us as we made our way through the congested streets.

"Fire! Fire SABOT!" Pinkston ordered, indicating to his loader, Pfc. Artemio Lopez, that he wanted a tank-killing SABOT round loaded next. A High Explosive Anti-Tank (HEAT) round was already in the tube.

Stewart planted the sight reticle squarely on the back slope of the tank on the right. The gun switch was set to MAIN, the ammo switch to HEAT. When Stewart heard the fire command, he squeezed the triggers on the gunner's handles and the 51-pound HEAT round rocketed out of the tube at more than 4,500 feet per second.

"Contact! Tanks! Frontal! Out!" Pinkston barked into the radio to let all of Charlie Company know that we had found the tanks that earlier that day we had set out to kill.

It was 3 April 2003, and the 3rd Infantry Division (Mechanized) out of Fort Stewart, Georgia, was advancing quickly on Baghdad less than two weeks into Operation Iraqi Freedom. We had already traveled farther and faster than any armored unit in history, fighting determined Iraqis most of the way, and were now knocking on Saddam Hussein's palace gates.

But first we had to clear pockets of resistance south of Baghdad that we feared would come back to bite us in the butts if we did not render them combat-ineffective, that is to say, kill them.

As commander of Charlie Company of Task Force 1-64 of the division's 2nd Brigade Combat Team, I was given the job of taking my tank company through the suburb of Mahmudiyah to kill any Iraqi tanks or other armor we found. Charlie was the only tank-heavy company in the task force. Alpha Company, a tank company, got a platoon of infantry from Charlie Rock, the mechanized infantry company, and gave it a platoon of tanks. That mixture gave the task force more versatility. But the task force commander, Lt. Col. Rick Schwartz, kept Charlie Company intact. We were to be his knockout punch with our 14 tanks and one Bradley fighting vehicle that served as our fire support vehicle.

Through the first two weeks of the war, Charlie Company was often third in the task force line of march. The exception was at our first battle at a place called Objective Rams, where we ran into several hundred near-fanatical Iraqi fighters that our intelligence reports had told us were not there. Now we would have another chance to live up to our company motto: "Cobras lead the way." It was a last-minute mission, but the orders given by Schwartz were clear and succinct: "Find tanks and kill them."

This is what we as tankers train to do: kill tanks before they kill us. We spent six months in the desert of Kuwait getting ready for this.

But the training we did there was for traditional tank warfare, shooting and killing the enemy at distances of 1,500 meters or more. Now we were being ordered to go into a city with restricted maneuver areas, multistory buildings, and tight corners; perfect tank-killing ground for small groups of fighters who knew where the Abrams was most vulnerable. Few Charlie Company soldiers were trained for urban warfare, none in tanks. It was just not something that tankers did. A few of the officers got a quick lesson or two in urban warfare at the Armor Officer Basic Course at Fort Knox, Kentucky. But they were on foot when they did that, not in a tank.

Not since World War II had there been tank battles in cities involving American forces. There were tanks at Hue City during the Vietnam War, but that was largely American tanks against North Vietnamese infantry. Tank-on-tank warfare in an urban environment was not something any of us expected to see. Or wanted to be a part of.

We were exploring new territory here, literally and figuratively. Even though we did not realize it at the time, we were about to take all the modern doctrine of tank warfare and stand it on its ear. But what we were to discover this day about ourselves, and about how to fight with tanks in urban areas, would help convince division officials just a few days later to make the final push on Baghdad. And it would set new standards for the use of tanks in a city fight.

We got the tank-hunting mission shortly after noon on 3 April. We crossed the Euphrates River about 10 that morning after it was secured by the division's Task Force 1-15 in what appeared to have been a tough but eventually lopsided battle. Destroyed Iraqi vehicles were scattered all along the eastern approaches to the bridge, many still burning. And the smoking bodies of dead Iraqis littered trenches and bunkers on both sides of the road. Prisoners were still being rounded up as we drove through.

By late morning we moved into Objective Saints south of Baghdad and were set up at a crossroads next to a canal in the middle of potato fields. We had little opposition getting there, but at the crossroads found a single soldier with an AK-47 dutifully manning his post. When he raised his rifle to fire at S.Sgt. Jason Diaz's lead tank, the soldiers killed him with a quick burst from one of the machine guns.

We dubbed the crossroads Checkpoint Cobra. It was to be our home for the next few days. Just to our east, in the middle of Objective Saints, the brigade set up shop at the intersections of Highways 1 and 8 leading into and out of Baghdad.

Not long after we arrived, Schwartz called me to the task force Tactical Operations Center (TOC) and told me he wanted the company to attack south that afternoon to see what kind of forces were in the area. We were to move out about 1:30 p.m. We were in the lead, with our infantry heavy company, Charlie Company of Task Force 3-15, accompanying us.

To differentiate between the two Charlie Companies, we were known as Cobra; the other was Charlie Rock, or simply Rock.

I chose my second platoon to lead the company that day. Normally, my first platoon was my point platoon. I referred to the platoons as Red (first), White (second), and Blue (third). But on this day several of first platoon's tanks were having mechanical problems, and it was not at full strength. Third platoon carried much of the fight in an earlier battle, and I wanted to give them a break. It was time for second platoon, under the leadership of 1st Lt. Jeremy England, to lead us into what would turn out to be one of the key battles of the war.

When we left on the mission early that afternoon, Cobra was on the right side of Highway 8 and Charlie Rock on the left side of the divided highway. The roads in Iraq can be terribly frustrating for those of us accustomed to some rhyme or reason in our highway systems. You can be driving down an eight-lane divided highway in Iraq and all of a sudden it narrows to two lanes of deeply rutted asphalt. A few miles beyond that it might open back out onto a decent highway or it might just disappear forever.

As we drove south on Highway 8, the road began to narrow and peter out. We were getting fired on by an occasional dismounted Iraqi fighter, and every so often a rocket-propelled grenade would be launched in our direction. But enemy contact was generally light and ineffective.

I sent England and Pinkston ahead to recon the road when we got to a built-up area north of Mahmudiyah that did not show up on the map. Schwartz made it clear he did not want to get stuck in the city after dark but we also needed to press on with our mission.

"There's a fork in the road," England radioed me. "Do you want me to take a right or a left?"

The left side looked more troublesome, with three- and four-story buildings and narrow streets where it would be easy for fighters in windows or on rooftops to shoot down or drop grenades on us.

"Go right," I told England. It turned out to be a most propitious decision.

We had no satellite photographs of the area and were being guided only by our maps and hand-held Global Positioning System (GPS) devices.

Then England came on the radio again: "Sir, the road ends here."

"What do you mean it ends?

"It ends. There's no more road."

I moved up to take a look for myself. It appeared we were in the middle of farm fields. We knew where we were and where we wanted to go; we just were not sure how to get there. The maps and the roads had absolutely no correlation to one another. What was on the map was not on the ground, and vice versa.

As we were trying to figure out how to get back to Highway 8, we were still being peppered by small arms and RPGs. They were more a nuisance than a danger, because we were being fired on from considerable distances. We were in open terrain with a good view of everything around us. When we took fire, we sent it right back, usually in industrial strength quantities, mostly with machine guns. But occasionally, when we spotted a vehicle with weapons, a main gun round would take it out.

Finally, England radioed that he saw a bus traveling down a road to the east of our position. It was across an open field, and there were concerns about getting stuck in soft ground. Pinkston's tank, with Pfc. Justin Mayes in the driver's hole, plunged ahead and made the crossing first. When he did not get stuck, the rest of us followed.

It was about 3 p.m. when we got back on Highway 8. We knew the headquarters of the Medina Division's 14th Mechanized Brigade was just a few miles to the south. We were told before the war that this brigade would likely capitulate early in the fighting and its headquarters and armor might be taken without a shot. We even planned an elaborate ceremony with each of the task force company commanders playing a role. But, like so much of the intelligence we received during the war, this also proved faulty.

The task force's primary mission was to destroy units of the Medina Division and here was a perfect opportunity to do it. But it was getting late in the day and we still had to make our way back through some built-up areas before dark. I radioed Schwartz and asked if he wanted us to continue moving south, or turn around and head back north through Mahmudiyah.

He thought the town was too much of a chokepoint and we would run the risk of getting stuck in there. We were all familiar with the book "*Black Hawk Down*," and many of us had seen the movie version of what happened to a handful of American soldiers caught in the middle of an unfriendly city and surrounded by thousands of enemy fighters. That was Mogadishu, Somalia, in 1993. This was Mahmudiyah, Iraq, in 2003. We had no desire for a repeat performance a decade later.

As we moved back onto Highway 8, the road made a wide left turn and began pulling us back into built-up, populated areas.

Everywhere we looked were photographs and paintings of Saddam. Hundreds of people were in the streets, most of them in civilian clothes, many armed with AK-47s and RPGs. They would spot us, fire off a burst or two, and then run down one of the many narrow alleys to escape our guns.

Within minutes of pulling back onto the highway, England saw a man get out of a car with an AK-47 and take aim at his tank. He was quickly killed by machine-gun fire.

Another car, this one with six men, stopped not far from Pinkston's lead tank. The men jumped out and began unloading weapons from the trunk. Pinkston opened up with the .50-caliber machine gun and Stewart with the 7.62mm coaxial machine gun, killing all but one of them at the car. One Iraqi began running for a nearby bunker. He never made it. Stewart walked the tracers up to him and through him, felling him in mid-stride.

The farther Charlie Company advanced into Mahmudiyah, the more small arms fire we received. The volume of fire increased from the rooftops and windows of apartment buildings that loomed over us. Some of the tank commanders were still outside their hatches. The vision blocks inside the tanks greatly restricted our view, but with all this overhead fire it was dangerous to even peek out of the hatch.

"Get your ass down before you get shot!" Stewart yelled at Pinkston, who was so concerned about getting stuck in an alley or a side street he did not realize he was getting shot at.

After the road made its wide left turn, it swept back to the right around a corner. Just as Pinkston's tank turned the corner, Stewart saw the two T-72s.

England's tank was only a few meters behind Pinkston's but was not yet around the corner when the distinctive hollow "Boom!" of the Abrams main gun echoed among the stucco buildings. That was followed quickly by Pinkston's spot report of contact with enemy tanks.

At that instant England came on the radio to me: "Cobra Six, this is White One. We got tanks!"

"What do you mean you have tanks?" I asked, incredulous that we suddenly found ourselves fighting tanks in these tight quarters.

The infantry often refers to urban combat as a knife fight in a phone booth. For us, it was more like a gunfight in a phone booth. I thought he was mistaken and had seen BMPs or something else.

"I've got T-72s in the street!" he shot back.

The sound of a main gun round was enough to convince me that he was right.

Stewart's first shot hit the back slope of the T-72 sitting on the right side of the street. The extra fuel drums on the back exploded, sending flames and black smoke shooting high into the late afternoon sky. The tank's turret popped off, and the engine was knocked to the other side of the street.

The brass AFCAP of the M1A1 HEAT round was ejected from the tube, hit the deflector with a clang, and fell into the catch on the floor. Lopez quickly loaded another round. But instead of the SABOT that Pinkston called for, it was a HEAT.

An Iraqi T-72 tank destroyed in Mahmudiyah by Charlie Company gunners. (*Jason Conroy*)

The SABOT with its depleted uranium penetrator is the round of choice for killing tanks. We started the mission that day with many of the tanks battle-carrying SABOT because we anticipated fighting tanks. When we encountered trucks and bunkers, many tank commanders shifted to HEAT rounds, which are more effective against those targets because of the high explosives content. Now facing tanks, Pinkston's tank had HEAT more easily accessible in the ready rack than SABOT.

Pinkston saw the round go into the main gun's breech but decided to let it go rather than have Lopez try to remove it and try to dig up a SABOT. There was a second tank that needed to be killed and he did not want to waste any time.

But before Stewart could fire the second round, the T-72 on the left fired its 125mm main gun.

Pinkston said later he never saw the tank fire, but others behind him did. The round sailed high and to the left of Pinkston, whose tank was still moving forward. It then flew over Sgt. 1st Class Ray White's tank, which was third in the column, and exploded against a building behind it.

S.Sgt. Ben Phinney, just behind White's tank, was still out of the hatch. He saw the tank round hit the building, then heard an AK-47 round bounce off the back of the hatch cover, which was propped open. Sparks from the ricocheting round flew over his head and Phinney and his loader, Psc. Derrick Hemphill, quickly dropped inside the tank. Someone above and behind them was firing and had gotten a bit too close for Phinney's comfort. He gingerly reached behind him and closed the hatch, buttoning up inside.

Stewart fired another HEAT round at the second Iraqi tank. It hit the turret, but there was no massive explosion like the first.

England's tank pulled up close to Pinkston's.

"Alpha section! One round SABOT! Move out and fire!" England ordered.

Sgt. Chris Freeman, the gunner on England's tank, squeezed the trigger and the SABOT round sliced into the second T-72. It exploded in a flash of fire and smoke, sending fragments of steel clattering down the street.

England's loader, Spc. Mark Gatlin, pumped another SABOT round into the breech.

At that instant, Pfc. K.C. Brons, the driver of England's tank, looked to his right. There, in an alley, was another T-72. It was so close he thought he could almost reach out and touch it. The tank was no more than 25 feet from him. He could see the rear slope and the fuel drums stored there. The gun tube was pointing in the other direction and the alley was so narrow the gun could not be traversed left or right.

Brons told Freeman about the tank on the right. Freeman traversed the gun tube in that direction but could not see anything in the sight, even on its lowest magnification, 3-power. The tank was too close for him to be able to clearly identify it as a tank. He could tell he was looking at something metal, but he could not be sure what kind of metal.

"Back up!" England ordered when he heard Brons' pleas.

England confirmed it was yet one more T-72.

Freeman was not even sure he could shoot from this range. There was nothing in the manuals about it. He had never trained to fire main gun rounds this close to anything, much less another tank.

England gave the order to fire, Freeman squeezed the triggers, and the Iraqi tank erupted in a cloud of flame and white-hot debris that rained down on the Abrams.

Ray White's tank spotted a T-72 in an alley to the left as it pushed north. His gunner, Sgt. Cullie Alexander, fired a SABOT round and that tank virtually disintegrated. Its engine was knocked out of the main body and its turret was popped and sent spinning off into the air. The next day the turret was found nearly 300 meters away, on top of a three-story building.

Pinkston kept his tank moving forward through the flames, smoke, and ammunition cooking off inside the destroyed T-72s. This one small section of Mahmudiyah was now a hellish inferno. The heat was intense; the smoke thick and black and greasy with the smell of diesel. And still we could see people standing out in the streets, watching all this happen.

The kills knocked the T-72s backward and sideways just enough

Two burning Iraqi T-72 tanks in Mahmudiyah on 3 April 2003, as seen through the vision blocks of U.S. Army tank Charlie Six-Six. (*Matt Larimer*)

to give our tanks a path as we continued to push north to link up with a platoon of Charlie Rock, which was waiting at the north end of the city.

Pinkston and his crew were finding other tanks hidden in alleys or parked on side streets as they drove on. One tank was even inside a parking garage.

Pinkston and England passed the burning tanks and approached another corner. As they rounded it, Stewart spotted the front slopes of more armored vehicles.

"I've got more vehicles!" he called to Pinkston.

Stewart was ready to fire again. Pinkston was ready to give the order. They were not sure what was in front of them.

Stewart kept looking through his sight, straining to see if it was enemy or friendly.

"No! Wait!" he finally called. "It's a friendly."

"We've got Bradleys in front of us. We've got Bradleys in front of us," Pinkston radioed back.

The Bradley fighting vehicles of Charlie Rock came into view. The platoon's two lead tanks were out of the inferno and into relatively safe terrain.

But two of the platoon's tanks were still back in the city. White's tank stopped just short of the flames and shot another T-72 off to the right. At least four tanks were burning now, some of which may have been double-tapped by crews that were leaving nothing to chance.

Phinney's tank was the last in the platoon. Just as Pinkston reported he had Charlie Rock in sight, Phinney looked to his right through the vision blocks and saw two large drums of diesel mounted on the back of a T-72 that somehow the three tanks ahead of him missed.

"There's a tank!" he yelled to no one in particular.

Phinney grabbed the manual override on the turret and took control from Sgt. Steve Ellis, the gunner. He put the gun tube on the T-72, almost literally. The end of the Abrams gun tube could not have been more than five feet from the Iraqi tank.

"Are you sure it's not a Bradley?" Ellis asked.

"It's a tank! Shoot it!"

Ellis fired a SABOT round and the fifth T-72 took a fatal blow, this time from point-blank range.

Phinney released control of the turret to Ellis as the tank moved on. Pfc. Jeremy Menery, the driver, was maneuvering around the burning tanks when Ellis came over the radio: "I've got another one!"

"Are you sure it's a tank?" Phinney asked.

"It's a tank!"

"OK! Fire!"

This T-72 was about thirty meters away down a side street. A SABOT round killed it instantly.

I was directly behind Phinney's tank, looking for targets, as it fired. But the pace of the column was picking up so we could get the company through the kill zone. I spotted one tank in an alley but did not have time to shoot and radioed its location back to

An Iraqi T-72 tank destroyed on the road to Baghdad by Task Force 1-15 of the 3rd Infantry Division (Mechanized). A dead Iraqi soldier lies to the left. (*Jason Conroy*)

third platoon, which was trailing me. One of its tanks killed the final T-72.

The entire tank battle in the streets of Mahmudiyah lasted less than five minutes. In that brief span, Charlie Company tankers killed seven T-72s and two BMPs. At times we were firing from point blank range. No one ever heard of such a thing, much less done it. It was like the gunfight at the OK Corral with tank main guns. The fastest gun wins. We had done some quick reaction training in Kuwait before the war, but not at these distances. We had practiced at 1,000 to 2,000 meters. Anything less was considered dangerous.

The impact, and significance, of what we did in Mahmudiyah did not begin to sink in until after we got back to Checkpoint Cobra. And for some Charlie Company soldiers, it may be years before they fully understand the importance of that day.

It was not so much that we killed tanks in the first major tank-on-tank engagement of the war, but how we killed them. We shot main gun rounds at enemy tanks at distances that would be considered too close for a handgun fight. It was unprecedented. There were no manuals for this, no training programs anywhere to teach a tanker how to go into a city and be able to recognize enemy tanks, instantly react to that contact, and get off kill shots before he has time to realize what was happening.

In some ways we had a bit of luck going with us that day. Because of the direction in which the Iraqi tanks were oriented, we later decided their commanders believed we would be coming in from the north, moving south on Highway 8. Had we done that, we would have driven directly into their guns. And we would have done that if I had told England just a few hours earlier to turn left instead of right.

By skirting the city's west side, we avoided the main avenue of approach and came in from the south, unintentionally catching the Iraqis by surprise. Call it fate, the hand of God, or simple blind, dumb luck, we were in a better position to kill the Iraqis than they were to kill us.

But much of that was a result of the quality of Charlie Company's soldiers, especially the second platoon soldiers who on this day led us through a nasty little fight that could have been disastrous had they not demonstrated the aggressiveness and initiative that they did. I could tell from their radio transmissions they were pumped up and excited. But they never lost their composure and adapted to difficult and dangerous situations quickly and with a professionalism that made me proud to say I was a part of the company.

Pinkston's crew in the lead tank was especially critical in getting us where we had to go and aggressively engaging the Iraqis so they did not have time to respond to our attack. But all of the second platoon crews and TCs played key roles in this fight. They were able to adapt quickly to a difficult and dangerous situation and kill the enemy before he had a chance to kill any of us. Fighting in these close quarters was not something for which we had been trained, but Charlie Company soldiers responded as if it was something that was second nature.

The fight at Mahmudiyah was one of the more important of the war because it demonstrated to us and our commanders that we could take tanks into the city, fight in close quarters, and defeat a determined enemy. It was a fight that led the way to downtown Baghdad in the days to come.

Some weeks later, a national weekly news magazine tried to downplay our accomplishments by saying that the T-72s in Mahmudiyah were killed by smart bombs dropped from Air Force jets. The article marveled at the accuracy of the bombs, being able to find tanks hidden in narrow alleys.

If there were Air Force jets in Mahmudiyah that day, they were flying awfully low, were wearing tank treads, and firing 120mm HEAT and SABOT rounds. No Air Force jets took out those tanks. The Cobras led the way into Mahmudiyah, and back out, killing Iraqi tanks along the way.

Our mission was so successful that the following day we would drive south once again, this time finishing off the Medina Division and its equipment. And although we did not know it then, those two successes set the stage for something we were told we would never do—take our tanks into downtown Baghdad and the heart of Saddam Hussein's empire.

2

ROCK OF THE MARNE

IF there were any arguments among planners at the Pentagon and at U.S. Central Command over which division to use as the spearhead for the attack on Iraq, they must have been rather muted. The decision undoubtedly was one of the easiest they had to make before or during the war. Getting to the fight quickly with a considerable amount of punch was what the 3rd Infantry Division was designed to do and what its soldiers were trained to do. The division already had a full brigade combat team (BCT) on the ground, another had just completed a six-month tour in Kuwait, and a third was scheduled to head to the region in March 2003. The 3rd Infantry Division (Mechanized) was the obvious choice.

Based at Fort Stewart on Georgia's southeastern coastal plain, the division had kept much of its focus on Kuwait and Iraq since Operations Desert Shield and Desert Storm in 1990 and 1991. Its brigade combat teams were rotating in and out of Kuwait on six-month training cycles. Despite peacekeeping missions to Bosnia and Kosovo, the division was still considered the iron fist of the 18th Airborne Corps's Contingency Force. Its soldiers know if there is a flare-up anywhere in Central Command's area of responsibility, which includes most of the Middle East, and if the brass thinks armor or mechanized infantry is the appropriate response, soldiers of the 3rd pack their gear and head for the airport.

Division officials spent years refining their go-to-war timing and short-notice flyaway, sail-away capabilities. In August 1990 it took the Fort Stewart division, then known as the 24th Infantry Division (Mechanized) before its 1996 reflagging as the 3rd, more than a month to get its soldiers, tanks, Bradley fighting vehicles, and tons of equipment out of Georgia and into Saudi Arabia by ship for Operation Desert Shield.

But within a year of returning home from 24th's successful campaign in the desert, the division, under the command of then–Maj. Gen. Barry McCaffrey, developed a plan to provide some armored muscle for light fighters such as the 82nd Airborne Division or the 10th Mountain Division that might be quickly sent to world hot spots. The concept of "Division Force Packages," as it was known, was designed to get soldiers, 70-ton M1A1 Abrams tanks, and Bradley fighting vehicles anywhere in the world on just a few hours' notice. The concept remained virtually intact for the next dozen years, and by 2002 the division was prepared to send a variety of "force packages" depending on the need.

There was an "Immediate Ready Company," a "Division Ready Force" that featured a company-plus sized element, and a "Division Ready Brigade." But these packages were rarely used. The better plan was to put the heavy equipment into position ahead of time and simply fly the soldiers to the equipment. The result was prepositioned stocks of equipment in and around the Middle East. Some equipment was on ships and some in Kuwait and Qatar.

By the end of 2000 Kuwait and Qatar were home to large storage facilities for this heavy equipment. Those facilities could each house 115 tanks, 60 Bradley Fighting Vehicles, 100 M-113 armored personnel carriers, and 20 155mm self-propelled Paladin howitzers. Ammunition, food, and fuel were stored nearby. All the soldiers had to do was get off the plane with their personnel gear, jump into their vehicles, collect their ammunition, grab some water and food, and they were ready for war.

By late September 2002, the 3rd Division's 2nd Brigade Combat Team, of which Charlie Company was part, arrived in Kuwait and set up shop in a desert encampment, or *kabal,* about sixty miles northwest of Kuwait City. The Spartan Brigade under command

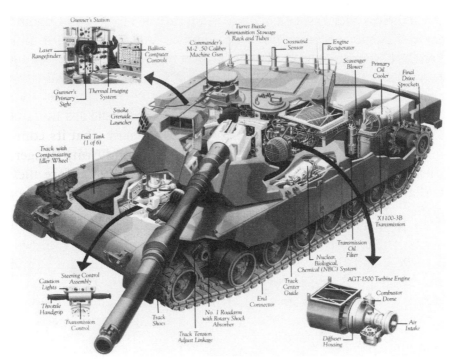

The M1A1 "Abrams" main battle tank. The 7.62mm coaxial machine gun is located just to the right of the main gun tube when looking from back to front but cannot be seen in this diagram because of the cutaway section. (*General Dynamics*)

of former West Point professor Col. David Perkins of Keene, New Hampshire, was there for six months of training in what was called Operation Desert Spring. Ostensibly the exercise was to provide for the security of Kuwait against possible predations by Iraq.

But even then it was quite evident from news reports that we were rolling inexorably toward a confrontation with Iraq and Saddam Hussein. The only question was whether the final showdown and ultimate solution would be political or military. As our later training demonstrated, military planners were already developing scenarios for what would eventually be our push into Iraq.

As the 4,300 soldiers of 2nd BCT were getting accustomed to life in the desert and starting their training routine, the 3rd BCT was returning home. The 3rd Brigade, or Sledgehammer Brigade, had just completed its six-month stint of coping with sand and heat in the trackless and impossibly inhospitable Kuwaiti desert as part of the same Operation Desert Spring. By the time it headed home, the 3rd BCT was well acquainted with the subtleties of the terrain along Kuwait's nearby border with Iraq and with the numerous idiosyncrasies of the prepositioned equipment.

Division officials knew it would take little to turn the 3rd Brigade around and send it back for the fight. That's exactly what its commander, Col. Daniel Allyn, a former paratrooper and Army Ranger, warned soldiers and their families could happen even before they had a chance to get reacquainted with one another and the soldiers had time to change their socks or grab a quick beer.

The 3rd Infantry Division is a split division. Its 1st and 2nd Brigades and many of its supporting units, including division headquarters, are at Fort Stewart, about 40 miles southwest of the port of Savannah on Georgia's east coast. Fort Stewart is the largest military installation east of the Mississippi River. Its 280,000 acres of swamplands and sandy pine barrens stretch over five southeastern Georgia counties. The nearby ports in Savannah and Brunswick, Georgia, and Jacksonville, Florida, plus the Hunter Army Airfield landing strip in Savannah, home of the division aviation brigade, make the post ideal for quick launches of forces overseas.

The division's 3rd Brigade is based at Fort Benning, Georgia, 270 miles west of Fort Stewart on the Georgia-Alabama border. The separation is more annoying and time-consuming for division officials than for its soldiers. And the split is not significantly detrimental to the unit's mission since the entire division can't train together anywhere in the United States.

The 3rd Division's other brigade combat team, the 1st, or Raider Brigade, was already prepping for its turn in the desert in March 2003. The 4,500 soldiers under the command of Col. Will Grimsley were scheduled to replace the 2nd BCT, at least on paper. However, there were serious doubts throughout the division that the 2nd BCT would be going home in March as planned.

By the end of the year, the division would have nearly 9,000 mechanized infantry and armor soldiers who had trained intensively in the desert over the past nine months and were ready to go to war. And with the 1st BCT preparing to head to the Middle East, the 3rd Infantry Division could put more than 13,500 combat soldiers on the ground by early in the year. No other division, Army or Marine Corps, could match those combat-ready numbers.

The 2nd BCT planned to complete most of the more demanding aspects of its training, including a brigade live-fire exercise at night, by Christmas 2002. The brigade had two tank battalions, 1st Battalion, 64th Armored Regiment, and 4th Battalion, 64th Armored Regiment, each with forty-four Abrams tanks. The other maneuver battalion, 3rd Battalion, 15th Infantry Regiment, had 44 Bradley Fighting Vehicles. For training in Kuwait and later during the war in Iraq, the battalions were task-organized. In other words, they included scouts, intelligence, engineers, artillery, and other assets that are not normally part of the units. As a result, each battalion was referred to as a task force.

While brigade commander Perkins had no combat experience, all three of his task force leaders were combat veterans of Operation Desert Storm and the 24th Infantry Division.

Lt. Col. Rick Schwartz of Alexandria, Virginia, commander of Task Force 1-64, was the son of a Vietnam veteran and a former elementary school teacher. He was a tank company commander in this same battalion during the Gulf War and was awarded a Bronze Star for valor.

Lt. Col. Philip DeCamp of Atlanta, Georgia, commander of Task Force 4-64, also was a tank company commander with the 24th during the war.

And Lt. Col. Stephen Twitty of Spartanburg, South Carolina, commander of Task Force 3-15, was a special assistant for operations to McCaffrey during the war and later served as his aide.

When it became apparent to division officials that the 3rd Infantry Division would play a key role in the war, they saw an opportunity for some international exposure. If the division was going to lead the charge into Baghdad, why not take advantage of a golden opportunity to make it a household name among an entirely new generation of Americans who for the most part had no idea who or what it was.

The 3rd has a long and distinguished history, dating back to

World War I. It was there that it picked up its nickname, "Rock of the Marne," for repulsing German attacks at the Marne River.

During World War II it participated in five D-Day invasions and had among its ranks one of the country's most decorated and recognizable soldiers—Audie Murphy, a Medal of Honor winner who later went on to a long, if somewhat lackluster, movie career.

In 1958 the division returned to Germany, where it served as one of the frontline units in the Cold War. It was to remain there in that capacity for 38 years, out of sight of much of the American public and out of mind. Its lone foray outside the European theater came when the 3rd Brigade was sent to Saudi Arabia in 1991 to fight with the 1st Armored Division.

Fighting not far to the west of that brigade during Operation Desert Storm was the unit the Germany-based division would replace at Fort Stewart in a few years, the 24th Infantry Division (Mechanized). It was not so much a replacement as it was a reflagging of the division. The 3rd Infantry Division's flags, battle streamers, and lengthy history were simply moved to Fort Stewart. The troops that had been in the 3rd Infantry Division in Germany became the 1st Infantry Division and remained in Europe. The 24th's colors were sent to Fort Riley, Kansas, where it became a hybrid division, part active, part Army National Guard.

Although the 24th gained some notoriety during the Persian Gulf War, its public identity could not come close to matching that of the 101st Airborne Division with its "Band of Brothers" cachet. Nor did it have the swagger of the 82nd Airborne Division with its jump boots and maroon berets. Even the 10th Mountain Division had a higher public profile because of what it did in Afghanistan in the hunt for Osama bin Laden and al-Qaida terrorists.

But the 3rd Infantry Division labored in anonymity for those outside the Army. This operation, even before it had a name, was a chance for it to shine and become a part of the national consciousness.

That public education about the division would be accomplished through daily reports sent back from the training grounds of Kuwait and the battlefields of Iraq by the hundreds of print, television, and radio journalists who were to be placed with American military forces in what the Pentagon referred to as "embedding the media." It was the first time since Vietnam journalists would be given a relatively unobstructed view of the battlefield, of how America's military sons and daughters earned their money and how tax dollars were spent. Division officials quickly embraced the idea of embedded journalists, and the unit's commander, Maj. Gen. Buford C. Blount III, was among those who liked the idea.

Division officials saw the embedding program as a means of getting soldiers their due in a campaign that was expected to set historical precedents. They saw it as a way of reviving the unit's history, largely unknown to all but military historians and soldiers who served with the division, and to make the "Rock of the Marne" greeting when soldiers of the unit salute officers as familiar as the 1st Cavalry Division's "Garry Owen, sir!" By the end of the Iraq war, the cross-hatched division patch with its alternating light and dark stripes, which some soldiers sarcastically refer to as "the broken television set," could be as recognizable and revered when worn as a combat patch on the right uniform sleeve as the "Screaming Eagle" of the 101st Airborne or the "AA" of the 82nd Airborne.

Blount seemed at times to be a shy and retiring man, uncomfortable around notebooks, cameras, and tape recorders. Some in the media referred to him as "Mumbles" for the habit he had of occasionally lowering his voice and talking into his chest. His staff said he preferred to surround himself with a few close confidants who could argue with him and tell him when he was wrong. He was unpretentious almost to a fault. When he would occasionally invite journalists to lunch at his mess tent in the desert, they invariably found lunch waiting on their plates: two peanut butter and jelly sandwiches on white bread and a bag of potato chips. He was fond of simple things and did not mind who knew it.

Blount had no previous combat experience. But he was a tanker, or "tread head" as those of us in armored units sometimes refer to ourselves. He understood what the Abrams and Bradleys could and, more important, could not do.

He brought one other skill to the job: he understood something of the Arab mentality. He had served as the armor plans and operations officer for the National Guard Modernization Program in Saudi Arabia and was familiar with the region, the people, their customs, and their religion.

Getting any sense of the people or the customs of the region was out of the question for us. We were there to train and there were only limited opportunities to escape the confines of the *kabals.* Our training schedule was so packed for the first few months in Kuwait that we had little time to do anything but tend to our tanks.

As Cobra Six, the commander of Charlie Company, Task Force 1-64 of the 2nd Brigade Combat Team, it was my job to ensure that the focus of my soldiers stayed on that training and not let them think too much about the future. Things were still too uncertain. But that was difficult. These were bright soldiers with more access to the news from back home through satellite telephones and the Internet than soldiers have had in any other war. They knew what was going on. They could see through any efforts to tell them anything but the unvarnished truth. So I did not try. I just told them to take advantage of the training they were getting, that it might come in handy some day soon. It might save their lives and the lives of their buddies.

For the most part, they heard the message. Maybe it was the lack of distractions way out there in the desert. Maybe it was the fact that many of the younger soldiers seemed to be growing up and maturing as they learned about themselves and the equipment they would have to rely on if we went to war.

I had confidence in them as professional soldiers and as men. They would listen when they were told something because they wanted to listen and learn. But it was not always easy. At times it had been a difficult task getting Charlie Company ready to go to war.

3

THE MAKING OF
CHARLIE COMPANY

THE Charlie Company I took to war in March 2003 was not the same Charlie Company I had taken command of little more than a year earlier. Many of the faces were the same, and the dedication and professionalism of the senior noncommissioned officers and platoon leaders remained much as it was before my change of command on 8 February 2002. But in the intervening year, the soldiers attained a singular focus about their jobs that I did not see when I took over the company. They matured in that year, as had I as a commander. They became confident, if not cocky. They were ready to take on anything the Iraqis could throw at us so we could get to Baghdad, get rid of Saddam Hussein, and then go home.

I came to Charlie Company from a staff job with 1st Battalion, 64th Armor Regiment. I was the S-3 air, coordinating tactical air movement in and out of the sectors in which we operated during exercises. The whole time I was on the battalion staff I was waiting for company commander's job to open up. That is the dream and the purpose of every line captain in the Army. It is our chance, maybe the only one we'll ever have, to lead men and see what we're made of as officers.

I was familiar with Charlie Company only to the extent that it was part of the battalion. It is difficult to see what a company is really made of until you take command. Charlie Company was not what it appeared to be. Things were going on behind the scenes that I discovered only after I got involved in the day-to-day routine of the unit.

That was all part of being a commander, though, and I was prepared to deal with it. I had seen life on both sides of the Army fence, first as an enlisted soldier, serving as a crew chief on Apache helicopters, and now as an officer. And growing up in Apalachin, N.Y., I was around veterans most of my life. My father, Gary Conroy, was a sergeant with the 25th Infantry Division in Vietnam. My maternal grandfather, Rudy Sigler, served with Adm. Bull Halsey in the Pacific during World War II and was on the *U.S.S. Missouri* for the Japanese surrender. My paternal grandfather, Cyril Conroy, served in the Army during World War II.

Charlie Company in Kuwait prior to the start of Operation Iraqi Freedom. (*Jason Conroy*)

I considered becoming a helicopter pilot when I became an officer in 1995, but instead opted for tanks. I found tanking to be challenging but not difficult. I never struggled with any of the concepts and enjoyed the problems we were given to solve. I also began to get enamored with the idea that if I ever went to war, I wanted to go surrounded by seventy tons of steel and armor. The more I saw of the capabilities and survivability of the M1A1 Abrams tank, the more confident I became of fighting a war in it and coming home alive.

My first assignment was in Germany with the 1st Armored Division's 1st Brigade. The division, then under the command of Maj. Gen. Bill Nash, went to Croatia in December 1995 to prepare to cross the Sava River into Bosnia-Herzegovina as part of an international peacekeeping force. I was a platoon leader with 4th Battalion, 67th Armor Regiment with the additional assignment of serving as the rear detachment S-1. For several months I was a courier, flying between Germany and Bosnia every ten to fourteen days. In late August 1996 I was deployed to Bosnia where I served as the 1st Brigade liaison officer (LNO) at division headquarters in Tuzla.

As the LNO I had the opportunity to travel throughout Bosnia. Things were still tense there as well as in neighboring Croatia and Serbia. The tension was especially noticeable in the Zone of Separation (ZOS) between the warring factions. If it was difficult for the American public thousands of miles away to sort out the differences among Croats, Serbs, and Bosnian Muslims, it was almost as difficult on the ground.

What struck me most about Bosnia was the absolute hatred each side had for the other. At times the hatred was almost palpable. There was an ugly, evil sense to it that you could almost reach out and touch. But at other times I would see these very strange relationships between Croats, Serbs, and Bosnian Muslims. I would see one person from one faction and a relative from another faction meet in the ZOS on a Saturday or a Sunday and express absolute love for one another. But the rest of the week they would be throwing rocks at each other. To see how they interacted despite their political and religious differences provided a foundation for me to later understand how the Sunni and Shia sects of Islam could be so much alike yet so different.

Watching Nash deal on an almost daily basis with the local citizens from different factions also provided a learning experience that I would use when Charlie Company eventually got to Baghdad. Nash was as much politician and diplomat as he was a military commander. While he was trying to enforce the ceasefire and take care of his troops, he was working to empower the local citizens to positively transform their local and national governments. He was trying to give those citizens what they needed to help themselves. The U.S. forces were there merely as guardians of the peace, not as occupiers.

We were there to help them make their lives better, not to control them. I believed that what was in their best interests was in our best interests. That was something not everybody understood. But it was a lesson I carried with me to Baghdad, and it would later help us keep the peace in our little corner of Iraq after Saddam's regime fell. An Abrams tank draws a lot of attention, but sincerity and quiet diplomacy can have far more impact on people who truly want to better their lives.

When it came time for me to take command of Charlie Company, I harbored no misgivings. I had served as a platoon leader and later as a first lieutenant, was Battalion Maintenance Officer (BMO) with 1st Battalion, 37th Armor Regiment in Germany. As BMO I had ninety-plus soldiers under my leadership. I used that time to prepare myself for command. By the time I got to Fort Stewart in July 2001, I was ready to command a company. I had prepared for it and was eagerly anticipating it.

I was not prepared, however, for the numbers and types of Uniform Code of Military Justice (UCMJ) charges with which I initially had to deal. The first heady rush of command had not even worn off when I found myself swamped with paperwork dealing with issues of drug use in the company. We had six soldiers who had tested positive for drugs. That quickly grew to thirteen when I started running random urinalyses almost every other week. That was more than 15 percent of the company.

The drugs used ran the gamut from marijuana to Ecstasy to cocaine. One soldier even tested positive on a urinalysis for the animal tranquilizer Ketamine. Known on the streets as "Vitamin K,"

"Special K," or "cat Valium," the drug is used legitimately to tranquilize animals. But in humans it reacts much like PCP and is regularly abused at clubs and rave parties.

I was concerned because when people are working on a complicated and dangerous piece of machinery like a 70-ton tank, a moment of inattention or sloppiness could easily get someone killed. I had heard stories about the Army back in the '70s and the rampant drug use and was thankful I was not in that Army. I thought the all-volunteer Army virtually eliminated the drug problems. I was not naïve about drug use, but I was stunned at what I found.

I knew I had to put a stop to it as soon as I could. It was either rehabilitate these guys or get rid of them because there was no room for drug use in an armor company. For me, it was also an issue of the pride of being a soldier—a soldier doesn't smoke pot, snort cocaine, or take Ecstasy. It was beyond me to understand why these guys were doing this after joining the Army. I knew I could clean up the company alone. But it did not take me long to find my biggest ally, 1st Sgt. Jose Mercado.

First Sergeant Mercado got to Charlie Company the same day I took command. My change-of-command ceremony was on 8 February 2002. Mercado's change-of-responsibility ceremony was the following day. He came to Charlie Company from Korea and had as little tolerance as I for any kind of drug use, sloppiness, or negligence. A native of Quebradillas, Puerto Rico, Mercado was a twenty-year veteran of the Army and was exactly what I was looking for in a first sergeant.

He was a veteran of the Persian Gulf War so he knew what combat was all about. He was a strict disciplinarian, physically fit enough to outlift and outrun most of the younger soldiers, and neat almost to a fault. He demanded cleanliness and proper military dress and bearing, no matter what the conditions. Even during the war, it became a matter of pride among us and helped maintain discipline when he insisted Charlie Company soldiers shave daily and wash as frequently as possible.

He was one of the most religious soldiers I have ever met. He went to Mass every Sunday and sometimes during the week. But he

Charlie Company's first sergeant, Jose Mercado. (*Jason Conroy*)

was also one of the most profane men I have ever been around. Not even my drill sergeants at Fort Dix could outdo First Sergeant Mercado in profanity. There were times in Kuwait when he would go to Sunday Mass then return to the company area and find something not to his liking. He would launch into a string of expletives and invectives that startled even me. I would look at him and say, "First Sergeant, didn't you just come from Mass?"

He would smile and say something like, "Well, sir, we can't let the soldiers slack off just because it's Sunday."

Mercado was tough on the soldiers but had their best interests at heart. He believed there was a good chance we were going to war and he wanted the soldiers to be tougher than anything the Iraqis could throw at them. He was, in my view, the quintessential first sergeant. He became a close friend and a trusted ally as we worked through those early, dark days of getting Charlie Company clean and ready to go to war.

First-time drug users were given a chance to rehabilitate. But if a soldier came up hot on a urinalysis one time, he invariably came up hot a second time, no matter how much rehab or counseling. When the second-time offenders started popping up, we shifted our focus to be more efficient in getting them through the legal system and out of the Army to minimize the impact they were having on other soldiers in the company. It did not take long for the entire company to get the message and soldiers began turning in the users. There was a new sheriff in town with some new rules. But it wasn't just one new sheriff; there were two, the first sergeant and me.

Within six weeks the offenders were identified and started going through the UCMJ process. The majority of the drug users were out of the company by May. Because we were handling them so efficiently, I was being given soldiers from other units who had drug problems. I was expected to deal with them. As with our own unit, we either rehabbed them or got rid of them. There was very little middle ground.

We had a few soldiers with drug problems who worked through them and straightened themselves out. I talked to them at length about their future and what a less-than-honorable discharge would mean in civilian life. Something I said must have hit home because they went through the rehab process, cleaned up their acts, and ended up being top-notch soldiers during the war.

I sometimes wondered what I had gotten myself into with Charlie Company. Much of the first thirty to forty-five days of my command was spent dealing with legal issues rather than training. I spent a good portion of each day dealing with paperwork, the Army's Criminal Investigation Division, the judge advocate general, or the military police. I was intent on getting rid of those few guys who were detrimental to the company. They were sapping the morale of the other soldiers and were truly dangerous to be around. They were taking away from what we needed to be focused on: combat readiness.

Once the drug users were removed and we finally got to Kuwait, Charlie Company was focused. Some of the guys we ended up getting rid of would not have made it through the war because they lacked that focus. A line company, whether armor or infantry, is a complex organism. With all the combined arms firepower at its disposal, that company is often more than the sum of its parts. Because we would be at the very tip of the spear in any combat operation, it was necessary for that company to function well as a team. I was not comfortable with the team I took command of in February 2002. By mid-March, when we had cleaned house, I was getting a better feeling of just who Charlie Company was and what it could do.

However, I still did not know what kinds of fighters were in the company. The soldiers gave me some hope in late February 2002 during what is known as Marne Focus, an exercise designed to prepare the 2nd Brigade for a month-long rotation at the National Training Center (NTC) at Fort Irwin, California. Charlie Company was the Opposing Force, or OPFOR, for Marne Focus. We did well. I saw a number of young soldiers with a great deal of potential. They shot well and maneuvered well in their tanks. They possessed good individual tanking skills. How we put that together as a company was another matter.

I thought I would get a better read on the company's ability to fight in May 2002. We were scheduled to go to the Joint Readiness Training Center at Fort Polk, Louisiana, for small unit training. Instead, we were sent to the NTC in March to serve as the White Cell detail for the 2nd Brigade during its rotation in the desert that was its preparation for Kuwait and Operation Desert Spring later in the year. White Cell is the name given to the unit that stays behind in garrison at Fort Irwin during training to focus on administrative and logistics issues so the larger unit can focus on training.

As the White Cell detail, we essentially had to make sure everything was in place for the brigade. We were responsible for what is known as the RUBA, or Rotational Units Bivouac Area, sometimes referred to as "The Dust Bowl." It was our job to keep the RUBA clean and to handle other chores such as running the phone center, laundry facilities, and vehicle wash rack. If there was a fuel spill, we had to clean it up. We inspected the cleaning areas and latrines, provided refueling and maintenance teams for the lights throughout the RUBA, and handled trash collection and separation.

It was not a glamorous job, but one that has to be done to ensure the brigade is able to focus on its training. But while there I was able to use some of the downtime to begin building the foundation for a war-fighting company. We trained crews in the Tank Crew Gunnery Skills Testing, which cross-trains them so they know how to do every job in the tank. We went through the Unit Conduct of Fire Trainer, in which we worked on specific skills for the gunners and tank commanders. We did six-mile marches in the desert with full packs while wearing our gas masks and biological-chemical suits.

It was at the NTC that we began to come together as a company, to build a foundation for our deployment to Kuwait later in the year. We got to know one another through daily company barbecues, pickup basketball games, and friendly competition in just about everything else we did. Instead of being a group of individual solders, we became a company.

By the summer of 2002 we were beginning to focus on Kuwait and our role in Operation Desert Spring. About that time a new battalion commander took over. He, in turn, began to focus our efforts on Iraq, particularly on one of the Republican Guard divisions, the Medina.

Lt. Col. Rick Schwartz was quite familiar with 1st Battalion, 64th Armored Regiment, generally referred to as the Desert Rogues. Short and slight, Schwartz looked more like the elementary school teacher he once was than the combat warrior he became during the Persian Gulf War when he fought in this same battalion. He taught as much as he commanded, challenging us to find our own solutions to problems. Despite his diminutive stature, Schwartz brought with him intensity and prescience about what we might do and where we might go.

One of first things he did was to set up a secret Iraq war room in the battalion headquarters. He stocked the room with old Iraqi uniforms and weapons. He gave us satellite maps that showed entrenchments, motor pools, and other areas of interest. We had information about morale and the sizes of individual Iraqi army units and where they were deployed in the country. Schwartz included information about the history of Iraq and Saddam, about the languages and the religion and how they affected what the Iraqi army might or might not do. There was material on how the Iraqis fought, or at times did not fight; how they used their artillery and maneuvered their tanks. If there was information available about the Iraqi military, Schwartz tried to get his hands on it and make it available to us. He did not believe in training for the next field exercise. He believed in training for the next war and he was convinced that war would be in Iraq. His insight gave us a chance to see what we would face in Iraq before we even got to the region.

My focus that summer was getting my tank commander (TC) and gunner combinations solidified so once we got to Kuwait we could concentrate on training and not have to worry about making numerous crew adjustments. Because of the soldiers cashiered out of the Army with legal problems, we had a number of young tankers who were inexperienced and had yet to prove themselves but who I thought had potential. The TC-gunner combination is the most crucial on the tank. If those two do not get along or communicate well, that tank can end up being more of a liability than an asset. We began promoting a number of our Specialists E-4 that had potential to Sergeants E-5 and put them in the gunner's seat. We knew we would have some growing pains, because they were all new to the position.

In my gunners I was looking for soldiers who, despite their relative youth and lack of time in the Army, had the maturity to deal with stress and responsibility. These soldiers would be my main shooters and killers, responsible for what goes downrange from the 120mm main gun and the 7.62mm coaxial machine gun. We looked at personalities, background, experience, and ability to deal with subordinates on the crew, particularly the loader and driver.

Working with the first sergeant and the platoon leaders, we tried to put the less experienced gunners with more experienced tank commanders, and vice versa. S.Sgt. Randy Pinkston, a lanky, easygoing Texan, was the gunner on my tank. When we started making moves, we gave him his own tank and assigned Sgt. Scott Stewart, who had just recently been promoted to that rank and was relatively inexperienced as a gunner, to Pinkston's tank. I moved Sgt. Nathan Malone, a short, muscular weightlifter from St. Louis, into the gunner's seat in my tank because I needed someone I felt could fight the tank on his own if I was busy directing the company. Malone was quiet but tough and had the maturity and the experience I needed to fill in as my replacement. He was the kind of guy who was always looking to improve himself.

I selected the rest of my crew for the same reasons I picked Malone. Spc. Matt Larimer, a tall, quiet Pennsylvanian, was my driver. He was young but kept his head about him. And my loader was Spc. Paul Helgenberger, a native of Micronesia who had an older brother in the division's 3rd Squadron, 7th Cavalry Regiment. Like every other crew, mine went through some early growing pains. But once we got in synch I only had to tell them something once and they did it and did it well. And when I was busy leading the company, which was often, they fought the tank on their own.

We even went so far as to look at language issues among the crews. We had a number of Spanish-speaking soldiers in the company, and for several English was still a difficult second language. For example, Psc. Jose Campos was a native of Costa Rica while Pfc. Fausto Trivino, was a native of Ecuador. Both were more comfortable speaking Spanish than English. We recognized language could be an issue and wanted to eliminate it before it cropped up on the battlefield.

Campos, who was in his mid-thirties and worked as a cook at a restaurant in New York several years before joining the Army, came to us straight from basic training. Trivino was in his early twenties but was married; his wife back in Savannah was expecting their first child.

Because Campos and Trivino were having language problems, I tried to find spots for them on tanks where language would not be a major issue. I put Trivino into a tank commanded by S.Sgt. Jason Diaz. Diaz was of Puerto Rican descent but grew up in New York City. He was one of the best gunners in the battalion and I knew he would have no problems mentoring Trivino. The move turned out to be a good one for Trivino. It gave him more confidence in what he was doing and how he handled himself. The only non-Hispanic in that tank was Spc. Chris Shipley, a native of Arizona who would later play a key role in our first run into downtown Baghdad.

I also moved Sgt. Jose Couvertier, another native of Puerto Rico by way of Hartford, Connecticut, into Diaz's tank. Couvertier was another of the recent promotions and did not have much experience as a gunner, so I wanted to put him with a more experienced TC. If they had to communicate in Spanish, so be it.

Campos ended up as the loader on a tank commanded by S.Sgt. Larrico Alexander, an experienced tanker and another recent arrival from Korea. Campos was the only Spanish speaker on that tank but meshed well with the rest of the crew, and language was never a barrier. Crew coordination and communication was not the problem with that tank. Mechanical issues plagued it throughout the war. It was never as effective as Alexander and I hoped it would be.

I looked at the crew changes and assignments more as a mentorship program. It was a matter of finding who could best train and mentor another soldier. We made the initial crew selections at Fort Stewart. I figured I could refine them once we got to Kuwait and started our intensive training. That would give me a better idea about what changes would have to be made.

By the time we began making final preparations for Kuwait in September 2002, I felt relatively comfortable with the TC-gunner combinations. There would be some tweaking, but not much. I felt our training in Kuwait would give me time to focus more on loaders and drivers and getting that mix just right. I wanted to make sure we had the best blend of experience, personality, and attitude in each crew. I wanted positives to offset negatives. I wanted one soldier's youthful impetuosity and bullheadedness to be balanced by another's maturity and experience. I wanted the best possible teams I could put together in the event we went to war.

4

OPERATION DESERT SPRING

WE arrived in Kuwait in late September 2002 and were greeted by unimaginable heat. Soldiers who had been here remembered the heat being bad, but complained it was far worse this time. Even in September the heat was well over 100 degrees during the day, often with a hot wind blowing that sucked the moisture right out of you. It cooled down only slightly at night. After setting foot in that heat, I hoped that if we went to war it would not be until after the weather cooled off. Trying to fight a war while buttoned up inside a tank without air conditioning and wearing a chemical-biological protective suit, would undoubtedly produce an inordinate number of heat casualties. I could not imagine what it was like for the 3rd Brigade soldiers who spent the summer training here. But I was to find out nine months later.

We drew our tanks, armored personnel carriers, Humvees, and a 5-ton truck and trailer at Camp Doha just west of downtown Kuwait City. Camp Doha is a sprawling, 500-acre compound of warehouses and offices near the port on the west side of Kuwait Bay. The facilities were provided to the United States by the Kuwaiti government to store the prepositioned equipment and house the offices from which the defense of the oil-rich emirate could be planned and carried out.

From Doha we quickly moved northwest into the desert near the border with Iraq. Our home for the next few months was a large, flat desert compound, or *kabal*, surrounded on all sides by sand berms built up for protection from Iraqis or terrorists or whoever might happen by. At that time there were four similar large encampments in the area. By the start of the war there were many more. Ours, which housed all of Task Force 1-64 and a few other units, was Camp Pennsylvania. It was a few miles to the west of Camp New York, where the 2nd Brigade Combat Team had its headquarters. There were also Camps New Jersey and Virginia stretched along a line about twelve miles west of Highway 80, which runs north and south, from Kuwait City to the Iraq border. The camps were named in honor of those states that suffered the most casualties and most damage from the terrorist attacks of 11 September 2001. The names were a constant reminder of one of the reasons we were here.

After a few days' housekeeping and vehicle maintenance, we launched into our gunnery training. We fired all of our weapons, from the 9mm Beretta handguns to the 120mm main tank guns.

S.Sgt. Jason Diaz (left) and Pfc. Fausto Trivino prepare 7.62mm ammunition for loading onto their tank in Kuwait before the start of the war. (*Brant Sanderlin/ Atlanta Journal-Constitution*)

Our master gunner, or Mike Golf, was S.Sgt. Jabari Williams. He had an easy smile and was soft-spoken but he knew his gunnery and he ran the crews through their paces on these tests. If they did not do it right, Williams made them do it again and again until it was done properly.

We started the tank gunnery tables with Table IV, the Tank Crew Proficiency Course, which is a dry fire exercise for the crews. We progressed through Tables V and VI, which are machine-gun qualifying tests. When it came time to shoot Table VIII, our scores improved markedly from what they were at Fort Stewart. Charlie Company tankers were absolutely destroying targets all over the range. They were dead-on accurate, and it became a source of much good-natured debate throughout the company about just who was the best shooter. Trash talking among the crews was a nightly event. It was good to see because the more they shot and killed targets, the more confident they became about their own abilities to do well on the battlefield. They were aggressive and merciless. When it came time to shoot Tank Table XII, the platoon live fire, we were just as accurate.

Just before the start of the war, we were also given the opportunity to set up a range to shoot live service rounds, those we would use in combat. Many of our soldiers had not fired live service rounds in training. They were used to firing training rounds, which have neither the same sound nor the same impact as service rounds. I wanted to get Charlie Company used to firing main gun rounds, especially those designed to take out enemy armor, because we were all under the impression that if we fought, it would be a tank-on-tank fight. We would be going against Iraqi armored vehicles or heavily fortified bunkers.

One aspect of our training that proved to be especially beneficial was a series of "cage matches" we set up not long after our arrival in Kuwait. These were like boxing matches between tanks, or a tank-on-tank gunfight. We would get a large patch of desert in northeastern Kuwait, put a tank at either corner, and let them go at each other. The idea was to see which crew was the most skillful in maneuvering the tank, and the fastest—and deadliest—on the trigger. I planned to give my young lieutenants and senior NCOs a great deal of leeway in how they would fight their platoons and I wanted them to get used to fighting as individual tanks and crews. We used the Multiple Integrated Laser Engagement System, or MILES, the laser-tag–like training devices, for this to help us figure out who won.

These one-on-one matches are not something in which tank crews normally engage. Tanks usually practice for platoon or company fights. But I had read an article in *Armor* magazine about the practice of individual tanks fighting each other and when I asked Schwartz about it, discovered he had read the same article. He said he had already decided to implement it battalion-wide. In retrospect these practice engagements proved very beneficial to us, especially at the battle for Mahmudiyah. The cage match allows the tank commander to fight at an individual level, without direction or guidance from above. Each cage match was a street fight, a shootout between armored behemoths. The guy with the most maneuverability and fastest trigger finger won. The other guy died. That's exactly what happened at Mahmudiyah. My second platoon soldiers were quicker on the draw and won the fight that day.

Among tankers it is a tradition to put names on the gun tubes. They are usually personal in nature. But in each company the gun tube names start with the first letter of the company name. Theoretically, all Alpha Company tanks would have names that start with A, Bravo Company with B, and Charlie Company with C. Exceptions can be made in rare instances.

At Fort Stewart the Charlie Company tankers named many of their tanks after beer. We had tanks named *Corona, Colt .45* and *Cold Beer.* But in Kuwait, in deference to the no-alcohol policy in the emirate, we had to forego the use of such names for fear of running afoul of host nation sensibilities. In fact, we initially were told that we could not put any names on the gun tubes.

When we pressed the issue and agreed to paint out the names if they became a problem, higher authority relented. We ended up with a variety of names. Some were patriotic, such as *Compliments of the USA* and *Courtesy of the Red, White, and Blue,* which was the name of my tank. We also had *Carnivore, Creeping Death, Call to Arms,* and *Case Closed.* Diaz's tank bore the name, *Cojone, Eh?,* a name he never fully explained; this proved to be a bit embarrassing when a photo of it turned up in a national news magazine after our initial run into Baghdad, where the tank was abandoned after being disabled by heavy enemy fire.

Tank names were changed at times, depending on who among the crew had the upper hand or was the most convincing debater. Pinkston changed the name on his tank to *Challenger II* after the space shuttle exploded, as a tribute to the crew members who lost their lives.

Still other tanks earned their names the hard way. That is how *Crash Tested* got its name. The tank commander was Sgt. 1st Class David Richard, a burly, likable native of North Dakota who spent four years in the Marine Corps before joining the Army. His gunner was Sgt. Anthony Marabello, a native of New York City recently promoted to his position and to the gunner's seat. They were two soldiers who could not have been more different. Marabello was a true New Yorker with an accent to match. He talked fast and did not think much of wide-open spaces. Richard, on the other hand, grew up on a ranch and barely tolerated cities. He was a hunter and a horseman and loved the outdoors. Despite their differences, the Richard-Marabello crew was one of my best.

But even good crews can have their troubles at times. After one of our early gunneries, Richard's tank was the last to leave the firing range. It was getting dark, and it was a long way back to camp for soldiers who were still learning their way around the desert. Sgt. 1st Class Brett Waterhouse, a by-the-book senior NCO, served as the range officer that day and hopped aboard with Richard for what they thought would be a quick trip back to Camp Pennsylvania.

The trip was anything but quick. The crew did not have a working Global Positioning System but felt they could dead-reckon their way back to the *kabal* without any assistance or headlights. We were not permitted to use a tank's headlights at night outside the camp. Without those lights to guide them, and with the lights from the camp washing out their night-vision goggles, they ended wandering around the desert. They knew they were near the camp, but were not sure just how near.

"Look for a berm. There should be a berm around here somewhere," Richard instructed his driver, Spc. Michael Donohue, over the tank's internal communications system.

"I think I see a berm," Donohue radioed back.

"Where?" Richard asked.

"Right there," Donohue replied.

And at that instant the 70-ton tank went almost perpendicular, with the front end and the gun tube pointed skyward as it rode up a twelve-foot-high sand berm. Just as quickly as it went up, it came crashing back down, gun tube first. The tank had found Camp Pennsylvania the hard way. Waterhouse, standing in the loader's hatch, crashed backwards, then forward, injuring his left shoulder. (The shoulder would bother him the rest of the war.) Marabello got the worst of it, smashing face-first into the gunner's primary site and pushing his teeth through his lips. Richard was bounced around but emerged unscathed

We occasionally practiced what we called "the great *kabal* break-out," an exercise to get the tanks out of the compound quickly in case we were attacked. This was the first time anyone tried breaking into the *kabal* and from then on the incident became known as "the great *kabal* break-in." And Richard's tank found its name. It was truly *Crash Tested*.

While we all laughed at Richard's misfortune—and we could do that since no one was seriously hurt—it provided another object lesson. The lesson essentially was that it's dangerous out there maneuvering a tank at night, whether in Kuwait or Iraq. When we went somewhere, we needed to have all our gear in proper working order and carry out a thorough precombat inspection, particularly of the hand-held GPS devices, or pluggers as we called them.

We seldom referred to our own tanks by the names on the gun tubes, though. That was for show. Instead, we used a simplified numbering system. There were four tanks to a platoon, three platoons in the company. Each platoon's tanks were numbered one through four. The number one tank was the platoon leader's tank. The number two tank was the platoon leader's wing man, and together they made up the platoon's Alpha Section. The number three tank was the wing man for the four tank, which was the platoon sergeant's tank. They made up the platoon's Bravo section.

Each of the three platoons was given a color code with a patriotic motif. First platoon was Red, second platoon White, and third platoon Blue. Thus, if we called "Red One," we were calling the platoon leader's tank in the first platoon. Red Four was the platoon sergeant's tank. The numbering system was the same for White and Blue platoons. The numbers and colors are standard operating procedures for tank companies to simplify radio communications and help in speedy identification of individual tanks.

Since 1st Lt. Shane Williams and I were part of the headquarters platoon, our tanks were simply Six-Five, also referred to as Cobra Five, and Six-Six, or Cobra Six, respectively. The personnel carriers were numbered differently. The first sergeant's PC was Charlie Seven-Seven since his call sign was Cobra Seven. The medic PC was Cobra Band-Aid.

Our training was moving ahead faster and with far better results than I had hoped. When we did force-on-force engagements, we always got the best of the OPFOR. Charlie Company soldiers were aggressive on the attack, something I encouraged throughout training. It was important to take the fight to the enemy; if a crew broke something on the tank while being aggressive, I willingly took the heat for it. Overall, I was pleased with what I was seeing.

When it came time for us to be the OPFOR for training in company-size operations, we hammered the other units. They often complained that we cheated. They could complain all they wanted though, because I know my soldiers ran them down and killed them. We were getting kills at long range, two thousand meters and more. We were going after the other companies and shooting them on the run as they retreated. The more Charlie Company practiced, the better it got. My soldiers felt like they were the best of the best. I'm sure many of the other companies felt the same way. But, for a commander, it is good to see that confidence and aggressiveness in a unit.

Many of the skills Charlie Company soldiers learned came from our time as the OPFOR. Our uncompromising maneuvering in training can be traced back in large measure to peer pressure. All of my gunners wanted to be the best. They prided themselves on being tank killers and first-rate trigger pullers. There was a great deal of satisfaction among them when we would leave an exercise and see the other unit's MILES lights blinking all over the battlefield. It reaffirmed the faith we had in ourselves as tankers and helped bring us together as a company. If we could do this to our fellow American soldiers, there was no telling what we would do to the Iraqis.

Any concerns I had during this time were more about individuals and specific skills they lacked. I was not worried about abilities to perform as a company. We began to feel we were unstoppable and certainly unbeatable as a company and as a task force. Even if we were outnumbered by tanks or soldiers, it was no big deal. We had the combined arms firepower to kill more of the enemy than he could kill of us. We felt we could beat anybody out there, especially the Iraqis, who cut and run during the Persian Gulf War and who some of our commanders felt would do the same thing this time.

Brashness and cockiness in the right doses can do a lot for a line company. But too much of either can create problems and cause deaths and injuries. I did not feel we were too brash or too cocky. Neither did I have a single doubt that we could not do the job, whatever that job might be.

Through the fall we remained very unsure about what was in store for us. My focus throughout training was that we were going to war at the end of it. I was more critical of Charlie Company soldiers when they made mistakes during the training in Kuwait than I would have been back in the States. I wanted them to know that mistakes on the battlefield could get them killed. The more I reinforced that in training, the less likely it would actually happen when people started shooting at us.

Some of the training exercises seemed a bit unusual. In one we were required to take our tanks through a narrow defile. On either side were steel pickets tied together with engineer tape. We were told this was low, swampy ground and if we got off the trail we would get stuck. What we did not realize was that while the overall plan was still in a state of flux, specific training exercises were being designed to prepare us for things we might face in Iraq. This particular exercise simulated what we actually encountered when we went through a narrow escarpment near Najaf on the road to Baghdad. Only much later would that become clear to all of us.

We worked on destruction of enemy observation and listening posts. We practiced crossing rivers on pontoon bridges, a feat we accomplished in riverless Kuwait by tossing pontoons out in the middle of the desert and pretending there was water around them by digging trenches on either side deep enough so that if a tank went off course, it would land upside down. And to further complicate the exercise, we did it in full MOPP gear, the Mission Oriented Protective Posture clothing and gas masks that were to be our defense against chemical and biological attacks. The intent was to make the training so tough that the real thing would not seem so difficult.

We also started thinking about collection of enemy prisoners of war (EPWs). Schwartz talked frequently of the thousands of Iraqis who surrendered during Operation Desert Storm and how the division was not prepared to deal with them. How would we deal with them this time if they started coming out of the desert in droves? Do we use duct tape to bind their hands or the plastic zip strips favored by military police? How do we segregate them? If we're moving quickly, do we have to leave people behind to guard them? Do we do as they did in the first Gulf War—simply disarm them, give them an MRE (Meal Ready to Eat), and point them toward Baghdad?

Virtually everything we did from September through December was with the mindset that we were going across the border into Iraq at some point. Normally, units sent to Kuwait train for Operation Desert Spring, the defense of Kuwait. The whole scheme of maneuver is defensive in nature. This time we were training for offensive operations, although we had no clue about what that mission was.

However, there were hints. In his briefings Schwartz kept hammering on the Medina Division. In December, he started discussing possible scenarios for an attack on Iraq. If we do something, this is what it might look at, he would say. But it was all very general. There was never anything definitive.

The brigade night live-fire exercise in mid-December finally gave us an opportunity to see how things might look when we were on the attack. The brigade had a three-kilometer-wide front and was really jammed together. It was tight, and we moved carefully, but that gave us a better understanding of how difficult it is to move a full brigade across the battlefield. The exercise also gave us invaluable experience maneuvering at night, something armor units rarely do at Fort Polk, the NTC, or even in Kuwait. This rare opportunity gave us insights into night maneuvers that paid dividends during the war.

In one portion of the exercise, we were ordered to take an old mining town dubbed Objective Mayberry. We were not to go into the town but were to roll up outside it on line and shoot with our main guns while calling in 120mm mortars. We followed that up with fire from .50-caliber and 7.62mm machine guns to give us practice in effectively massing our fires. But it was all done from the outskirts of town, never inside it. Tanks, we were repeatedly told, do not do urban warfare. It was too dangerous and there were too many ways a tank could get stuck or killed in there. The confined space did not give us enough room to maneuver the vehicles or traverse our gun tubes. The Abrams tanks were designed to be an offensive weapon and kill enemy tanks on the move at long distances in open country

It was about this time, just as we were wrapping up our live-fire training, that Charlie Company found itself in the uncomfortable glare of the international spotlight.

We knew there would be a number of journalists around if we went to war. We were told to prepare for it and saw the influx throughout our fall training. Their numbers increased the closer we got to the end of the year. At that time the 2nd Brigade Combat Team was just about the only American military story to which they were given access in Kuwait so they came at us in waves.

The Army started integrating journalists into the live fires for what were referred to as "test embeds." Journalists were queuing up in Kuwait City for a shot at becoming one of the permanent embeds but before any assignments there were test embeds, to see which of the journalists could handle living in the desert and filing stories and photos under incredibly austere conditions. Surprisingly, many could, and with very little whining.

I was not enamored of the idea of having reporters trail us everywhere we went. My initial reaction to the whole thing was that they were going to get in the way and detract from our mission. Having a journalist along meant one more person for whom I would be responsible but who I felt would not add to the combat-effectiveness of the company. I did not want to change anything we did, whether in training or combat, simply to deal with the media. We ended up doing that on several occasions during training, though, usually when the television stars and their producers started demanding our time and presence.

For the most part, when reporters came around I gave my executive officer, 1st Lt. Shane Williams, the job of media liaison. Like me, Williams was a former enlisted soldier. A native of Plant City, Florida, he got into the Persian Gulf War near the end with the 11th Armored Cavalry Regiment. Williams enjoyed dealing with reporters. He was a good storyteller and a gifted impressionist, and the reporters liked being around him.

But none of us was prepared for a tragedy that occurred during the 2nd Brigade Combat Team's final live-fire exercise. A French television crew, part of the media horde that descended, was headed by Patrick Bourrat, who was something of a legend in French television for his coverage of wars all over the world. I had limited contact with that crew, which spent much of its time around the task force tactical operations center (TOC).

On Saturday, 21 December, we were in the final two days of the exercise. Charlie Company tanks were involved in an operation in which we were to move through a lane, or breach, cut in a barbed wire obstacle. When a breach lane is opened, our tactics call for us to get through as quickly as possible so we do not become an easy target for antitank weapons or chemical or biological agents that could be dispersed around that chokepoint. Infantry is instructed to steer well clear of the breach because of the speed with which tanks move through. Once a 70-ton tank starts moving at high speed, it's tough to stop in a hurry.

On this day a number of journalists were watching the breach operations, Bourrat and his crew among them. Maj. Mike Donovan, the task force operations officer, escorted Bourrat, telling him where to stand and pointing out the danger areas. Then, just as the Red Three tank with the rather ominous name of *Call Yo' Chaplain* on its gun tube charged into the breach with dust flying everywhere, Bourrat ran out of the protected area and into the path of the tank.

The left front fender of the tank hit Bourrat and tossed him about fifteen feet into a pile of concertina wire. Larrico Alexander, the commander of Red Three, ordered the tank to stop immediately. But immediately can take some time with a vehicle that size traveling at 20 to 25 miles per hour. Medics were called and Bourrat was given immediate first aid. Alexander, a fun-loving soldier with a quick quip for anyone in earshot, took it hard. But I told him and the crew there was nothing they could do. They were doing exactly what they were supposed to do. There was just no time for anyone to react when Bourrat inexplicably ran into the breach lane.

The exercise was delayed briefly as a medical evacuation helicopter was called to take the injured reporter to a hospital in Kuwait City. Bourrat did not appear to be hurt too badly, and reports indicated he was badly bruised but suffered only four broken ribs. Saturday night, he called the task force and said he would likely leave the hospital the next day. But further tests run that night revealed a ruptured spleen and a damaged kidney. Bourrat's condition worsened quickly, and he died Sunday morning. We were shocked when we heard that, especially after first being told he had survived, was not seriously injured, and was expected to get out of the hospital that day. What made a horrific incident worse was that U.S.-French relations were already at low ebb because of France's unwillingness to support President Bush's position on Iraq.

The investigation that followed exonerated the task force. The soldiers were doing their jobs, just as they were trained, and had had no time to react. It was a tragic example of how quickly someone could get injured or killed out here even during training. It was a sobering lesson to many of the journalists who sometimes had a very cavalier attitude about dangers facing them in the coming war.

Not all our early media experiences were bad. Dianne Sawyer of ABC's *Good Morning, America* visited us just before Christmas. The soldiers enjoyed the exposure we got on national television. Trivino got to talk to his pregnant wife back in Savannah.

Another of our soldiers, Pfc. Maximiliano Guerra of Miami, was quite popular with the TV crews. Guerra had a younger brother, Gonzalo, in the task force's Alpha Company. A third brother, Alvaro, was scheduled to join them shortly. It was unusual to have two brothers in the same combat unit, but to have three was almost unheard of since World War II. The military frowns on such things and has since 1942 when five Sullivan brothers serving on the *U.S.S. Juneau* died when the ship sank after being torpedoed by a Japanese submarine. The Guerras were required to sign waivers to be able to serve in combat units at the same time, and the patriotism of the three made it a natural television story.

While these were distractions, they were welcome distractions. We had finished our training, and the soldiers needed a break from their mind-numbing daily routines. When the brigade-level exercise was completed and the bulk of our training was done, we were able to relax a bit at Christmas and enjoy a few days' rest after an intense three months. We were still very much unclear about what was going to happen. We talked among ourselves about being over here as little more than a show of force. We were the real-life muscle behind the ongoing diplomatic negotiations that many hoped would reach a peaceful settlement in Iraq. Many of us thought Saddam would give up and give in, or at least buy a little more time for himself. I think most of the soldiers were hoping for a peaceful solution, even though we were preparing for war.

Christmas night we gathered around a huge bonfire in the middle of Camp Pennsylvania. Just about every spare piece of wood we could find—packing crates, shipping pallets, and plywood—was thrown on the pile. The stack was at least 25 feet high by the time it was set on fire. The task force chaplain, Capt. Ron Cooper, donated several pounds of Starbucks coffee from his personal stash that he was never without. The coffee was brewed and set out in large, five-gallon containers. Capt. Joe Linn, the task force administrative officer, broke out cigars he received as a Christmas gift and passed them out to the soldiers. Cooper also handed out song sheets with the words to Christmas carols.

We stood around the fire, drinking Starbucks coffee, smoking cigars, singing Christmas carols, and thinking of home. That Christmas was filled with uncertainty for all of us. Were we going home? Were we going to war? Or would be stuck out here in the desert for months while politicians and diplomats wrangled and haggled over who was going to do what? We felt we had kept our end of the bargain. We worked and trained hard. We were ready to do whatever they wanted us to do. We just wanted them to tell us to do something. The last thing we wanted to do was sit around the desert and wait for someone to make a decision.

5

THE WAIT IN KUWAIT

BY 1 January 2003, we were well into a planned period of repairs and maintenance on the tanks, getting them ready for a war many of us were not yet convinced was going to be fought. We had not seen a plan, although we kept hearing bits and pieces about what we might be doing. At that time we were probably less informed about what was going on than most of our friends and families back home because of our isolation in the Kuwaiti desert. The Internet was a great source of news when we could get to it, but that was infrequently. Many times the best news came from soldiers who managed to get through to a loved one at home after standing for hours waiting for a telephone at one of the base camps. The families were getting news. We were getting rumors. But often it was difficult sorting out the fact from the fiction once it worked its way from family to soldier and then through the ranks.

So we waited, impatiently most of the time, as thousands of fresh troops and tons of equipment poured into the camps northwest of Kuwait City. In late January we were forced to pack up and leave our relatively comfortable digs at Camp Pennsylvania and move back to Camp New York. Much of what we owned was packed into military vans for storage or shipment home. We went to Camp New York with only what we would take to war with us if we went, and what we needed to be comfortable in the interim. We were crowded into tents with far less living space than we had at Camp Pennsylvania. Still, we had to start building a new infrastructure in this constricted environment while we continued to train because we did not know how long we would be here. Our new home was a few miles closer to Kuwait City and Camp Doha, but it was so crowded in all the camps that it was difficult to find a spot to be alone, much less move around. Going to the Post Exchange or trying to make a telephone call often proved to be all-day affairs.

Among the new arrivals in mid-January were soldiers from the division's 3rd Brigade Combat Team, back in Kuwait after spending more than six months training here during the spring and summer of 2002.

With the arrival of 3rd BCT, all that was left to fill out the division's three combat maneuver brigades was the 1st BCT, which originally was scheduled to be our replacement in March. But division officials were speeding up the timetable and were going to get that brigade here much sooner. Any hopes that they would replace us, allowing us to go home, were pretty much tossed out the window. Some of the soldiers were still hoping it would happen, including many in Charlie Company. I tried to get their minds off going home and keep them focused on going to war, but it was difficult given the uncertainty of the situation.

It was obvious to all of us something was brewing. The new troops, supplies, and equipment were everywhere. The level of activity along the trails that led to the camp and on Highway 80, the main paved road leading south to Camp Doha, was picking up noticeably. The rhetoric coming out of Washington and Baghdad also was increasing in intensity and frequency. Soldiers were smart enough to read these signs and know what they could mean for them. What I tried to impress on them was that it was in their best interests to have their tanks and all their weapons ready to go to war. Despite their longings for home, most of them threw themselves into the repairs and maintenance with the fervor of a sixteen-year-old polishing his new car for the first time.

If these were the tanks we were going to take into battle, the soldiers wanted everything on them to be perfect. If there was one minor problem or defect, there was tension. The soldiers wanted things corrected immediately. But the maintenance team was over-whelmed. And while the mechanics worked long hours, there never seemed to be enough time for them to fix everything that every-body wanted fixed.

It was not that the tanks were in bad shape. In fact, when we picked them up at Camp Doha in September, they were in far bet-ter shape than anything we trained on at Fort Stewart. But we drove them relentlessly during training. To a certain degree, we abused the tanks. But it was abuse only in the sense that we trained with them as if we were going to war. We skipped them off berms and ran them in the heat and the cold, and through dust storms and rainstorms, until just about any other tank would have croaked right there. They had been put through the wringer for the past four months. As had we.

But all that abuse was having a cumulative effect. Only a few had severe maintenance problems, but just about every tank had minor difficulties. If it was not badly worn road wheels, it was road wheel arms. If it wasn't road wheel arms, it was a torsion bar or a genera-tor or batteries. Since track, road wheels, and road wheel arms take the most abuse in a tank, special attention was paid to those items. A tank without track is not exactly useless, but it's not going any-where. And bad road wheels and road wheel arms can mean prob-lems for the track. But these were all problems that could be fixed with time and enough spare parts.

The air induction system in the Abrams is another critical com-ponent. Charlie Company soldiers were very meticulous about keeping the air induction system cleaned and free of the powderlike sand that worked its way into every tiny little crevice and stuck like sandpaper to every lubricated part. Whenever they got a chance, the soldiers would clean the precleaner, which filters out the big stuff, and blow out the V-Pacs, the large filters that keep the fine dust from getting into the engine. They knew from experience that a clogged filter will slow down the turbine engine before they real-ize it, causing it to overheat or freeze up.

At times the soldiers became very emotional about getting fixes for the tanks. They would do almost anything to get their tanks up and running. Sometimes they would pray. Sometimes they would even call in the chaplain to see if he could work some of his magic.

Chaplain Cooper was a tall, easy-going former Church of the Nazarene minister who could have gotten out of the Army before we were deployed to Kuwait but decided to stick with us when word got around that we might be going to war. He wanted to be with his soldiers. The soldiers, in turn, liked him because he always brought a sense of peace and rightness wherever he went. He helped give us a sense of balance to what we were doing and what we were about to do.

In October, my first platoon had its hands full with maintenance problems on its four tanks. The crews would spend hours and hours, often into the early morning, on the tank line working with the mechanics to get things running right. But at one point it got so bad that Sgt. Carlos Hernandez, the gunner on Red One and a first-rate mechanic in his own right, had had enough. He thought his tank, *Creeping Death*, the platoon leader's tank, was cursed. Or possessed by demons. Or both. He decided to seek help from a higher power.

About two o'clock one morning, Hernandez rousted Cooper from his cot and asked the chaplain to come bless all the first platoon tanks. It did not matter that Hernandez was Catholic and Cooper a Protestant. A groggy Cooper put on his glasses, slipped on his boots, and made his way to the tank line. He said a quick prayer over the tanks and then baptized each of the 70-ton vehicles. As he was splashing something on the tanks, the soldiers sniffed the air.

"Is that cologne, chaplain?" Hernandez asked.

"It'll work," a sleepy Cooper mumbled and went back to bed.

And it did work for a while. It was either that or the hard work of my mechanics, led by Sgt. 1st Class Solomon Ball, the mechanic team chief, and S.Sgt. Michael Williams, the maintenance NCO. Maybe it was a combination of efforts. It was not until the war that Red's tanks started having problems again.

For me, the bottom line was getting the tanks repaired. I would be satisfied if they could shoot, move, and communicate, and if the nuclear, biological, and chemical (NBC) protective systems worked. Everything else was a bonus. They did not have to be perfect. They just had to be able to kill Iraqi T-72 tanks and anything else we faced on the road to Baghdad.

We took a lot of our cues during this time from Schwartz, the battalion commander. He is one of those commanders always leaning forward, always looking for what is just over the horizon. He kept pushing us as if we were going to war at any moment because he knew it was easier to ramp down if it did not happen than it would be to ramp up. So we stayed keyed up, or at least as much as we could without having any clear sense of what might happen.

During January and on into February, I was especially hard on the soldiers about maintenance on the vehicles and personal discipline. I was getting tougher and tougher on them. Neither 1st Sergeant Mercado nor I tolerated sloppiness or laziness. I wanted to bring everybody back alive should we go to war. I did not know if I could do that, but I was going to do what I could to make it happen. I had served briefly as a casualty assistance officer during my time in Germany and experienced what the sight of a flag-draped coffin does to a family. I did not want any of the families of my soldiers to have to go through that. I felt if I were hard on them, they would be hard on themselves, and harder still on the Iraqis. And that gave them all a better chance of surviving this war.

We tried to maintain tight discipline during this time. Our training opportunities were limited, and the soldiers had a lot more free time with little to do except get into trouble. It was difficult finding trouble so far out in the desert with no alcohol and few other distractions. But if there is trouble to be found, young soldiers can find it. So we held a lot more formations and scheduled training than some of the other units in the division.

But it was maintenance that occupied most of our time. I stressed maintenance until the soldiers were sick of hearing about it. Many of them did not understand why I was so meticulous. They thought it was because I wanted to maintain a high operational readiness rate so it would look good on the records and impress higher command. But I was not doing it to impress anybody. I was doing it to have those vehicles prepared for war. We were the unit in theater at the time and would most likely be the first across the border. I wanted the tanks to be able to respond to that call.

A tank company is supposed to have an Operational Readiness Rate of 90 percent. We were consistently above 90 percent, despite the challenges of the dust and a lack of spare parts. We had plenty of time for maintenance but getting spare parts was always a problem. We felt the logistics folks were hoarding them for a war stock. Whatever they were doing with them, they weren't sending them down to us. And it would be that way throughout the war. My soldiers became very creative at "finding" spare parts. Ball and Williams the mechanic were incredible scroungers. They always seemed to be able to find parts, whether at Camp Doha or out in the desert.

Part of the maintenance included weekly checks on the tank NBC systems to make sure they worked. When I would pass the word to check the systems, someone would grumble: "We did that just last week."

"Well, do it again," I would tell them.

One of my biggest concerns was the possible threat we were facing from weapons of mass destruction. We did marches with heavy rucksacks at NTC and Fort Stewart in full MOPP gear to get soldiers used to the system. We were continually checking their canteens to make sure they had the proper NBC caps for them and that the drinking tubes worked. The caps were in short supply in theater, and while everyone had at least one, each was supposed to have three. I asked about the caps at every battalion-level meeting I attended. I felt it was my duty as Charlie Company commander to make sure my soldiers all had the proper equipment.

In late January, just as we were completing intensive maintenance on the tanks, the company went through one of those changes that left all of us concerned about unit integrity and the cohesion we built up over the last four months of training.

My third platoon, or Blue, had been under the leadership of 1st Lt. Courtney Jones since the previous March. The soldiers liked him, trusted him, and worked well with him. I was confident in his abilities as a platoon leader and was not worried about him taking Blue to war. Now, on the apparent eve of that war, Jones was yanked out of the mix and sent to battalion as an intelligence ana-lyst. There wasn't much we could do about it but grit our teeth and make the best out of what we thought would be a bad situation.

It turned out to be not nearly as bad as we expected. In fact, it worked out quite well for us. Jones' replacement was 2nd Lt. Erik Balascik, of Tamaqua, Pennsylvania, a 2002 graduate of West Point and only a few months out of the Armor Officer Basic Course at Fort Knox. He had had a brief stop at Fort Stewart before being shipped to us in Kuwait. He was as young and as green as second lieutenants come.

Rather than being disruptive as I had feared, the change in the platoon actually forced it to focus more on its training at a time when there were not a lot of training opportunities. Balascik was a bright, easy-going officer. He had all the basics of leadership and tanking. What he did not have was the experience of working with our soldiers in the desert or the knowledge that only years of tank-ing could bring.

But Balascik was a quick learner. He let his senior NCOs in the platoon know that he did not know it all and would rely a great deal on their experience and judgment. He took the tank com-manders aside and told them to tell him when he did something wrong. All he asked was that they not embarrass him in front of the soldiers. He was eager to learn and asked a lot of questions. Schwartz, the task force commander, talked to Sergeant 1st Class Richard, the platoon sergeant for Blue, and told him to work closely with Balascik. Richard, one of my more experienced and levelheaded soldiers, was skeptical of Balascik at first because of his inexperience and his age. Balascik was nearly fifteen years Richard's junior.

I had my doubts as well. But they went away after just a few weeks. The turning point was when Blue served as one of the opposing force (OPFOR) units in a training exercise with a unit from the division that had only recently arrived in the country. Blue was the only tank platoon in an OPFOR contingent that included engineers, infantry, and scouts. During the exercise Blue destroyed an entire company, captured a fuel train, and left MILES lights blinking all over the desert. After that, I had no concerns about Balascik or third platoon. I knew they would do just fine and would be able to handle anything I asked of them, which proved to be true just a few weeks down the road.

As we waited and waited in Kuwait for some word about something, it was obvious to just about everyone we were getting restless. To help take the edge off, we made several trips into Kuwait City. We got to dress in civilian clothes and feel almost normal again as we walked around the glitzy, immaculate malls that are all over the city. The soldiers got a chance to eat fast-food hamburgers, sip some Starbucks coffee, and buy Cuban cigars. It wasn't much, but after living for so long in the desert and focusing on nothing but our tanks and our training, these trips were a great stress buster and made us feel close to human.

Also during this time, the soldiers began receiving a series of anthrax and smallpox inoculations in the event those biological warfare agents were used against us. Again, everybody gritted their teeth and put up with it. And in an environment where no one was particularly fastidious except for 1st Sergeant Mercado, we suddenly had to become conscious of staying clean to prevent infection of the inoculation site and so we would not infect anyone else.

We were given a brochure listing smallpox inoculation "dos and don'ts." Don't touch the inoculation site. Wash your hands frequently. Don't let anyone touch the inoculation site or clothes that came in contact with it. Do not share a bed, bunk, or cot with anyone. Do not share clothes, towels, linen, or toiletries. Wear shirts with sleeves. Use bandages. Avoid rubbing. Avoid swimming—like there was anyplace to get wet in that big sandbox.

But staying as clean as the brochure cautioned was a physical impossibility. Dust and dirt were everywhere. The constant pounding of feet and tracked vehicles turned the grainy sand into powder as fine and white as talcum. When the wind blew, the dust coated everything from cots to laptop computers to every piece of clothing and gear we owned. And when it rained, that dust turned into a caking, cloying mud that was not unlike cement when it dried.

Still, we all managed to survive with just a few sore arms to show for it and no short-term adverse affects.

The issue of combat, and how we would deal with it, became a topic of frequent discussion among Charlie Company soldiers during this waiting period. Although there was a lot of posturing and tough-guy talk among the soldiers, I could tell there were serious concerns about how some of the soldiers would handle themselves when they came under fire.

Not many Charlie Company soldiers were veterans of the Gulf War. 1st Sergeant Mercado, Waterhouse, and Shane Williams were there, all as junior enlisted soldiers. The rest of us knew about war only as we saw it in the movies or on television.

So we spent a lot of time in January and February listening to Mercado and Waterhouse talk about what combat was like. Mercado did an excellent job relating his experiences in the Gulf War, providing great insights into how Charlie Company soldiers might react to the sight of dead bodies, or pieces of bodies, for the first time. We wanted the soldiers to be aware they would likely see things they would never see again, and never want to see again. We wanted them to think about it so it was not something that would cause them to freeze the first time they encountered them.

We also talked about being shot at, about artillery landing next to the tank, about the tank commanders being killed or wounded and how the crews should react. We talked about what they should do if the first sergeant or I were killed or seriously wounded. We talked about what Iraqi vehicles would look like when they were hit, with balls of flame erupting and turrets popping off. I had a bunch of the Gulf War videos we watched to acquaint the soldiers with that aspect of tank warfare.

I never had any doubts my soldiers and I would not be able to handle combat. What I feared most was getting hit with a chemical attack and losing a number of my soldiers. I went over in my own mind what decisions I might have to make. I was concerned about making the wrong decision, or a poorly timed decision, that would cost someone his life. I wanted to make sure before we went into combat that I had made every effort to get them the right equipment and the proper training.

We talked through all these issues at length. But what we never talked about through January and on into February was urban warfare. Combat in the cities was just not on our radar screen because of guidance from higher in the chain command.

After convincing ourselves that we would not go into cities, we began getting some signals that we might have to unconvince ourselves. Task Force 3-15, the 2nd BCT's infantry heavy battalion, conducted some training on military operations in urban terrain (MOUT). But 3-15 was infantry, and that is what infantry is supposed to do. We were tankers, and tankers just don't go into the cities. Tanks sit outside cities and pound the heck out of whoever is in there and let the infantry do the dirty work.

Charlie Rock, the infantry company from 3-15 added to our task force, also went through the MOUT training at a small mock village out in the desert. There were a few ramshackle, crumbling buildings there, but by no stretch of the imagination could that be considered a reasonable facsimile for urban terrain. Still, that was what the infantry did. Tankers did not because we had too few soldiers and lacked the necessary assets to both clear buildings and continue to fight the tanks. Even Schwartz reinforced the fact that if we went to war, the tanks would not fight in the cities. That was good enough for me and my soldiers.

Then, in early February, the division brought in a team of retired soldiers to talk to us about urban warfare. Blount, the division commander, was there, along with all the company commanders. My initial reaction was: "This is interesting, but I don't plan on doing this. This is not something we trained to do. And it's a bit late to be bringing it up now."

The more they talked, though, the more apprehensive I became. They talked about Somalia and Mogadishu and what happened there: how Humvees and armored vehicles bogged down and were shot up and killed in the streets, how communications were disrupted by the buildings, how it would be difficult to evacuate casualties by helicopter in the middle of an urban fight, and how any ground medical evacuation would be susceptible to more enemy fire.

I went back and broke the bad news to my soldiers: maybe we would be going into the cities. "We need to get real smart in a big hurry," I told them.

Because most of my soldiers were trained tankers, few had any experience dealing with urban warfare. My officers and I were given some brief sessions in MOUT warfare during the Armor Officer Basic Course at Fort Knox. But we were on the ground at the time, not in tanks. The idea of rolling a tank into a city and fighting there was a new concept for all of us.

We started doing some classes on urban warfare. The briefers at the division-level session handed out a compact disc with information on urban training and fact sheets on the inability of the main guns on the Abrams to elevate more than twenty degrees above horizontal or more than ten degrees below horizontal. I told the soldiers we would not be going in by ourselves but that we would most likely be used to grab a foothold so the division could expand out from wherever we stopped. We discussed supplies, or lack thereof, and getting casualties evacuated quickly and safely.

I knew we were proficient and trained to do what we were supposed to do—kill tanks and other armored vehicles at great distances. If we were in the open desert, Charlie Company soldiers could kill anything in sight. But we had not talked about urban warfare and civilians, about power lines and sewers, about humanitarian efforts. I drew from my experiences in Bosnia and tried to get them thinking about what life would be like if we ever went into a city.

The unwelcome prospect of urban warfare got us thinking about reconfiguring our load plan for tank main gun rounds. Each tank carries forty-two 120mm main gun rounds, seventeen of those in a hydraulically operated ready rack. We had a choice of three types of rounds: the M829A1 SABOT, the M830A1 HEAT (High Explosive Anti-Tank), or the M830 MPAT (Multi-Purpose Anti-Tank).

My initial plan was to go heavy on SABOT because we were expecting to fight armored vehicles in the desert. The SABOT is lighter than the other two at forty-eight pounds but it is considered a sure tank killer. It is a kinetic energy weapon. It has a depleted uranium penetrator that acts like a magic dart that slices through armor. It also has an extremely high muzzle velocity and goes into the target small but comes out big, sucking everything inside out with it. It is most effective on targets beyond two thousand meters.

Earlier models of the SABOT were referred to as the "Silver Bullet" during the first Gulf War because of their ability to take out any piece of armor the Iraqis put on the battlefield.

The HEAT round, weighing in at fifty-one pounds, is a killer in its own right and can take out everything from vehicles to bunkers to light armored vehicles. It is often used as a confirmation round after firing a SABOT. The SABOT will knock out an armored vehicle, but sometimes if the turret does not pop off, the vehicle is still operational. The HEAT round provides the explosives to set it on fire, pop the turret, and start the ammunition inside cooking off.

The MPAT round is the heaviest of the three: fifty-three pounds. Its great value is that it has a proximity fuse and can be used against ground or air targets. It is more of a penetrator than the HEAT round and is a great bunker buster. In some lengthy conversations with my master gunner, S.Sgt. Jabari Williams, we thought if we were going into cities, either by ourselves or in support of infantry, having a number of MPAT rounds would be helpful to punch holes in walls for the infantry to get through or to kill anything behind the walls.

Our initial load plan called for each tank to carry roughly fifteen SABOT, eleven HEAT, and sixteen MPAT rounds. Each platoon's Alpha section would be heavier on SABOT because they likely would be the first to encounter enemy armor. The Bravo sections would be heavier on HEAT or MPAT.

Our plan sounded wonderful in theory. But it fell apart in a hurry. The problem was that there was a shortage of MPAT rounds in theater. Someone apparently decided, as we had, that this war would be a reprise of Gulf War I, a tank-on-tank battle in the desert. MPAT rounds seemed to be an unneeded addition to the arsenal. But we did not find that out until we started to upload our go-to-war ammo.

On 22 February, the news that we would start loading our main gun ammo the next day sent a buzz through the company unlike anything else we had heard in a while. People were still not convinced we were going to war. But the fact that we were finally going to get our 120mm rounds after they had been stored away in the Ammunition Holding Area for all these months—presumably in case the Iraqis came across the border—got everybody excited. The discussions about who would carry what type of rounds, what each tank would battle-carry in the main gun, and what would be available in the ready racks only intensified. But it was good for us at that time. It got the soldiers refocused on going to war and took their minds off going home.

Our training was complete, we had our go-to-war ammunition, and we were getting psyched up and ready to go. Now all we needed was a plan. Within a few days we got the word again: pack up and move out. On 28 February we left the relative comfort of the terribly crowded Camp New York and moved out into an assembly area in the desert named Rogue Zero, the starting point on the road to Baghdad for Task Force 1-64, the Desert Rogues. It was there that we would get the plan that would take us to Baghdad.

6

THE PLAN: HEAVY METAL AND ROCK 'N ROLL

ROGUE Zero was nothing more than another patch of feature-less desert in a country overrun with featureless desert. It was slightly closer to Kuwait City than any of the other camps. On a good night, when the wind was not blowing and the dust was not swirling, far to the east we could see the string of lights along High-way 80. Directly to the west was Camp New York. A few miles to the north and west were Camps New York and Pennsylvania. To the South was Camp Virginia.

We knew when we left for Rogue Zero that there would be abso-lutely nothing there. No tents. No telephones. No latrines. No showers. No amenities of any sort. It was expected that we would live and work and sleep on the tanks until they called us and told us to execute whatever plan developed. But no one could tell us with any certainty how long we would be there. I became con-cerned even before we got to Rogue Zero that the soldiers would not be as prepared as I wanted them to be if we had to spend weeks battling the elements before we were turned loose on the Iraqis.

The weather was getting warmer as we headed into March. But the nights were still cold. And the desert windstorms, or *shamals*, can get downright nasty at that time of year. We had already experienced a few, and they were not pleasant.

It was tough enough to work in that environment, much less sleep. I wanted my soldiers to be well rested before they went to war. They could not do that on their vehicles. If we were called to fight, it would be in everyone's best interests to have well-rested soldiers. The bits and pieces we were hearing about the attack plan called for us to drive twenty-four hours at the start of the war, and I wanted my soldiers fresh before we made the push across the border. Of course, the first sergeant and I wanted the same thing. There was no reason to make life harder than it already was.

Shortly before we moved to Rogue Zero, I made a run to Camp Doha to see if I could put my hands on some tents. We were short of crew tents, as was every unit in the task force. We were told to not bring them with us from Fort Stewart, that tents would be waiting for us in Kuwait. They were, but looked like large circus tents, were relatively permanent structures, and could not be moved. We needed something smaller that could be moved quickly.

I took two of my best scroungers with me, Sergeant 1st Class Ball and Staff Sergeant Williams, the mechanic, and we spent the day poking around the base, asking questions and nagging people until they got sick of us. Finally, late in the day, we found one warehouse with a bunch of tents that were to be thrown out. We checked them out and found most had one or two small holes in them, but that was not going to bother us. We found two relatively serviceable general-purpose medium tents, stuffed them in the back of our Humvee and headed back to the desert. I told the supply people to put them on my property books and I would deal with them later.

The tents were a real boon for us. We used one for our command post, where we could serve hot chow and set up our maps that would lead us north to Baghdad. I also put a DVD player and TV in there so when soldiers had some downtime they could watch movies to relieve some of the boredom and stress. It was good for them to be able to sit down for an hour or so and watch a movie and not think about where they were or what they were about to do. We also built showers and latrines and put up a volleyball net. There was no reason to keep stress elevated to unreasonable levels.

By early March, planning for the invasion of Iraq was well into its eighth month. Unknown to us, it started back at Fort Stewart in July 2002, when a group of about fifteen planners under the guidance of Blount and the division G-3, Lt. Col. Peter Bayer, began putting together various highly classified scenarios that were all designed to take out the Iraqi regime. The planners did not know what other assets would be in theater if the fight came so they developed a wide variety of plans that called for us to fight with everything from a single brigade to an enhanced division.

Blount, the division commander, challenged the operations group early in their planning to be creative and innovative. He advised them that it was likely the division could go to war with either less than a full complement of forces, or with far more responsibility than a division is normally given. He wanted the planners to get out of the comfort zone of doing things the way the Army and the division normally planned and not to be afraid to take risks with their schemes and concepts. By the time we left for Kuwait in September, the planners were running full-bore.

It was a virtual given that the 3rd Infantry Division would be at the center of any fight. But how that fight would be configured was the big question. There was a lot of tension among the planners over the uncertainty of who would be here and how ready we could be when the President made whatever decision he was going to make about Saddam Hussein.

The 2nd Brigade Combat Team was already in theater and had been training here for some time. The planners even gave some thought to keeping the 3rd Brigade Combat Team in Kuwait instead of sending it home in the fall. But the uncertainty of the situation precluded that, and the 3rd BCT's soldiers went home to Fort Benning. Some were home for more than three months, but a few managed only six weeks with their loved ones.

In January and February we were told that the 2nd Brigade Combat Team would focus its efforts in the vicinity of the airfield at Jalibah in south-central Iraq. It was much the same ground our predecessors, the 24th Infantry Division (Mechanized), fought over and won decisively a dozen years earlier. Schwartz, as a young company commander, had been among those soldiers and now was being asked to retake the same ground.

Some versions of early plans involved the entire division and were oriented on Nasiriyah and the destruction of the Iraqi 11th Infantry Division. That was seen as an infantry fight supported by division artillery and attack helicopters. The 3rd Brigade Combat Team, an infantry heavy brigade, was assigned the task of taking out the 11th Division and securing the Highway 1 bridge across the Euphrates. The 2nd BCT would then cross the river and drive straight north to take on the Medina Division, an armor division of the Republican Guard. That was to be the main fight, an armor fight, a fight for which we trained and prepared.

The Medina Division was scattered throughout the suburbs leading into Baghdad from the south. Our fight would not be an open desert fight as was the last war. The terrain would be somewhat restricted because of the small towns and other built-up areas. There were also a large number of small agricultural canals and irrigation ditches in the area that made cross-country movement impossible and forced us to travel on roads. But it was not something that gave anyone cause for great concern at the time. There were still no plans to send the 3rd Infantry Division's armor into major urban areas, including Baghdad.

The thinking was that the destruction of the Medina Division south of Baghdad would force Iraqi commanders to shuffle other Republican Guard Divisions defending the gates of the capital. That, the planners felt, was one of the key elements that would bring about the downfall of Saddam Hussein and his regime. We could move faster and with more firepower than his forces. Once the Medina Division was destroyed and Iraqi units started repositioning to bolster the defenses of Baghdad, we could take advantage of the confusion, slip through the seams, and beat them to the stronghold of Saddam's empire.

The planners reasoned that the 3rd Infantry Division and whatever other assets it would have could never destroy all of Saddam's military. But they believed that if we took away one of his key divisions, the Medina, he would be forced to move others, making them vulnerable to attacks from the air. If the Medina disappeared, we would be sitting at the gates of Baghdad before Saddam or his commanders had time to react.

But they also knew that the further they got into the campaign, the murkier it got in terms of how the Iraqis would react to what we were doing. The enemy always has a vote in how these things go, so there were no assurances the Iraqis would respond as they did during the Persian Gulf War, with mass surrenders. If Saddam decided to withdraw his forces to Baghdad and slug it out there, the plan was for the Army's V Corps forces west of the Tigris River and the Marine Corps forces on the east side of the river to secure objectives around the city and create a noose from which there would be no escape. When that was accomplished, we would run armor raids into the city to destroy or seize enemy forces and key installations to hasten the regime's fall.

At the end of January and during the first week of February, the division's senior leadership went to Germany for a simulation-based exercise to work out kinks in the plan with V Corps, which would be our higher headquarters during the war. Some of the plans were developed with the idea that multiple Army divisions, the 3rd, the 4th, the 1st Cavalry, and the 101st Airborne, would be in on the attack as part of V Corps. We kept hearing about the 4th Infantry Division out of Fort Hood, Texas, trying to get in through Turkey. But the Turks did not approve of that and toward the end of the exercise the word went out that V Corps would most likely have only the 3rd ID, 101st Airborne Division, and 3rd Armored Cavalry Regiment available to go to war.

V Corps and the division began to rethink how they were going to carry the fight to the Iraqis. One option was to keep the 3rd Infantry Division south and west of the Euphrates River. That was considered but was not fully developed as a plan because of the belief that additional forces would be in theater and part of the attack. If those forces were available, the 2nd Brigade Combat Team would be able to attack directly north on Highways 1, supported by the 1st BCT attacking to our west along Highway 8 toward Baghdad once the Euphrates River Bridge at Nasiriyah was taken.

The final decision was to keep the 3rd Infantry Division west and south of the Euphrates River during the first phase of the operation, which for the division was code-named Operation Cobra. The name seemed fitting to us since that was Charlie Company's nickname, but I know we had absolutely no influence on the choice.

Under this plan, the 1st Brigade would drive north from its tactical assembly area in northwestern Kuwait and take the airfield at Jalibah. The 3rd Brigade would bypass Jalibah en route to Tallil and the Euphrates. The 2nd Brigade would make a wide sweep into the southern desert of Iraq and come up behind the Medina Division. The 1st Brigade, an infantry heavy brigade, would support our fight against the Medina Division. Gone was the plan for a frontal assault on the Medina Division. Now, we were looking at a variation of the "Big Left Hook" during the first Gulf War, when the 24th Infantry Division and 101st and 82nd Airborne divisions swept into Iraq from the west and south, trapping enemy troops in Kuwait.

It was difficult then for the Iraqis to track units in the far western desert because Special Operations forces and air strikes took out their listening and observation posts early in the fighting. It would be even more difficult this time. If the division did not cross the bridge at Nasiriyah, the Iraqis might know we were out there in the desert, but finding us would be a problem.

Instead of a frontal assault on the Medina Division, the plan now called for an enveloping maneuver. The purpose, however, was the same: destroy one of the premier divisions in the Iraqi Army and send a message to Saddam and his henchmen. We hoped that message would hasten the downfall of the regime and the capitulation of the Iraqi military, sparing the destruction of Baghdad and the loss of thousands of civilian lives.

The 2nd Brigade Combat Team was responsible for destroying the Medina Division with its 211 tanks, 293 armored personnel carriers, and sixty-nine towed artillery pieces. We would be outnumbered and outgunned nearly 3–1. The brigade had just seventy tanks and sixty Bradley fighting vehicles. But the belief was that our firepower was so superior to their outdated armor and ammunition—degraded by a lack of spare parts and years of wear-and-tear—we, in combination with our air strikes, would significantly reduce their effectiveness. For Task Force 1-64, the Desert Rogues, the focus was on the Iraqi 2nd Armor Brigade, which had ninety tanks (most of them T-72s), fifty-six armored personnel carriers, and twenty-one BMPs.

Whatever solution the planners looked at, they knew the Iraqis were no match for us in terms of firepower, manpower, and resources. By the first week of February, division planners finalized their schemes and were working on operations orders.

The big problem with the new route we would take was terrain. There were few roads, dirt or otherwise, out there. It was trackless desert, with lots of deep *wadis* and shifting sand. Getting to where we needed to go would be difficult and time-consuming. But it was not considered an insurmountable obstacle. It would just require more from the men and the machines. Perkins, the brigade commander, said it was not unlike Hannibal taking the elephants over the Alps. "Only in this case the Alps are deep *wadis* and the elephants are 70-ton tanks," he was fond of saying.

It was apparent from the maps and the briefings that supply and communications lines would be stretched to the breaking point. The 2nd BCT would start its attack into Iraq from southwestern Kuwait, far removed from its brother brigades. To complicate matters further, the brigade would be divided into two combat elements: Heavy Metal and Rock 'n Roll.

Heavy Metal would include all the brigade armor: seventy tanks, sixty Bradley fighting vehicles, and an assortment of M113 armored personnel carriers. It would make a tough, direct, cross-country dash to a spot in the desert south of the city of Samawah called Objective Martin. The Rock 'n Roll element contained all the wheeled vehicles in the brigade and would take a southerly, circuitous route along a more navigable stretch of desert that included some dirt and paved roads. The two elements would link up at Objective Martin. In total, the brigade would have more than 2,000 vehicles going across the border.

In addition to Heavy Metal and Rock 'n Roll, there would be a Task Force Wadi, made up of engineers to help clear the way through the berms and over and around tough spots in the desert. There would also be a Team Fix, well stocked with mechanics and spare parts to get us through this first tough stretch of desert.

Enemy contact was expected to be minimal or virtually nonexistent along both routes. No heavy opposition was anticipated until we got near Karbala, about sixty miles southwest of Baghdad. We might see some Iraqi forces in the vicinity of the holy city of Najaf, north of Samawah, we were told, but they would most likely be reconnaissance troops.

The size of the area we had to cross just to get into position to fight was daunting. It was nearly 300 miles of difficult desert. If you were to impose that area on the eastern United States, it would cover most of Tennessee and Kentucky along with parts of North and South Carolina, Georgia, Alabama, Arkansas, Missouri, and Ohio. The run to Objective Martin was to be a twenty-hour-plus dash across the desert, a full-throttle run into the heart of enemy territory.

Fuel, food, and water were the primary concerns for this first leg of the invasion. The planners developed the maneuver concept first, and then figured out how to support it. Units were told that every vehicle that crossed the berm into Iraq was required to carry a minimum of five days of fuel, food, and water. I spent a lot of time talking with 1st Sergeant Mercado about load plans, what to take and what not to take. While I dealt primarily with the combat aspects of the company, he focused on supply and maintenance issues.

When I told him about the five-day minimum supply that was being recommended, he immediately said he thought it best we take at least ten days' supply. We would have food and water stashed in every conceivable nook and cranny of our vehicles, and looked not unlike the Beverly Hillbillies going to Baghdad, but the first sergeant was insistent that we not put the soldiers at risk of running out of food or water.

What we did not know then, and would not find out until much later, was that the "just in time" logistics plan the Army was trumpeting was based on the division having enough cargo trucks to haul the necessary supplies to the front. Division officials already were scrounging up virtually every bulk fueler they could get their hands on in Kuwait to accompany us to make sure the combat vehicles would not run dry. But many of the cargo carriers we were counting on for other supplies were not yet in theater and would not arrive until long after we got to Baghdad. Planners tried to anticipate how quickly and how far we would travel and how hard it would be to get logistics lines established. They knew it would be difficult, but it proved to be even more difficult than anyone imagined.

Throughout the planning, training, and run-up to the war, speed and power were continually emphasized as the keys to victory. The faster we got to the gates of Baghdad and sat out there with our gun tubes pointed at Saddam's regime, the more likely it was to collapse. The regular Iraqi army, full of conscripts, was not considered a significant threat. The Republican Guard and Special Republican Guard forces might present more of a challenge. But even if they fought, their two-decades-old Soviet weaponry was no match for what we could put on the battlefield. And the Iraqis had shown a predilection for turning and running, or surrendering when confronted with the superior firepower we brought to bear on them.

Veterans of the Persian Gulf War were never particularly impressed with the fighting abilities of the regular Iraqi soldier. During one of our exercises in December in which we simulated attacking a fortified position, Schwartz was on the radio directing units into attack position. Once they were ready and the firing began, Schwartz said that the enemy forces, "being the good Iraqis that they are, will probably turn and run."

To certain degree, we hoped Schwartz and the others who told us that there would be mass surrenders and defections were right. But we were primed for a fight. And the fight for which we were primed was a tank fight, either in the desert or in relatively open terrain where we could move and shoot and kill the enemy. Visions of the potential pitfalls and disasters of urban warfare all but faded for most of us. We were tankers, ready for a gunfight at two thousand meters. We did not expect, and did not want, a knife fight in a telephone booth.

7

SAND AND FURY

WE spent the first week of March 2003 learning to cope with the miserable weather that spring brings to Kuwait and southern Iraq. In a place where the weather is usually predictably bad, the spring of 2003 seemed far worse than normally bad. High winds from the north and west, blowing dust and sand, and rain were all part of the bad weather equation. The locals called these rapidly changing conditions *shamals*. We called them a pain in the butt.

When a *shamal* blew through, you could count on every piece of gear you owned getting a good dousing of sand and grit. Computers, cell phones, and DVD and MP-3 players were often rendered useless if they were not wrapped in plastic. Weapons were coated with it inside and out and required almost constant cleaning and maintenance. The sand sifted through every little crack and crevice in tents and vehicles. At nights we would have to sleep with goggles covering our eyes and scarves around our noses and mouths to keep from breathing in the dust. It was bad enough inside the tents, where dust hung in the air like a thick, brown mist. Sleeping outside was out of the question.

One of the more irritating aspects of the *shamals*, and potentially dangerous, was that at times the dust got so thick that our pluggers, the hand-held GPS devices, were useless. We could not pick up satellite signals that enabled us to pinpoint where we were or where we were going. In a trackless desert such as this, the pluggers were vital to our existence and survival. Without them we were literally and figuratively lost. At times we simply shut down all movement and hunkered down until we could get a reading on the plugger.

Our medics, S.Sgt. Mark Strunk and Spc. Shawn Sullivan, kept busy washing sand out of eyes and dispensing medication for the chronic sinus infections that plagued us during the *shamals.* The weather would go from naggingly cold to hot and then back again, often accompanied by the wind, the dust, and the rain. My soldiers were relatively healthy, but months of living in the desert made us all susceptible to sinus and eye infections.

There seemed to be no real pattern to the *shamals.* They often popped out of nowhere, presaged only by a dusty sky to the north or west and a fresh breeze. The night of 11 March was promising to be a bad one. The winds picked up and it started raining. But what we thought would be an ordinarily bad night quickly turned worse. And not because of the weather.

Just as we were preparing climb into our sleeping bags for the night, I received a radio call from the task force S-1, Capt. Joe Linn. He had some unsettling news for me.

"We're bringing a couple of media out to you," Joe told me.

"You're doing what?" I exclaimed.

Linn explained that a reporter and photographer from the *Atlanta Journal-Constitution* were being embedded with us for the war. Linn said the reporter, Ron Martz, had spent time with the task force, including Charlie Company, for a few days back in December. I only vaguely remembered him, being so focused on training at the time that I chose not to deal with the numerous journalists sent out to the company. I had given Shane Williams and 1st Sergeant Mercado the responsibility of taking care of him.

This was absolutely the last thing I expected, or wanted. I knew the division was high on the Pentagon idea of embedding several dozen journalists for the war, putting them with units so they could be up "close and personal" with the soldiers as we battled to Baghdad. But I thought they would go to task force level, or higher. And I thought it unlikely that Charlie Company would have any media assigned to it because of the incident in December involving the death of the French reporter.

My team was set. My soldiers were primed and ready for war. Throwing another unknown and untested element, or two of them, into the mix that did not add to my combat-effectiveness at this point had the potential to upset what I felt was a delicate balance. Every one of my soldiers had his job to do. I did not have anyone to spare to ride herd or serve as nursemaids to two journalists. Besides, I was wary of the whole concept of embedded media. But the orders came from above and as any good soldier, I had to salute and march on. Still, having media assigned to us was a little like being ordered to take the anthrax shots; there was nothing I could do about it but grit my teeth and try to make the best out of what I thought could become a bad situation.

As it turned out, Martz and Brant Sanderlin, the photographer, wound up being welcome additions to our little band of warriors. Sanderlin was on his first combat assignment but bonded easily with the soldiers because he was not much older than most of them. He grew up in North Carolina hunting and fishing and was comfortable living and sleeping outdoors. Martz was a former Marine with a lengthy list of combat assignments dating back to Central America in the early 1980s. He had been reporting on soldiers and Americans at war before some of my soldiers were born. He also had covered the Persian Gulf War and spent time in Bosnia and the Middle East. He was the senior citizen of our group. We thought the first sergeant was an old man at the age of forty. Martz was sixteen years his senior.

After Joe Linn's radio call, we scrambled around and found a couple of cots and a spare piece of plywood that Martz and Sanderlin could use for a desk. We set them up in the back of the command post tent where they had some shelter and access to generator-furnished electricity. We were not sure how they would fare in the austere conditions to which we had grown accustomed. But they quickly adapted to life in the desert and within a few days became part of the fabric of Charlie Company.

As the war progressed, Martz and Sanderlin became the only link my soldiers and I had with our families back home. Through their

Brant Sanderlin, the photographer from the *Atlanta Journal-Constitution* who accompanied Charlie Company during the war, files photos from the desert south of Karbala using a laptop computer and satellite telephone. His "desk" is a stack of MRE cartons. Filing was seldom this peaceful. He frequently filed while under fire. (*Brant Sanderlin/Atlanta Journal-Constitution*)

daily reports and photographs, and occasional use of their satellite telephones, our families could track our progress and see and read how we were faring. Neither the journalists nor I realized until after the war how important this was to our families.

On 12 March, the day after Martz and Sanderlin joined us, the entire task force gathered on a small rise near Task Force 1-64's TOC. Schwartz wanted to get the task force together one last time before the war for what he called a "So Help Me God Service of Reflection." He wanted the soldiers to think about what they were about to do and to rededicate themselves to their country and to the cause on which they were about to embark.

It was almost like a pregame locker room pep talk. Schwartz used the front deck of his tank as a stage with the task force arrayed around him in an open box.

"You are at the defining moment of your lives," Schwartz told the nearly 700 soldiers assembled before him.

He talked about all of us missing birthdays and anniversaries, of giving up Christmas with our families, of giving up many personal moments we would never be able to get back. But he said we were doing this not for ourselves, but out of a sense of duty and a selfless service to others that bound us together.

"You are God's ministers of justice," he intoned. "As God's representatives, know those weapons systems are being used for His justice. There are ten million people out there waiting for freedom from tyranny. That's why we are here."

It was clear from Schwartz's speech that war was in the offing, possibly only days away. There were no more pretenses about us being there for a training exercise or to defend Kuwait. We were going across the border and were heading for Baghdad to take out Saddam Hussein and his regime.

Near the end of the ceremony, the soldiers raised their right hands and in unison repeated their oath of enlistment: "I do solemnly swear that I will support and defend the Constitution of the United States against all enemies, foreign and domestic. . . ."

When it was over, Chaplain Ron Cooper performed a full immersion baptism ceremony for eight soldiers. He and some other soldiers had dug a small pit, lined it with plastic, and filled that with water for the baptisms.

This was another indicator that the soldiers knew we were getting close to heading north. God was becoming an important factor in their lives and their hearts, more so than ever before for many of them. It did not matter if they were Catholic, Protestant, Muslim, or Buddhist. Services were available for all faiths and many took advantage of the opportunity before the war to make things right with their god. They knew they might not have a chance once we crossed the border.

We hiked back to the company area and continued with our preparations. We loaded small arms ammunition for our M-16s, M-203s, and M-9s into magazines, clips, and pouches. We unsealed the first of two sets of new-style MOPP gear and went through the process of making sure it all fit and everyone knew how to put it on. The new style was known as a JSLST, for Joint Service Lightweight Integrated Suit, and we had had minimal training on its components before it was issued to us in the desert. The JSLST had a pair of charcoal-lined pants, a charcoal-lined jacket with a hood that went over the top of the protective mask, heavy rubber boots, and gloves. The training was necessary so the soldiers knew how to align the various pieces of the suit to ensure a good seal against biological or chemical agents.

We were required in training to be able to put the mask on and get a good seal in eight seconds or faster. The requirement for getting into the pants, jacket, and protective boots was eight minutes. The pants and jacket were not a major problem. But the boots were a real pain for most of us. If we went across the border in MOPP gear, the speculation was that it would be level II, meaning we would be wearing pants, jacket, and boots. Level IV, full MOPP gear, adds the protective mask and gloves. At MOPP-II we would already be wearing the items that consumed the most time to don. We would only have to put on the mask and, if necessary, the gloves, if we were hit with biological or chemical weapons.

That night one of the worst *shamals* any of us had seen yet swept through Rogue Zero. Like the others, it came virtually without warning. Our tents were popping and snapping and seemed on the verge of being torn loose from their moorings and sent sailing out into the desert night. A fine film of dust hung in the air inside even the most tightly buttoned-up tents, and just about everyone went to sleep that night with goggles and scarves over their eyes and mouths.

It was a total blackout condition outside. Move away from the tent to relieve yourself, and you ran the chance of getting lost if you wandered more than a step or two. One soldier with the task force did just that. He walked for more than a mile before he stumbled on another unit's tents and took refuge for the night. It was another one of those nights when we could do nothing but wrap ourselves in our sleeping bags and wait for morning.

But morning brought little respite from the wind or the dust. The storm abated slightly just before dawn, but regained intensity around 8 a.m. and continued through the day. If this was what we would have to fight in, the soldiers would have a tough time, as would the machines. But not as tough as the Iraqis would have it. We had technological advantages that would help us deal with the weather. It was just a matter of being able to deal with the misery factor that the weather brought with it.

The weather was on-and-off lousy in the week leading to war. During the bad days we survived. During the good days we worked on the vehicles and checked and rechecked our equipment.

Even in the midst of this measured preparation for war, there occasionally was some glimpse of humanity, some little bit of hope for the future for all of us. Pfc. Fausto Trivino, who had been waiting for some time for news about the birth of his first child, was denied what was termed "baby leave." We were so close to the war that the brigade canceled all such leave. Trivino took the news better than most soldiers would, but we wanted to make sure he had an opportunity to find out about his wife and first child before we went across the border.

Getting to the telephones at Camp New York or Camp Virginia was a near physical impossibility because of the crush of people waiting to use them. We decided to send Trivino back to Camp Doha so he could stand in the telephone line there, where there were more phones. On 16 March, a Sunday, Trivino and 1st Sergeant Mercado headed back to Doha before dawn.

Trivino quickly learned that he was the father of a baby girl, Alejandra Isabella, nearly twenty-four hours earlier. He was floating the rest of the day. To celebrate, he brought two buckets of Kentucky

Fried Chicken back to camp. And it did not matter one bit to him that he waited in line nearly four hours to get it.

Finally, on 17 March, we were given the order to break camp and move into forward assembly areas near the border. We were to take with us only what we would need for the war. The rest would be put into containers and either shipped home or kept in Kuwait. Our carefully constructed and maintained latrines and showers were dismantled and either burned or buried. Schwartz wanted us to leave no trace behind, no indication that we had been here. He wanted the desert returned to its natural state, which was to say, bleak and barren.

The following day I gathered the company together for a few last words of encouragement. The first sergeant spoke first. He reminded the soldiers of why we were there, and of September 11.

"There was no pity when they did that and I don't expect any here," he said in a way that was both a challenge and an order. "If he's got a uniform on, we blow him away. If he's got a weapon, we blow him away. But whatever we do out there, the idea is to all go home together."

I did not feel the soldiers needed any more encouragement or inspiration. They were pumped up and ready to go. There was little I could do at that point to get than more ready. I just wanted to reinforce the reasons we were here, and to give them something that might get them through the early stages of the war.

I reminded them to take care of each other on the battlefield; that we wanted to go home with everyone we deployed with. I also reminded them to clearly identify their targets to make sure we were killing combatants, and not civilians. Our war, I told them, was not against the Iraqi people, but against Saddam and his regime.

"What we're asking you to do is go out and kill the enemy. Identify the enemy and kill him," I said, knowing full well that is exactly what Charlie Company soldiers would do if given the opportunity.

When I finished my speech on 18 March, Charlie Company gathered around me in a group huddle as the soldiers often did after a formation. S.Sgt. Jabari Williams, our spiritual leader, led us in a quick prayer. Then, in unison we shouted: "Cobras lead the way!" and Williams topped it off with a shout of "Game on, baby!"

Schwartz came down to the company that day to go over our plan and talk to the soldiers before we headed into attack positions. He reminded them it would be a long, tough battle to Baghdad. And because of all the civilians who would be in and around the battlefield, he cautioned them to be sure of their targets. "You have to be absolutely sure that the kill decision is absolutely the right decision," he advised them. But he also asked them to take care of each other. "When all is said and done, all I ask is that you take care of your brother Cobras."

That afternoon we packed up, and the following morning, 19 March, we moved out, southwest of Rogue Zero for our tactical assembly areas. Once again, our movement was slowed by a fierce sandstorm. The pluggers were useless at times, and navigation was extremely difficult. There were also the mechanical problems that bedevil any armor task force on the move. Red Three, the *Call Yo' Chaplain* tank of Larrico Alexander, was getting a new engine and arrived late. Red Two, the *Cojone, Eh?* tank of Jason Diaz, broke down and needed some quick fixes on the way to our Tactical Assembly Area (TAA).

Heavy Metal set up in a position code-named Metallica. It was within sight of the five-kilometer exclusion zone on the Kuwait side of the border. There was a fifteen-kilometer exclusion zone separating Kuwait and Iraq established at the end of the Persian Gulf War that until recently was patroled by United Nations forces. In addition to the five kilometers on the Kuwait side, there were ten kilometers between the border and where Iraqis were allowed to operate.

While we set up at Metallica, Rock 'n Roll was a few miles to the rear in an area code-named Rogue One. We would wait in these positions, making our final preparations, until we got the word to head north. The President had given his "Get out of Baghdad in forty-eight hours or we're coming to get you" speech directed at Saddam, and the clock was ticking.

It was clear to all of us at this point that there was not going to be a lengthy air campaign preceding the ground war as there was in Operation Desert Storm. Six weeks of bombing kicked off the war twelve years earlier. Now, it appeared there would be a short air war followed by a lengthy ground war. In fact, G-Day, or Ground Day, was scheduled two days after A-Day, or Air Day, the start of the air campaign.

The 2nd Brigade Combat Team Spartans would be the focus of the fight for the 3rd Infantry Division. Within the brigade, Task Force 1-64, the Desert Rogues, would often lead because we were armor heavy and had been in theater longer than Task Force 4-64, the other armor heavy task force. Task Force 3-15, the brigade's infantry heavy battalion, would lead us across the border, taking out Iraqi outposts where there were any and clearing the path.

The Task Force 1-64 lineup was Wild Bunch, Charlie Rock, and the Cobras. We batted cleanup in the battalion's three-company lineup. Wild Bunch and Rock would go into a fight first and fix the enemy. Then we would finish up the attack with our armor knock-out punch. That was our alignment as we sat at Metallica waiting for the word to go, waiting for the air war to start. We didn't have long to wait.

At 5:25 a.m. on 20 March, as soldiers were beginning to stir from their vehicles and start their morning routine, we began hearing a low, droning sound coming from the east. It was a deep hum, not unlike the sound an unmanned aerial vehicle makes. We looked up as the sound got louder. There, just a few hundred feet above us, their rocket engines glowing red against the still-dark sky, were several Tomahawk cruise missiles.

Soldiers came out of their vehicles, pointing to the sky, whooping and hollering and cheering the start of an air campaign we heard was being called "Shock and Awe." We were not shocked, but we certainly were in awe as the cruise missiles streamed overhead the next few minutes, several dozen in all. Now we knew things were serious.

When the show was over, we went back to work. Throughout the morning of the 20th, we focused on getting every last little thing ready to go across the border, which we felt would be in about two days. There was no real sense of urgency, no wild scramble to find parts we needed. We felt we had time to get done what needed to be done.

A few hours later, that all changed.

The afternoon of 20 March was bright and hot. Many of us had just finished a quick MRE lunch and were looking forward to the evening meal, a hot meal that would be sent out to us, our last hot meal before we crossed the border. We were cleaning weapons, writing last letters home, or just taking time to stretch out in the sun for quick nap. Sanderlin had come out to shoot pictures of the last-minute preparations.

It was about 1:30 p.m., and I was in the middle of briefing the platoon leaders on a subject that in retrospect was one that was probably best left unmentioned. For several weeks we were getting intelligence reports that indicated certain Iraq units would surrender *en masse* as soon as the war began. An elaborate document was drawn up listing fifteen articles of capitulation to which Iraqi commanders had to agree in order to be eligible for the benefits contained in them, the major one being they would not be killed. The articles of capitulation included agreements on such things as pulling down all Iraqi flags and displaying white flags. All armor and mechanized vehicles were to be parked in the motor pool and pointed in a certain direction with the gun tubes over the back. There could be no acts that might remotely be considered hostile.

Many of us were starting to believe capitulation was a real possibility. Or maybe we just wanted to believe. Perkins, the brigade commander, gave a detailed briefing that morning on possible capitulations to the twenty-five or so media that would accompany the brigade into combat. He seemed as convinced as anyone that capitulations might happen.

"We think the regular army will capitulate but the Republican Guard will not," Perkins told them. "This is the new way wars are being fought."

Those who capitulated would be allowed to keep their side arms. The idea was to make these capitulating Iraqi soldiers the nucleus of the new security force for the country once the old regime was ousted. The capitulation plans were so elaborate we even developed an elaborate surrender ceremony in which all of the company commanders in the task force would participate.

Although we first heard about possible capitulations in early January, we never saw anything concrete until 20 March. I was skeptical about the whole thing. I did not think it was possible to have all this done by the time we crossed the border. It was neither reasonable nor logical. Still, higher command held out that hope to us.

It probably would have been better for all of us had no one said anything about possible capitulations and mass surrenders. When the news got out to the troops, it seemed to take the edge off a bit. It planted a seed in our heads that this was going to be a walkover, at least until we got close to Baghdad. Not only would there be mass capitulations, intelligence briefers told us, there would probably be little resistance until we got through the Karbala Gap and began approaching Baghdad.

Originally primed for a fight, we were now primed for waves of EPWs. It was not a good mindset to have heading off to war. By the end of the war the document with the formal articles of capitulation became a popular souvenir; something everyone wanted to take home to remind them of what did not go right. Or to use them as toilet paper.

As I was briefing the platoon leaders and platoon sergeants on this, an explosion suddenly reverberated across the desert. We all looked around, trying to figure out what was going on.

"That must be the artillery prep going on," I told them and went back to the briefing.

The division artillery was supposed to start firing at Iraqi observation and listening posts, but I thought to myself: "Jeez, that is not supposed to happen until later in the day." I told Malone to call the task force TOC and ask if they knew the source of the explosion.

A few seconds later, we heard a second explosion, this time closer. It shook the ground and sent shock waves bouncing across the sand. The battalion radio net came alive with chatter. I sent the soldiers back to their tanks and told them to prepare their crews to go to MOPP-IV and prepare to move across the border. Something was obviously going on.

Soldiers from Charlie Company, Task Force 3-15, scramble for their chemical-biological protective suits on 20 March after a Scud missile was shot down nearby, raising fears of a possible chemical attack. (*Brant Sanderlin/Atlanta Journal-Constitution*)

Then we heard the sirens start to wail. Quickly the word came over the net: go to MOPP-IV: possible chemical attack. It was the first time since we arrived in Kuwait and started preparing for war that I felt real fear. I could taste it in my mouth as I struggled with the cumbersome JSLST suit. And I could see that same fear on the faces and in the eyes of my soldiers as they clawed at the plastic wrapping in which their suits were stored. The fear was there because none of us knew what was happening. The soldiers did not have to say anything. It was clear they knew this was serious.

This was my worst nightmare, the thing I dreaded most about the war: the chance that we would get hit with biological or chemical weapons—"slimed," as the soldiers called it.

Seeing all those Charlie Company soldiers scrambling around, trying to get into their protective gear, made me think that someone on the intelligence side let us down in a major way. Not only was I frightened for my soldiers and myself, I was angry that we were being fired on and were not already in MOPP-II, jacket, pants, and boots. We had previously requested permission to go to MOPP-II but were denied because the JSLST has about a six-week life span once they are taken out of the packages and higher command wanted to maximize their use. The intelligence analyses indicated we were safe from chemical or biological attacks where we were.

I ordered the tanks to scatter out into the desert in case we started taking incoming artillery or missiles. As they began moving, White One, the *California Dreamin'* tank of 1st Lt. Jeremy England, commander of second platoon, threw track and was dead in the desert. He could not move anywhere, and it was too dangerous to get out and get the track back on.

As everyone began buttoning up inside the tanks, Sanderlin climbed on top of my tank looking for shelter. He was dropped off at our position without his mask or JSLST. If we really were under attack and about to get slimed, he was a dead photographer.

"Find a Bradley and get in there!" I shouted at him. He was offered a spot in a Bradley, which has an NBC protective system. But he chose to get in the medic's personnel carrier because he thought he could get faster medical care there if we were slimed.

I turned from those distractions and sent an order over the radio net to put out the M22 Automatic Chemical Agent Detection Alarm and be prepared to use the M256 Chemical Agent Detector Kit. The M22 is a small, handheld device that can detect the presence of mustard and nerve agents from several hundred yards. The M256 can test for a variety of nerve and blister agents that might be used against us.

The mere fact that we even had to break out these kits and get into our MOPP gear made me angry. It was as if we had been personally attacked. The Iraqis had taken what until then had been largely an abstract idea for most of us and made it personal. I remember thinking: "The audacity of these people to shoot at us when we're here to liberate them."

For the next thirty minutes we sweated profusely, soaking our boots and uniforms as we waited inside the suits inside the tanks for some word on what happened. Finally, the word came down: it had been a false alarm. The first of the two explosions we heard was a SCUD missile being intercepted overhead by a Patriot missile. The second explosion was when the SCUD warhead hit the ground. It was an unsettling few moments for all of us. But it was also an object lesson. We learned how quickly we could, or could not, get into our MOPP gear. And although we had a few laughs at Sanderlin's expense after the fact, he learned not to go anywhere without his JSLST.

Shortly before dark, 1st Sergeant Mercado led the chow wagon out to us for what would be our last hot meal until we got to Baghdad. We gobbled down a plentiful supply of meatballs, red beans and rice, succotash, and canned peaches. Then the soldiers strolled back to their tanks, calling to each other: "Stay safe" and "See you on the other side."

As Jeremy England, the first platoon leader, trudged through the sand back to his tank, he said with an upbeat smile: "It's time to get this thing done."

Then we hunkered down to wait and see what the night would bring. There were no orders to move, no orders to attack. We would just wait and watch and listen. And we would reflect once again on what we were about to do.

I was extremely confident in the soldiers of Charlie Company. They knew their equipment. They knew the enemy. They knew each other. And they knew what they had to do to get home. What they did not know was how they would react the first time they came under fire. No soldier ever knows that. It is something they wrestle with in their own minds before they go into battle for the first time.

I had made my peace with God and my wife, Susan. I felt that if it was my time to go, that was it; there was nothing I could do about it. I had gone to Catholic Mass just a few days earlier and after that I felt I had a clean soul. If it was my time, it was my time. I had no problem with that because I knew Susan and my two daughters, Ashlie and Amanda, would be taken care of.

About 8 p.m., Maj. Rick Nussio, the task force executive officer, called officers and senior enlisted with the Rock 'n Roll element together for a quick briefing back at Rogue One. By the lights of a

Humvee, he quickly outlined the situation. The oil fields at Rumaylah were on fire, set by retreating Iraqis, and G-Day was being pushed ahead by a day. There would only be one day of the air campaign.

"That was one of our triggers to go early," he explained. The trigger had now been pulled. As Nussio spoke, the division artillery began laying down its preparation fires. At Rogue One the troops cheered them on. We sat on our tanks and watched as explosions from the 155mm artillery shells lit up the night sky with bursts of red and white.

Shortly after that Schwartz called us to his tank to brief us on what would take place over the next few hours. The first thing he told us was that all operations and movement orders were to be given in Zulu time (Greenwich Mean Time, which was three hours earlier than local time). The idea was to simplify things for everyone at the Pentagon in Washington, at Central Command headquarters in Tampa, Florida, and at the Coalition Force Land Component Command headquarters in Kuwait, where the ground war would be run. Supposedly, we would all be on the same time clock. Great in theory, lousy in execution, especially coming at the last minute as it did. Zulu time did nothing but confuse everyone. At times, orders were given in Zulu time. Other times, they were given in local time. Sometimes they were given both in Zulu and local time. Half the time we had no idea what time it was. It was irritating at the outset and continued to irritate us throughout the war. We were never as confused about anything as we were about Zulu time.

Schwartz said we were going across at 0300 Zulu. We would go in MOPP-II because of the scare earlier in the day. The order of march would be Wild Bunch, Charlie Rock, and Cobra. We would be eating dust all the way, but we were ready to go and get this done. Schwartz would take his tank with Wild Bunch. Maj. Mike Donovan, the task force operations officer, would have his tank with Charlie Rock. Perkins and his staff plus the Fox television news crew shadowing him would follow Cobra into Iraq.

The name of the operation, we were told, would be Operation Iraqi Freedom. When we first heard it, we all looked at each other quizzically. Operation Iraqi Freedom? There was a general consensus that it was rather wimpy for something of such significance. We thought it would grow on us once we heard it enough. It didn't.

I gave the order to Charlie Company that we would go with our normal order of march: first platoon, second platoon, and third platoon, Red, White, and Blue into Iraq. I would be behind Red. Red Two, Diaz's tank, would lead us across the border. We would go with gun tubes alternated, one to the right, the next to the left, actively scanning all the way to Objective Martin. No one could sleep much after that and about 2 a.m. Zulu, 5 a.m. local, on the 21st, we began creeping toward the border. We would go through on Lane 10, Rock 'n Roll would cross on Lane 11, just to our south.

I sat on top of my tank, feeling the chill through my MOPP suit, watching the night sky light up, listening to the radio reports. No one could sleep. We had an AM-FM radio tuned to Voice of America and just about every hour they would broadcast a wailing siren, indicating a SCUD launch. The sound sent chills down my spine. I looked over at Hernandez on Red One, who was listening to the same thing. He would shake his head, and I would shake mine. It was going to be a long night, and a longer day ahead.

Then, over the task force radio net, came the words that put all of us on instant alert:

"Contact! Tanks!"

8

FIRST FIGHT: COBRAS LEAD THE WAY

EVERY piece of intelligence we received prior to the war assured us there was little to be concerned about when we crossed into Iraq. The Iraqi army was not supposed to be anywhere near the border, at least not in numbers that would pose a serious threat to us. There might be a few soldiers in observation or listening posts, if they survived the overnight artillery prep, but not much more. Sheep, camels, and Bedouins were all we were supposed to see on our drive to Objective Martin.

Yet here, just minutes before we were to go into Iraq, the brigade radio net was exploding with reports of enemy contact. We heard the low boom of the tank main guns, first on the radio, hollow thumps that cut through the ever-present static and told every tanker who heard them that 120mm rounds were being fired and we were engaged. Then the sound of those main gun rounds came echoing across the desert and mingled with the steady chugs of the 25mm chain guns on the Bradleys. Task Force 3-15 was either heavily engaged, or there were a lot of young soldiers out there with very itchy trigger fingers. If it was going to be like this all the way to Baghdad, it was going to be one hell of a fight.

About thirty minutes before we crossed, Perkins came clanking

up to us in his M113. He had just come back across the border
from where he watched 3-15s fight and wished us all well. It was
just a small gesture, but it meant a lot to my soldiers and me. It
meant that higher command was thinking of us. There was nothing
more we could do now.

By 3 a.m. Zulu, 6 a.m. local time, we began our move into the
demilitarized zone. Despite the muted morning light, it was difficult to see more than a few feet in front of the tank because of a
thin, patchy fog that hung just above the ground. All the gunners
were scanning with their thermal imaging sites, looking for hot
spots and enemy contact, looking for something Task Force 3-15
might have missed.

But there was not much out there to see. A few Kuwaiti border
guards were up early, smiling and waving as we went by, as if this
invading force was something they saw every day. We passed several large, white buildings with "U.N." emblazoned on the side in
black paint, indicating these were observation posts and shelters for
the United Nations troops that had been here since the end of the
Gulf War. But the U.N. troops were long gone, fleeing weeks earlier
as it became apparent that there would be a war.

On the Iraqi side of the demilitarized zone, we saw a border post
that had been obliterated by artillery fire. We also ran across a
boneyard, a junkyard of tanks and other armored vehicles
destroyed in the Gulf War or abandoned just after it. Some of the
equipment looked to be in good condition and the sight of it popping up in the TIS gave more than a few of my soldiers a quick
shot of adrenaline. We watched carefully for any movement as we
continued on, but there was nothing. It was a graveyard of long-
dead armor. We figured Task Force 3-15 in its nervousness and
excitement got into a fight with a bunch of dead tanks. Better to do
that, though, than sit back and wait to get shot at.

The border crossing was terribly anticlimactic after the excitement of the previous day and night. No one had slept much over
the past few days and once the soldiers began to realize this portion
of the intelligence analysis was correct, that nobody was in front of
us for miles, they began to relax. It was not unusual over the next
twenty-plus hours for drivers to fall asleep in their holes in the

front of the tanks even as their vehicles bounced across the desert. Gunners, loaders, and TCs also nodded off with regularity as we drove northwest to Objective Martin along what was known as Route Hurricanes.

Our goal was to get to Martin as quickly as possible. There would be two quick fuel stops along the way. Martin was to be a brief tactical pause to allow the Rock 'n Roll element to catch up and for all of us to refuel once more, get something to eat, and perhaps grab a few minutes' sleep.

Route Hurricanes took us west to a village called Rudhaim that showed up on the map but apparently no longer existed. It was just open desert where the village was to have been. There, we turned north onto Route Sixers. Once on Sixers we headed straight for Objective Martin and what we hoped would be a much-needed rest.

Rock 'n Roll was traveling directly behind the Heavy Metal element along Route Hurricanes after we went through separate breach lanes. But when we turned north for Martin, the wheeled vehicles continued west on Route Tornadoes because the terrain on Sixers was too rough.

Route Tornadoes took the wheels west along a series of deeply rutted dirt roads to a village called Shawiyat. At that point, a decision was to be made whether the task force would turn north or continue following the road southwest to Salman, another village in the middle of nowhere. When the westerly route was drawn on a map, it looked like a giant penis extending southwest into Iraq. The wags at battalion called it "The Bobbitt," after the former Marine, John Wayne Bobbitt, whose angry wife took a knife one night and severed his "love commando." The choice was whether the wheels could "cut off the Bobbitt" if the terrain permitted, thereby shortening their trip to Martin. Going around the Bobbitt would take longer but would be easier on the vehicles, which were already taking a beating. Higher command opted for the longer route, and the Bobbitt remained intact.

Route Sixers was as unforgiving a trip as any of us had ever been on. It seemed to last forever. It was long and miserable, with deep *wadis* and thick sand that we ground into a fine dust that left all of us choking and coughing. Every tank crew had to stop at some point along Sixers and blow the sand and grit out the tanks' V-Pacs so the turbine engines would not seize up.

The closer we got to Martin and the longer the desert beat on the tanks, the more mechanical problems we had. Blue One, Erik Balascik's tank, had a generator problem. He jumped into the loader's hatch of Blue Two and pressed on. Red Three, Larrico Alexander's tank, had a recurrence of its engine problems and broke down just before we got to Martin. Charlie Six-Five, Shane Williams' tank with Jabari Williams as TC for the first leg of the move, also was having troubles. Shane was in a Humvee in charge of Charlie Company's wheels in Rock 'n Roll.

White Four, Sgt. 1st Class Ray White's tank, had the worst of it. The tank's fan tower, which cools the transmission oil, broke about thirty miles from Martin. When the tank overheated, it simply shut down and refused to move. White Three, S.Sgt. Ben Phinney's tank, hooked up and towed White Four into Martin. White Four put the gun tube over the back, and Ray White and his crew closed themselves up inside, sweating and eating dust all the way into the objective. They were lagging far behind the rest of the battalion, pushing through the desert on their own in the middle of the night. At one point they had to stop and blow out their V-Pacs like everyone else. But unlike everyone else, they were alone, two Abrams and two crews in the middle of a dark and desolate desert.

Red Four, Sergeant 1st Class Waterhouse's tank, got to Martin and then turned around and went back to give Red Three a tow. We wanted to make some quick repairs that we hoped would get Red Three running again. But it needed more repairs than we could manage in the little time we had.

Our plan was to put the broken-down tanks on heavy equipment transporters (HETs) and bring them into Martin for repairs. But the HETs were overwhelmed and were having problems making it through the deep sand. Our next option was to use our M-88 tank recovery vehicle to bring in the disabled tanks. But the M-88 also broke down en route. Waterhouse ended up towing Alexander's tank back to Martin and on to our next objective, Rams, a few hours to the north. Phinney did the same with Ray White's Red Four.

The M1A1 Abrams tank is a particularly finicky creature. When it's good, it's an awesome monster of a weapon. Its 1,500-horse-power gas turbine engine can push it cross-country at more than thirty miles per hour. On the road it can hit speeds of more than forty miles per hour. It can carry more than 500 gallons of fuel in its tanks and travel more than 265 miles before refueling. Its laser sights and TIS enable it to find and kill enemy targets at up to three thousand meters. Its 120mm smoothbore cannon can be fired and is dead-on accurate even while the tank is on the move, day or night. There is no tank anywhere in the world with the speed and power of the Abrams.

But if the Abrams starts having problems, there are times you curse the day you ever decided to get into tanking. If something is wrong on the tank, it will shut itself down to prevent further damage. Often, there is no clue as to what went wrong. Finding the source of the malfunction can take a few minutes or a few days, depending on your level of experience. My mechanics, most of whom spent their military careers tinkering with these beasts, could spot problems faster than the experts who designed them.

If someone on the tank could tell the mechanics what the problem sounded like, how it felt, or how it smelled, they could sort it out in a hurry. And they could figure out ways to fix things that are not in any manual. In one instance they used a coat hanger and electrical tape to fix a wire that shorted out in one tank. I frequently told the mechanics to do whatever they had to do to get a tank up and running. I did not want to know what they were doing or how they were doing it. I just wanted it fixed and I wanted those tanks ready to fight. These guys were incredible shade-tree mechanics. It didn't matter what was wrong. Just show them a problem, let them stomp around and bitch and moan for a while, and usually within hours it would be fixed.

Charlie Company tanks were not the only ones with problems. Road wheel arms on tanks throughout the task force were shearing off because of the rough terrain along Route Sixers. Schwartz, the task force commander, had his starter go out and we gave him the last one in our inventory. Donovan, the task force operations officer, was also having trouble and his tank broke down just a few hours later, right in the middle of Objective Rams, blocking a bridge.

It took my crew in Charlie Six-Six about twenty hours to cover the 225 miles from the border to Objective Martin. We arrived about 2 a.m. local time. In the distance, a few miles to our northeast, we could see the lights of Samawah twinkling through the shimmering desert dust and haze. I wondered if the people of Samawah knew we were sitting out here. Or, more important, whether the Iraqi soldiers knew we were here. And if they did, were they running and hiding or getting ready to defend their homeland?

We saw no troops and very few civilians along Route Sixers. Rock 'n Roll saw some of both in Salman, and captured several prisoners on a paved road just a few miles north of the village. Did they have cell phones? A radio to report our presence?

First Sergeant Mercado told me later that Salman was so primitive it looked almost biblical. There were a few cars and trucks about, but very little that spoke of civilization. There was virtually no acknowledgment of the presence of Americans in their midst as Rock 'n Roll moved through the village. The villagers seemed neither happy nor upset that tons of American firepower was moving through their peaceful, isolated little piece of the desert. When I arrived at Objective Martin, I did a quick inventory of my combat power and found the company was down two full tanks, Red Three and White Four. Two more, Blue One and Charlie Six-Five were not in the best of shape and were marginal if we were to get in a tough fight. That left only ten fully operational tanks and the Bradley fire support vehicle. We had not fired a single round, and no one had fired at us, and already Charlie Company was down a platoon of tanks.

I ordered the crews to blow out the V-Pacs once again, do what maintenance they could, clean their weapons, get something to eat, and, if possible, grab some rest. We were all dog-tired. The lack of sleep and the pounding we took along Route Sixers made our knees and backs ache as if someone had been beating on us with a base-ball bat. We were dusty, dirty, and starting to smell.

I tried to get the brigade's Team Fix to work on some of my tanks since their mechanics carried more spare parts than mine. But I could not raise Team Fix on the radio. I tried to use the FBCB2 to communicate with brigade, but had no luck with that, either. The FBCB2 was one of the technological marvels of this war. At times, it made life a lot easier for commanders. The Force XXI Battle Command, Brigade and Below, as it is known, is a small, satellite-based computer monitor that fit inside my tank. With the FBCB2, I was receiving up-to-the-minute information about what was going on all over the battlefield. I was able to monitor the disposi-tion of enemy and friendly forces, identify targets, and send e-mails requesting logistical support. The problem trying to use it at Mar-tin was that so many people were logging onto the system, it was too slow to do us any good. Team Fix was out of reach. It was up to Charlie Company to make its own repairs.

We did what we could, refueled, checked our weapons again, and prepared to move out for Objective Rams.

Objective Rams was another one of those desolate pieces of desert that seemed to have no real military value. It was a few miles southwest of the city of Najaf, a Shiite Muslim holy city of about 400,000 that was said to house the tomb of Ali, a cousin of Muham-mad. The desert around there was once rich farmland, but years of water diversion for projects favored by Saddam had left the Shiite farmers with their own version of the dust bowl.

As we moved north to Objective Rams, 3/7 Cav was to create a diversion by crossing the Euphrates at Samawah and then driving north on Highway 8. The intent was to convince the Iraqis that the whole brigade would cross there when, in fact, we would continue along the west side of the Euphrates on Highway 28. The brigade would move into and clear Objective Rams, which is in sight of Najaf, so V Corps and division-level assets could set up there as we pressed forward. Again we were told no major resistance was expected at either Rams or in Najaf.

Each task force within the brigade was given a different portion of Rams to clear. The Brigade Reconnaissance Team (BRT) was pushing eight to ten kilometers in front of us and some long-range surveillance and Special Operations teams were said to be in the area. If our guys were out there with eyes on the objective, we figured whatever intelligence we were getting would be solid.

We moved out of Martin about 10 a.m. local time on 22 March. Rock 'n Roll caught up with us and we were now at full strength as a company, except for the two tanks that were being towed. Those tanks could still fight; they just could not move on their own. We hoped to be able to repair them once we got to Objective Rams. But that was assuming the objective would have little or no enemy opposition and we would have the time we needed.

The movement to Rams was about thirty-five miles. Because of the perceived lack of a threat, we moved in a task force column along Highway 28, a paved road that was supposed to be two lanes but was barely wide enough to accommodate a twelve-foot-wide tank. The highway ran through the middle of Objective Rams and contained two key checkpoints that the task force was to secure: Checkpoint 274, a small bridge near what appeared to be a cement plant or processing facility of some type, and Checkpoint 278, a crossroads a few miles north of the bridge. Everything else on Objective Rams was flat, gone-to-seed farmland. Throughout the objective area were low dirt and sand berms running at both parallel and right angles to the road.

About an hour out of Martin, things began to change. Samawah was too well defended, and a decision was made not to send the Cav across there. Instead it continued north along the west bank of the Euphrates but ran into a larger than expected enemy force, slowing its advance. Division planners did not expect such heavy contact so soon.

Perkins called Schwartz and told him Task Force 1-64 now had full responsibility for clearing Objective Rams to enable the rest of the brigade to move forward. Our mission was to sweep through the objective, clear it of enemy activity, and create some space for follow-on units to operate. We were told to be aware that a long-range reconnaissance unit was in the area but radio contact with it had been lost, and no one was sure where they were.

About three miles from Rams, Schwartz came over the radio

with specific missions for each of the companies in the task force. There were three key objectives: a radio tower, the cement plant and bridge at Checkpoint 274, and a berm complex farther north that led into Checkpoint 278, the crossroads. Rock, the infantry company, was to clear the tower and the processing plant, with Wild Bunch moving up to take control of the plant once it was secure. We were to support Rock, then push out to the west side of the objective before moving north through the berm complex toward the crossroads. The attack was to be a "sequential with multiple objectives," a classic "movement to contact." We were not sure what was out there or what we would find. But after months of waiting, and miles of dusty desert, we were keyed up and ready for a fight.

We ran through a quick radio rehearsal and, less than two miles from the objective, moved off the road into battle formation. The soft sand and berms slowed us some, but what was to have been a movement to contact instead became a race to contact. Everyone was eager to fire that first shot and get that first kill. Tanks were cutting in front of one another because the restrictive terrain was funneling them into narrow lanes. Cobra and Wild Bunch tanks quickly became intermingled. It was late afternoon by this time and with the sun going down and the dust in the air restricting vision, there was far more confusion than I expected or anyone wanted.

Wild Bunch and Charlie Rock surrounded the radio tower and started clearing the buildings but found only a few workers there. Charlie Company pushed forward to the processing plant and moved into attack positions. Red was in the lead. But it had only three operating tanks. Red Four was towing Red Three and was running dangerously low on fuel. White moved out to the west while Blue swung around to the east.

As Blue was moving into position, Anthony Marabello, the gunner on David Richard's Blue Four, saw movement to his north beyond a conveyor belt that carried materials into the processing plant.

"Cobra Six, Blue Four," Richard called.

"Blue Four, Cobra Six."

"Cobra Six, I've got a group of individuals here. I think there's about fifteen. They're all in black."

"Are they workers?"

"I don't see any weapons. They're holding up a blue flag."

I told him to let them surrender. I called the report up to Schwartz, but while I was on the net with him I heard Richard call in and say the group had just fired two RPGs and AK-47s at them.

"Can I engage?" he asked.

"Roger, engage."

Blue Four and the Blue Three tank of S.Sgt. Germell Milton opened up with .50 caliber and 7.62mm. The Iraqis were staying behind the berms, rising up slightly to fire a few rounds, then ducking back down. Blue was having a tough time spotting them behind the berms so I ordered White to roll up the Iraqis' right flank and get into a better position to shoot them.

Red One gunner Carlos Hernandez also saw the Iraqis behind the berm.

"They have weapons," Hernandez radioed to his TC, 1st Lt. Roger Gruneisen.

"You sure they have weapons?" Gruneisen asked.

"They have RPGs."

Gruneisen called me asking for permission to engage.

"Cobra Six, Red One."

"Red One, Cobra Six."

"Cobra Six, we have dismounts in front of us with weapons. Can we engage?"

"You sure they have weapons."

"They have weapons!"

Hernandez was continuing to scan. He could clearly see the faces of Iraqis with the ten-power magnification on his gunner's sight.

"Red Two, this is Red One Golf," Hernandez called to Diaz, indicating he was the gunner for Red One. "They have RPGs."

Red began pumping .50-caliber and 7.62mm rounds downrange from both the coaxial machine gun and the M240 on the left side of the loader's hatch. There were about a dozen dismounted fighters four hundred meters to the front of Red trying to hide behind sand berms and firing wildly back at the tanks with AK-47s. White also began engaging the Iraqis.

During training, the normal fire command for the TC, once enemy troops have been clearly identified, is "Fire." Although at times this seemed like a training mission, the regular routines were often not followed. Ben Phinney, in White Three gave one of the most succinct and to-the-point fire commands in that first fight. As Phinney's White Three came on line, still dragging the immobilized White Four, Sgt. Steve Ellis, Phinney's gunner, called over the radio: "I've got troops!"

Phinney did not hesitate.

"Hose those fuckers!" he barked.

It was not gunnery standard, but it worked.

Ellis flipped the gun select switch just above his head to coax and began firing 7.62mm rounds at the Iraqis. Psc. Derrick Hemphill, the loader, did the same with the M240 from his hatch while Phinney fired the .50 caliber from the TC station.

Because of the volume of fire we threw at the Iraqis, they were reluctant to peer over the tops of the berms. They seldom took time to aim before they fired. This was especially true of those who fired RPGs. They would often hold the RPG above the berm and, without looking, fire it in our direction. It was a technique the Iraqis used throughout the war, usually with little success. Only on occasion did they get lucky and score a hit on the tanks, though it did little damage to the Abrams armor.

There was a certain unreality to all this for many Charlie Company soldiers. We had spent so many years in simulators practicing for this, and so many years shooting at pop-up targets, that it was almost as if this were not real combat, but a video game on which we would be graded. No main gun rounds had been fired yet, and loaders were outside their hatches firing the M240s. TCs were also outside the hatches, firing the .50-caliber machine guns or M-4s. They seemed almost impervious to the enemy fire being directed at them. The incoming fire was desultory and badly aimed. However, there was enough of it, especially the RPGs, to cause serious problems if some Iraqi got lucky.

The Iraqis quickly decided they had had enough. The AK-47s

and RPGs hit the ground and hands went in the air. One of the Iraqis started waving a white flag instead of a blue towel while others began stripping off their uniforms and putting on civilian clothes they carried to the battle in small, plastic grocery sacks. This puzzled us at first. We thought these were regular forces, who for some reason may have figured it was better to be taken prisoner in civilian clothes than in uniform. They may even have thought we would consider them noncombatants if they were in civilian clothes. But there was not much chance of that with all the weapons around their positions.

As the Iraqis started surrendering, some came running toward Richard's tank. He fired a few warning shots over their heads with his M-4. They all hit the dirt and started taking off their shirts to show they had no weapons or explosives on them. They stayed there until Charlie Rock's infantry came up to take them prisoner and move them to the rear. We had thirteen prisoners and a number of bodies in the ditches. Several soldiers from White got off their tanks and began moving through the ditches, helping process the prisoners and checking on the wounded.

With Diaz in the lead, Red moved across a small bridge and toward the intersection. I told Blue to follow Red while White continued working the ditches and bunkers near the bridge. We received reports from some of the EPWs through an interpreter that reinforcements in white pickup trucks were headed into our area. It was relayed to me and I passed it on to Diaz so he could watch for them.

Couvertier was peering into his TIS when he saw trucks coming down the highway directly at Red's lead tanks. They were white Toyota pickup trucks, crammed with soldiers carrying AK-47s and RPGs.

"I've got a white truck," Couvertier radioed to Diaz.

Then, in quick succession: "I've got another. I've got another. And another."

Diaz was out of the hatch, looking ahead. About one thousand meters to the front he could see vehicles coming his way, flashing their lights. He got on the radio to Gruneisen.

"I've got trucks in front of me. White trucks."

"What's going on?" Gruneisen asked.

"They've got weapons and they're jumping out of the truck and there's some kind of machine guns in the back of the truck," Diaz replied.

Gruneisen radioed me.

"I've got white trucks coming down the road flashing their lights at me."

"Can you tell if they have weapons mounted on them?"

"We've got guys in the back with machine guns and they've got a large-caliber machine gun on top of it."

Gruneisen requested permission to engage with the main gun.

"Roger, engage."

"Fire!" Diaz ordered.

Couvertier had already flipped the gun select switch to MAIN and the ammunition select switch to HEAT. He centered the sight reticle on the lead truck, double-checked it, and then squeezed the triggers on the palm switches.

The fifty-one-pound round went hurtling toward the lead pickup at more than 4,500 feet per second, rocking Red Two only slightly but sending a resounding "Boom!" across the desert that caught many Charlie Company soldiers by surprise. It was the first main gun round of the war fired by the company.

The trucks were fewer than four hundred meters from Red Two when it fired, and it took only an instant for the HEAT round to strike the first truck. It exploded in a brilliant flash that lit up the early evening sky. Remnants of the round and pieces of the first truck then tore into the second truck, exploding it as well. Both were ripped into mangled, smoking strips of metal that the next day were barely recognizable as truck parts.

The AFCAP was ejected from the gun, hit the deflector with a clang, and then fell into the catch in the floor. Trivino quickly loaded another HEAT round.

Red One was in the loose dirt and powdery sand on the left of Red Two, nearly side-by-side. Red One was carrying what was to have been the ceremonial first main gun round fired in the war. The HEAT round was specially marked for the occasion by the contingent of Hispanic troops in the company. They signed their names on the round, affixed a Puerto Rican flag, and added a salutation in Spanish to Saddam that roughly translated said: "Up your ass, motherfucker."

Hernandez fired the ceremonial round next and another truck exploded. It had taken no more than five seconds for Charlie Company to turn the first three trucks in the convoy into smoldering ruins of jagged metal. The soldiers who were in the back of the trucks were now smoking shards of flesh scattered alongside the road. The soldiers in the remaining trucks began bailing out, heading for the sand berms and bunkers on both sides of the road.

Despite the quick kills of the first three trucks, more trucks and soldiers kept coming down the road. And Couvertier and Hernandez kept shooting them as quickly as they appeared. Even Waterhouse's Red Four, still towing Red Three, got into the fight. Waterhouse kept his tank on the road to keep from getting bogged down in the soft sand but had enough clearance for Sgt. Phillip Riley, the gunner, to destroy one of the trucks with a HEAT round.

Within minutes, fifteen trucks were destroyed; the remaining Iraqis scattered into the desert, taking up positions to fight us with small arms and RPGs. They were outnumbered and outgunned, but these Iraqis who were not even supposed to be here, according to the intelligence reports, were fighting with a fanatical intensity none of us expected.

At one point my gunner, Malone, said he saw Iraqis crawling up to tanks to get a better shot with an AK-47 or RPG. That was unthinkable. A single soldier with only a rifle or RPG single-handedly taking on a tank? It was like taking a knife to a gunfight. It was the first time we saw it, but would not be the last. These definitely were not your Gulf War Iraqis, who were ready and willing to surrender for some warm clothes, an MRE, and a chance to go home alive. These guys did not seem to care if they died, and they must have known they would die going up against tanks with only rifles and grenades.

As the fight continued, the company was on line with Red in the middle, White on the left flank, and Blue on the right flank. Because of the threat of Iraqis trying to come around our right flank, I requested support in that area. Charlie Rock moved up to provide security but was stopped by berms and low, swampy ground.

Many of Charlie Company's loaders and TCs were still outside their hatches, firing M-4s and 9mm pistols at the Iraqis creeping close to them. What looked like a red tracer round flew out of the Iraqi lines and exploded between Richard's tank and mine. A spray of rocks and dirt blast the front of his tank.

"What the hell was that?" Richard said to no one in particular.

"Sergeant Richard," said his driver, Pfc. James Pyle, "an RPG just landed about thirty feet in front of us."

It was not so much a surprise as it was a wake-up call to Richard and other TCs. I told them it was time to exercise more caution about how often they would be out of the hatch and exposed to enemy fire.

Darkness was quickly overtaking us at this point, and we began to discuss covering for one another while the drivers switched to their night sights, and TCs and loaders got out their night-vision goggles. It takes only five minutes or so to do it, but it meant that during that time, a tank's driver, loader, and TC were occupied with something other than fighting the enemy. We coordinated it so one platoon at a time went to their night sights while the other two platoons provided covering fire.

The longer the fight went on and the darker it got, the more evident it became that the Iraqis had no concept of our night-vision capabilities. After dark they started walking around as if they thought the night shielded them, and that we could see as little as they. They obviously did not know about our TIS, which let us pick out hot spots all over the battlefield even on the darkest nights. It was not unusual after dark for an Iraqi to get up from behind a berm or step outside a bunker in the middle of the fight, apparently thinking we could not see him.

When the Iraqis finally figured it out and went to ground so we could no longer see them, I called a ceasefire because we were expending a lot of small arms ammunition on very few and difficult-to-hit targets. After just a couple of minutes, we started seeing hot spots out in front of us again. By that time a mortar mission I had called in earlier was ready to fire.

The soldiers said later that they saw one soldier get out of a bunker and start walking across their front, west to east, almost staggering as he went. Our soldiers watched him go.

"Should we shoot him?" some of the second platoon soldiers asked.

Their TCs demurred.

"Let's see what he does."

He did not do much. 1st Lt. Jim Hock, who was in charge of the Bradley Fire Support Vehicle (BFST, pronounced B-fist) from 1st Battalion, 9th Field Artillery Regiment attached to Charlie Company for the war, had called in the 120mm mortars from the task force mortar platoon. One of the targets was the bunker the Iraqi had just left.

As the soldiers watched, a 120mm mortar round sailed in, hit the Iraqi in the shoulder, drove him to the ground, and exploded. There was a blinding flash in the TIS, then nothing. The Iraqi disappeared, literally vaporized in front of their eyes.

The radio came alive with chatter from soldiers who were both shocked and titillated by what they had seen.

"Holy shit!"

"Did you see that?"

"The fucker just disappeared."

Mortars hit all around that bunker, destroying it and the four or five Iraqis who were in it.

Fuel was becoming a problem for all of Charlie Company's tanks. We had transitioned from a long road march directly into a movement to contact and now were involved in an hours-long fight that threatened to drag on into the night.

Waterhouse was so low on fuel that he was forced to shut down his tank several times to make sure he did not run out. When he did that, other tanks had to cover him because his tank was also having battery problems, and he could not operate the TIS or traverse the gun tube without the tank running.

The entire task force was facing fuel problems. Fuel was available back near the bridge, which was now secured, so Schwartz started rotating companies back to get gassed up and grab a quick breather before getting back in the fight. Although we were still engaged, I rotated platoons back to refuel, giving those tanks still towing tanks a chance to drop off their loads before returning to our positions.

Some of Charlie Rock's vehicles were stuck in swampy low ground east of the road, and I sent White to provide security as the soldiers worked to free them from the muck. Once the rest of the company was fueled up and rearmed with small arms ammunition, we pulled back to just south of the bridge to get further guidance. Perkins and Schwartz came up to discuss where we were to go from there. The emphasis was on getting Highway 28 cleared to the intersection and keeping it open until Task Force 4-64 moved through later that night. The plan was to put Task Force 1-64 tanks and Bradleys on both sides of the road to provide a security gaunt-let through which 4-64 could move. We could not move far off the road because of terrain limitations so a sweep on line through the area was impossible.

As I was briefing my platoon leaders on the plan, an explosion just across the road from us showered us with sand and debris. We all scrambled for our tanks, thinking we had been targeted by incoming mortars or artillery. I called the task force TOC and asked if they knew what it was, but before they could reply the engineers radioed in to say it was a controlled explosion of a main gun round that had gotten stuck in Red One's gun tube and had to be dis-carded. The engineers apologized for not telling us what they were doing, but it was a bit late by then. If we were not nervous by then, we were now. After that the engineers did a better job letting us know when they were going to blow up something.

We lined up and moved down the road in two columns with Charlie Company in the lead, followed by Charlie Rock and Wild Bunch. It only took us a few minutes to get there, and along the way we were engaged by some of the Iraqis behind a large berm to our right; we returned fire until the area was secure. We also received some incoming rockets fired from Najaf. We saw red streaks and thought at first they were antiaircraft tracers. But all of a sudden things started exploding behind us as we moved toward the intersection. No one was injured, but twelve rockets of some sort landed near enough to us to keep us all on edge for the rest of the night.

When we finally got to the crossroads, we could see the lights of Najaf on a rise to the northeast. The city was nearer than I thought it would be, but we had more pressing concerns closer to us. There was a small, ramshackle police station on the southeast corner of the intersection. Two light poles with two low-watt bulbs on each cast just enough light to illuminate the crossroads and make us an inviting target. The road was elevated slightly from the fields and berms around us and it was easy enough without the lights to see us silhouetted against the night sky.

With support to our rear, I arrayed the remaining three tanks from Red on each of the roads leading into the intersection. Red One was facing west, Red Two north, and Red Four northeast, toward Najaf. I put my tank in the middle of the intersection.

Waterhouse requested permission to clear the police station. When it was granted, Larrico Alexander, who jumped into the loader's hatch on Red Four, volunteered to do it, as did Riley, the gunner. This is not something tankers normally do and are not trained to do. But since Rock's infantry was tied up elsewhere, we could not wait for someone to come up and do the job for us.

Alexander and Riley went in, searched the few rooms in the building, and came out to report that whoever had been there was gone. When they got back to the tank, I told Waterhouse to have his crew shoot out the lights. Alexander, standing out of the loader's hatch, decided to shoot it out with his M-4. Noncommissioned officers who TC tanks do not spend a lot of time training on M-4s. It showed that night. Alexander fired several rounds but failed to hit the light.

"Shoot the damned light!" soldiers were calling out to him.

Waterhouse pulled out his 9mm with a laser sight and hit the light with his first shot. But the round did not penetrate a casing around the bulbs. Riley, a former Alabama National Guard soldier with a slow drawl and a quiet, easy way about him, finally grabbed the M-4 from Alexander.

"Give me that damned rifle," he said.

Riley sighted, fired one shot, and the lights shattered. The night went black.

"It just takes an old country boy to do this," Riley drawled, handing the rifle back to Alexander. It was a few weeks before the jokes about Alexander's marksmanship ended.

No one slept much again that night. We were on the northern edge of the American advance into Iraq, looking out into no-man's land. It was incredibly tense. Everyone buttoned up inside the tanks and stayed there. The gunners were seeing hundreds of hot spots in their TIS. But many of them were three thousand meters or more away on the road leading out of Najaf, and we could not tell if they were carrying weapons. It appeared at times that some people were planting mines on the road, but we could not be sure. We reported the sightings to the task force but there was justifiable concern about us going down the road and getting ambushed. We were told to simply to monitor the situation.

There was not much time to reflect on what we did that day. With the enemy out there, there was too much to risk if we lost focus. But I was more than pleased with the way the soldiers performed in their first action. They were as aggressive as I thought they would be. They were as accurate with their gunnery as I knew they would be. No one panicked, despite the confusion inherent in every battle. If they erred they did so on the side of caution, making sure they had clear targets before they fired, and making sure those targets were armed enemy fighters.

We were beyond tired, running on adrenaline and nerves, but we were still together as a company. Our first fight was a success. We had defeated a determined enemy force and had not had any Charlie Company soldiers killed or wounded. And while we would not get a full battle damage assessment (BDA) until the next day, the task force destroyed fifteen vehicles and killed about 150 enemy fighters.

Even though Objective Rams was said to be devoid of enemy soldiers, we found plenty of them. They fought hard and tenaciously, almost fanatically at times. We did the mission we were given and cleared the objective so other forces could move into the area. This piece of Iraqi dirt now belonged to us, at least for the time being, and V Corps and the division rear could begin to push its assets forward. We did not anticipate the fight, but it was a fight we needed, a fight that prepared us for what was to come in the days ahead.

9

THE NIGHT IT RAINED MUD

THE morning of 23 March was bright, sunny, and cool. About 6 a.m. Task Force 4-64 began moving through our positions at the crossroads and pushing north on Highway 28. We turned over the honor of being the 3rd Infantry Division unit farthest north so their soldiers could secure the road for a logistics convoy that was scheduled to move through later in the day. For a few brief moments, we were able to relax, and for the first time since we left Kuwait some of us got a chance to shave, brush our teeth, and grab a few bites of an MRE.

Based on the events of the night before, we knew we could not relax too much where we were sitting. We had good visibility and clear fields of fire to our east and northeast, where Najaf could be clearly seen on a low ridgeline a few miles away. The west was another story. A cluster of buildings about a half-mile from the intersection blocked our view and provided perfect cover for someone to move in with a heavy machine gun and hit our positions before we could react. We did not clear the area the night before, so early in the morning I sent second platoon out to sweep it.

Jeremy England's second platoon was still down one tank. Ray White's White Four was in for repairs, but I figured the other three could handle whatever was out there. We saw some hot spots in that area during the night but they were not enough to be overly concerned about. Our main focus was northeast and Najaf, where the bulk of the fighters had come from the day before.

The three tanks moved out in a column, with England in the lead, Pinkston behind him, and Phinney bringing up the rear. There was a rock quarry out there with a number of junked vehicles in it, a mosque about three hundred meters off the road with some low buildings around it, and a few other two-story stucco houses with flat roofs that were typical of the structures in that region.

Phinney saw some people coming out of one of the buildings and started maneuvering to the north to get a better view. As England's tank drove by the building, he reported he was taking fire from a heavy machine gun or some sort of air defense artillery (ADA) weapon.

Brons, England's driver, quickly threw his tank into reverse. "Look out! I'm backing up!" he yelled. The 70-ton tank lurched backward.

Justin Mayes, driving Pinkston's tank, did not have time to react, although Scott Stewart was able to traverse the gun tube just enough to keep it from getting caught between the two tanks as they collided with a resounding metallic *thonk.*

The crews in both tanks were thrown about inside, their senses momentarily scrambled. They were not sure if they'd been hit by an RPG or an antitank round. It took a few seconds for them to realize the tanks had collided. There was no serious damage and Pinkston had his tank back out of the way.

"They're shooting out of the building," Phinney told Ellis, his gunner.

"All right, I've got them," Ellis calmly replied and fired a HEAT round into the second story of the building.

Pinkston began firing on the building with coax, and then hit it with another HEAT round.

All three tanks were lighting up the building with their machine guns before England got a report that soldiers were seen running out of one of the buildings and in the direction of the quarry. He ordered his driver to take the tank off the road in pursuit but as he did they plunged into a swamp. The tank was mired and could not move. So much for the pursuit. It took a few hours to get England's tank out of the muck. By that time Charlie Rock's infantry had come up and cleared the rest of the surrounding buildings.

I had just finished dealing with England's situation when I got a radio call from third platoon's Balascik. He was quite upset and said third platoon had almost shot and killed one of our own soldiers.

Spc. Joshua Metheny, one of the Bradley fire support team crew, had gone out into the field east of our lines to dig a hole, squat over it, and relieve himself. It was primitive, but life was often reduced to the basics out there. (Rather than squat in the sand, some soldiers used MRE cartons as toilets, others ammunition boxes. A couple of our tankers took a metal folding chair, cut a hole out of the seat, filed down the sharp edges, wrapped it with duct tape, and used that as their toilet. Mercado also had one of those, and he and I both made good use of it.)

Although Metheny told his Bradley crewmates what he was doing, no one else in the company was informed. Metheny was wearing his Combat Vehicle Crewman's helmet, which from a distance could be mistaken for an Iraqi helmet. In addition, he was squatting in one of the Iraqi trenches. When the crews of Blue One and Blue Two saw him, they began shouting for him to come out with his hands up. Metheny could not hear them because the CVC covered his ears, so he did not respond. One of the crews fired several rounds from their .50 caliber over the berm as warning shots. That got Metheny's attention. He dropped behind the berm on his back, hurriedly pulled up his pants, and tossed a few sheets of toilet paper into the air, shouting for a cease fire, that he was a friendly.

It took only a few seconds to sort things out and for Metheny to emerge unhurt. But he was thoroughly embarrassed by the experience of having his morning constitutional rudely interrupted. The word was passed that from then on anyone going out in front of our lines to take a dump was required to notify the CP of their position.

Balascik was probably more upset about the incident than Metheny, who later was able to laugh about it. Balascik was shaken, and I had to assure him that it was an honest mistake and he needed to put it behind him and stay focused on the mission.

By 10 a.m. we had moved about a mile east of the crossroads and set up on line in a deeply rutted farmer's field. Najaf and the ridge on which it sat seemed to loom over us. We were in a blocking position waiting for an Iraqi mechanized infantry unit called the Golden Brigade, which was reported to be moving south in our direction. The brigade's main avenue of approach was expected to be down Highway 28, where 4-64 was positioned. But if the Iraqis moved around the ridge to the east of Najaf, we were in position to stop them.

By mid-afternoon the threat of the Golden Brigade had been eliminated by an air strike that caught the mechanized unit out in the open. We never fired a shot, but could see smoke rising far to the north where the enemy task force was stopped. Once the threat was gone, we had time to refuel and rearm, get new V-Pacs for the tanks, and do some personal hygiene.

Charlie Company was the closest unit to Najaf at that point and we started getting groups of people coming out of the city asking for food and protection. Three young men, one of whom spoke relatively good English, offered their services as scouts or fighters. They said they came from wealthy families in Najaf and were tired of Saddam. They spoke openly of the disposition and size of Iraqi forces in Najaf. They said the Saddam *fedayeen* had moved into the city, and they and the Ba'ath Party loyalists were terrorizing the local population, forcing them and many others to flee.

They were so free with their information that we began to suspect they might be decoys, sent out to deceive us. As it turned out, much of their information was right on the mark.

While we were interrogating those three and feeding them with MREs, some U.S. Special Forces soldiers rolled into our position to take control of them. At the same time a group of about a dozen nomads started approaching our lines. They had pitched their tents nearby a few days earlier but were now fearful of moving anywhere since they were caught between the Iraqis and the Americans. We gave them MREs and told them to go back to their tents.

The crossroads we had secured the night before was now open and more civilian vehicles were moving in behind us to pick up the dead. We requested several times that it be closed but were not successful. First Sergeant Mercado and I were not pleased with the number of civilians allowed inside our lines. He suspected many of them were fighters who had escaped, gone home, and changed clothes before coming back to pick up their dead buddies. But he believed some had more sinister motives; that they were checking our positions and strengths and surveying the ground for future artillery or mortar attacks.

"If those guys had their shit together they'd be getting grids to this place and hit us with everything they got tonight," he harrumphed to anyone who would listen.

As usual, he was right. There were entirely too many civilians running around in our midst without anyone knowing why they were really there. They seemed to have an uncanny knowledge of the location of everyone who died the night before. Schwartz admitted later that his decision to open up the crossroads and allow civilians to pass through our lines to pick up the dead was a mistake. He said he should have shut things down completely and not allowed anyone in. It was a learning experience for all of us. Next time, we would do it better.

For a number of Charlie Company soldiers, this was the first time they had seen dead bodies, whether in a funeral home or on the battlefield. The dead we saw the day after the fight at Rams took on a yellowish, waxy appearance and bore an eerie resemblance to stuffed Saddam look-alike mannequins set out there as part of some elaborate movie set. They all had full, round faces and brushy black mustaches. Some bodies did not have a mark on them, and looked as if they were asleep. Some showed only traces of blood. But a few provided only the slightest hint that just a few hours earlier this had been a human being.

One body we found west of the road beside a berm looked as if it had been hit by a 25mm high-explosive round. It was virtually turned inside out. The face looked like a rubber Halloween mask with nothing behind it. What remained of the arms and legs were ripped away from the body and pointed in various directions.

People who came out from Najaf to pick up bodies would find whoever they were looking for, dump them in the back seat or the

The remnants of a pickup truck and a dead Iraqi fighter at Objective Rams following Charlie Company's battle on 22 and 23 March. (*Brant Sanderlin/Atlanta Journal-Constitution*)

trunk, then drive off, sometimes shouting at us as they went by, and occasionally throwing rocks.

In some instances, the removal of bodies struck a note with the sometimes-morbid sense of humor fighting soldiers develop. One taxi had a body in its too-small trunk with a leg sticking out. The driver tied a red bandanna around the leg of the dead man and it looked like they were signaling the car behind that they had a long load, just like a logging truck might do. Another taxi had a body in the back with the arm of a dead man sticking out. As the taxi bounced over the rutted road the arm would wave up and down. Some of the soldiers waved back as the taxi passed.

Many of the bodies we saw wore dark green Iraqi Army pants and black-and-white checkered headscarves. And just about every one of them had a thick wad of Iraqi 250 dinar notes in their pockets or near their body. Each note bore the likeness of Saddam Hussein. We learned later through one of the EPWs, a warrant officer in the Iraqi Army, that many of the fighters were militia, recruited from other areas of Iraq to come and kill Americans. Although the money paid them was virtually worthless in the world economy, it apparently had been enough of an incentive for these fighters to have attacked our tanks using pickup trucks and small arms. Sgt. Dan Pyle, one of my drivers and our admin specialist, spoke a little Arabic, and the task force S-2, Capt. Jason Ferrill, asked that he be sent back to the TOC to help interrogate the Iraqi. Pyle was able to get enough out of him for us to put some perspective on what happened here.

According to the EPW, someone was seen parachuting into the area a few days earlier, giving rise to the belief that either the 82nd Airborne or 101st Airborne was going to jump in. The Iraqis thought they were going up against relatively lightly armed paratroopers. They did not expect tanks. In addition, he said, many of the officers simply put their troops in position, then left and returned to the safety of Najaf. Even though the Iraqis came lightly armed for a fight with tanks, they still had plenty of small arms and RPGs. The task force engineers found large caches of weapons and ammunition when they searched the bunkers in the area.

About 5 p.m. we moved just south of the intersection and established a temporary defensive position until just before last light. Then I repositioned the company, this time over to the east side of the road, so the enemy could not see where we were setting up for the night. We had taken mortar and rocket fire the night before, and in light of the Iraqi capability of indirect fire, we were vulnerable if they had eyes on us; we stayed in the original position just south of the intersection. The intersection was a convenient landmark and target reference point and I wanted to be in a position where there were no significant terrain features that would allow their spotters to get a fix on us. We set up in a 360-degree company coil and had someone on TIS watch in every vehicle all night to prevent anyone from low-crawling through the fields and across the berms to get to us from the east.

By dark the logistics convoy and other division assets were moving up Highway 28 directly through the middle of Rams. There were thousands of vehicles, creating a massive traffic jam on the narrow road and kicking up clouds of choking dust. The worst part of it was that every vehicle had on its white lights instead of being blacked out. We were in a combat zone, and these drivers were acting like they were out for a quick trip to the supermarket. The string of headlights and tail lights stretched for miles; we knew they were visible to anyone in Najaf looking our way.

Mercado was livid. He was driving back and forth between the company area and the battalion maintenance area, riding herd on the mechanics and repairs to the vehicles, and could not believe that anyone would be driving through a tactical area of operations with white lights. It was almost as if the drivers did not realize that the road march portion of the operation had ended, and we were now in a fight.

"If those guys were smart, they would have grids to this road and would be hitting it right now. They could turn this into a real mess," he said, shaking his head in disgust.

Mercado was not the only one upset. All the task force leadership was complaining about the white lights but nothing could be done about it. Someone somewhere made a decision that the lights would stay on, apparently to help the vehicles move more quickly through the area.

About 8 p.m. I decided to stretch out on top of the tank's turret and grab a few minutes' sleep. What little sleep we had gotten the past few nights came while sitting inside the tanks. That was not sleep as much as it was tortured rest. We were cramped, cold, and uncomfortable. I wanted to stretch out, just for a few minutes.

My eyes were closed no more than ten minutes and I was just drifting off when I heard a *whoosh* and saw something fly over my head. That was followed quickly by an explosion that rocked the tank. A mortar targeting the convoy behind us had fallen short of its target and landed just behind my tank. I jumped up, keyed the radio, and brought all crews to REDCON ONE in the event we started taking more mortars. I wanted to be able to get out of there in a hurry. Thankfully, the rest of the night turned out to be uneventful.

The following day, Monday, 24 March, we pulled back to the vicinity of the task force TOC to be the Quick Reaction Force (QRF). Schwartz realized we had been out front fighting or on security since we arrived at Rams and wanted to give us a break from the front lines and its stresses. After we moved south on Highway 28, we set up across the road from the TOC facing west. A four-foot-high berm about fifty meters in front of us squeezed us back against the road, so we were strung out north to south. We had plenty of support on three sides of us and our only worry was to the west, much of which had been cleared by the engineers before we got there.

As the QRF we were responsible for responding to any mission the task force might get on short notice. Among the missions we received were a fruitless search for a SAM site that did not exist and a movement north by Red on Highway 28 through a thick fog to destroy a mortar position harassing the convoys.

The mechanics continued working feverishly, using every spare part in our inventory and cannibalizing other tanks that they referred to as "bitch tanks." They were able to get all our tanks up and running. We even got our M-88 tank recovery vehicle back, thanks to a new engine. It was an incredible effort, performed under extremely difficult conditions. I had a great deal of admiration for those guys. They seemed at times to be able to perform miracles on call.

For the first few days of the war, we were relatively lucky with the weather. We had good visibility, cool temperatures, and the only sand was what the vehicles kicked up. That changed the afternoon of the 24th. Another nasty dust storm blew in, buffeting the vehicles and making travel difficult for everyone. The pluggers were not working well with all the dust in the air and I was taking a chance getting lost just going the two hundred meters across the road to the TOC.

Martz and Sanderlin by this time were lobbying hard to get closer to the action. They spent the battle of Rams in soft-sided Humvees several miles from the battle and were not happy. They even went back to the task force to see if they could hook on with someone else who could get them closer. They had no luck. They were stuck with us, and we with them. I decided to put Martz in Mercado's PC and Sanderlin in the medic track to get them closer to the action as they requested.

The weather continued to be miserable through most of 25 March. The wind was up and dust was getting into everything. Despite that, I told Mercado to break out the generator and the Mr. Coffee. We had not had decent coffee for several days and I felt we all deserved a cup. I had a stash of Starbucks coffee left, and a package of chocolate biscotti I received from home some time earlier.

Before long I was sharing the coffee and biscotti with Mercado and Martz as we stood in front of one of the Humvees.

"I said before this started that if I'm going to war, I'm going to do it the right way, with Starbucks and biscotti," I told them.

They saluted me with their cups and we shared a quiet moment of civility in an otherwise hostile and forbidding landscape.

Throughout the afternoon, the wind increased and the visibility decreased. By 4 p.m. everything was bathed in a dull, orange glow as the setting sun was filtered through the blowing dust. We did not know it then, but it was a precursor of what was to come the following day just a few miles down the road.

The winds were gusting at times to seventy miles per hour, and the Humvees were rocking back and forth. It was difficult to walk upright, and everyone was trying as best they could to stay inside the vehicles and avoid breathing too much dust. Face scarves and goggles were a must for everyone.

Shortly after dark I was called over to the task force TOC for a briefing on a "be prepared mission" that had the task force going into Najaf. Visibility was so poor I had to use my plugger just to find the road.

Schwartz and Donovan were back at division rear getting orders to go up and relieve 3/7 Cav, which was engaged in a prolonged fight on the east side of the Euphrates. The Cav was running out of fuel and ammunition, and the division fuelers and supply trucks could not get up there without help. Task Force 1-64 was to clear the route, secure the bridges, allow the Cav to get back across the river before they got trapped on the east side, and make sure the resupply vehicles could move forward.

We were told the Cav lost two tanks and a Bradley to enemy action. A suicide bomber in a loaded fuel truck that rammed the tank reportedly made one of the tank kills. There was no word on casualties, but what appeared to be suicide bombings with fuel trucks put us all on edge.

As it turned out, the Cav did not lose the tanks as a result of enemy action. An Army study done after the war indicated that at least one of the Abrams was disabled by friendly fire from a Bradley fighting vehicle's 25mm cannon. The explosive rounds penetrated the engine compartment and killed it. There were no casualties but the tank was abandoned where it stopped.

That night we also learned that eleven Americans soldiers in a maintenance company attached to the 3rd Infantry Division had been killed and about a dozen taken prisoner when their convoy was ambushed in Nasiriyah. At least one of those captured was a woman, who turned out to be Jessica Lynch.

In addition, we received a message that the first sergeant from 1-64's Bravo Company, which was attached to Task Force 1-15, was seriously wounded in a mortar attack.

I was not a happy company commander when I left that meeting. The Iraqis were starting to use suicide bombers. We were losing friends, soldiers, and tanks. And the weather was the pits. Visibility was worse than zero: it was negative visibility.

I returned to the company area and began to brief my platoon leaders and platoon sergeants. I spread the map out on the hood of my Humvee, and in the glow of blue and red tactical lights I began to describe the next mission. I thought we would be allowed to ride the storm out here. I did not think there was any way we would move before morning. But just in case, I warned them: "You have thirty minutes to get ready. Be prepared to move at any moment."

Just then I saw some mud on the map and thought it came from my gloves when I opened it. I cleaned it off and returned to the brief. When I looked back at the map there was more mud. The more I tried to clean the map the muddier it got.

"What the hell?" I muttered to myself.

"It's raining, sir," someone said, "raining mud."

And it was. Mud was actually falling from the sky. Rain was falling through the dust storm, picking up dirt, and falling as wet, gooey mud. It was starting to coat everything. I moved the briefing under the overhang of one of the tank turrets and ran through the mission quickly. Charlie Company's objective was to secure two crossroads, Checkpoint Charlie and Checkpoint Charlie One. We were to deny all vehicle movement in and out of Najaf while the rest of the task force seized three bridges over the Euphrates to give 3/7 Cav an opportunity to get back to the west side.

"Remember to keep complete 360-degree security because you don't know where they are going to come from. These guys are fanatical. They are taking trucks and ramming them into our vehicles," I said, shouting above the wind.

About two hours later, around 11 p.m., we got the order to move. The weather was no worse, but it was also no better. We could not see a thing. The drivers were driving blind. Everything was being coated in mud. I could not read the grids on my plugger. Goggles were caked with mud. It was extremely difficult for our lead vehicle to link up with and follow the last of Charlie Rock's vehicles just a few feet in front of us.

All we could do was keep moving forward and hope we did not drive off a cliff or into oblivion. The first sergeant's PC with Sgt.

Andrew Coffman driving hit a ditch and nearly rolled over. Coffman, Mercado, Martz, and Spc. Shawn Sullivan, one of our medics, were bounced around inside pretty good.

We somehow managed to stay on the road and not lose anyone. Eventually, we were told to halt for the night. It was a relief to not have to move through that mess anymore. I set up a security plan so we could sleep in shifts but kept everyone at REDCON 1.5 for the night. The wind, rain, and mud were still pelting us, and we knew there were a lot of angry Iraqis out there who wanted to kill us. In the back of Mercado's PC, the first sergeant, Martz, and Sullivan settled in for the night as best they could in the terribly confined space.

"This is going to get nasty," Mercado said to no one in particular as he closed his eyes and tried to grab a few minutes sleep.

Nasty was not the word to describe it. It would be beyond nasty, something none of us could have imagined in our most wild and bizarre dreams, something we still have problems describing to anyone who was not there.

10

THE BATTLE FOR NAJAF

IF there is such a thing as an occasional glimpse of hell on earth, we saw it the afternoon of 26 March. It was the intersection near Najaf that would become known as Checkpoint Charlie.

The wind stopped just before dawn and stayed calm long enough to allow a biting cold to set in, hardening all the mud that gathered on our weapons and vision blocks. We spent several hours chipping the mud off the weapons, cleaning them, and making sure they were well lubricated before we moved out. No sooner had we finished at about 8:30 a.m. than the wind resumed with a frightening ferocity. With the wind came the sand and dust. It swirled over us and into the vehicles, fouling the weapons and once again limiting our visibility to just a few feet.

Charlie Company was last in the task force line of march. Wild Bunch, Charlie Rock, and the engineers were ahead of us, racing to secure the Euphrates River bridges to provide escape routes for 3/7 Cav. Intelligence reports indicated technical vehicles with machine guns and Iraqi fighters were closing in on the Cav from the north and south. We were to go to the intersection of two main roads on the southeast side of Najaf and set up a blocking position to deny all access into and out of the city and keep the road secured for the Cav to pull back through our lines. Because Wild Bunch and Char-

The intersection outside Najaf that was later named Checkpoint Charlie, seen as Charlie Company moved to secure it during a raging sandstorm on 26 March. Note the civilian bus with its front end ripped off, sitting in the middle of the intersection. It had been commandeered by local militiamen and, with civilians still aboard, rammed into a Bradley fighting vehicle. (*Jason Conroy*)

lie Rock were clearing the road ahead of us, I figured most of the fighting would be over by the time we got to the intersection.

As we moved along the road leading into the intersection, we began receiving mortar and small arms fire. Bunkers and fighting positions were scattered along both sides of the road. The closer we got to the intersection, the more fire we took. We could hear mortar rounds exploding, although the explosions were muffled by the wind and dust and almost drowned out by the noise of the tanks and our own suppressive fire.

Capt. Andy Hilmes, commander of Wild Bunch, would radio back that he was taking fire. Then Capt. Larry Burris, commander of Charlie Rock, would radio that he was taking fire. I don't think the Iraqis could see what they were shooting at because it was so windy and dusty, but they were firing at our noise. Rounds were pinging off the sides of tanks and Bradleys. It sounded almost like someone was throwing handfuls of gravel at us as we went past. Few of the enemy rounds found their mark. But one hit an engineer squarely in the chest as he was firing back at the Iraqis from the top of a PC. Were it not for his Interceptor body armor he would have been seriously wounded or killed. As it was, the impact merely shocked him for a few seconds, and he kept fighting.

Just a few moments before Charlie Company hit the intersection, Burris came over the radio: "They just ran a bus into my Bradley!"

I'm not sure what I expected to find, but I know I did not expect what I saw. The sun was setting as we pulled into the intersection and the dust was so thick that the afternoon turned red, as it had the previous day. The entire scene was bathed in an eerie glow that made us feel like we were at war on Mars. Sitting squarely in the middle of our objective was a civilian bus with its front end torn

Spc. Curtis Gebhard walks past the civilian bus that rammed into the side of a Bradley fighting vehicle, injuring several civilians, during the battle for Checkpoint Charlie. (*Brant Sanderlin/Atlanta Journal-Constitution*)

off. It was leaking oil and transmission fluid all over the road. Dead and injured passengers were scattered inside and outside the wreck. Militia fighters who came here from Baghdad and Karbala had commandeered the bus and ran it into Burris's Bradley. The Bradley was unscathed, but the bus was a mess.

When I pulled into the intersection, I saw First platoon and Shane Williams in Charlie Six-Five moving southeast on the main highway. Their instructions were to go straight through the intersection and continue on to a dirt road near a power plant that was to be Checkpoint Charlie One. But in the chaos of the fighting and with the limited visibility, they turned right at the main intersection and were heading in the wrong direction. I quickly got on the radio to Williams and Roger Gruneisen and told them to turn around and come back. We had information that a large enemy force was somewhere down that road, and we did not want to get into that fight just then because of the concern that we might push those Iraqis closer to the Cav, which was already in a tough fight.

Second platoon was supposed to orient to the southeast where Red had just gone. But when it saw Red heading in that direction, White went through the intersection heading for the power plant. Randy Pinkston in White Two, the lead tank, realized he was going the wrong way and turned the platoon around. I could barely see the tanks because of the flying dust but knew that they were having the same problems and the mistakes were understandable. Still, trying to get the tanks into their proper positions was a bit like herding cats at that point.

My main concern was Najaf, just a few miles to the northwest. I believed the bulk of enemy fire would come from there, so I tried to position my tanks to defend against it. I put Erik Balscik's Third platoon on that avenue of approach.

The two main roads at the intersection run roughly southeast to northwest, and southwest to northeast. We came in from the southwest and began setting up a tight, 360-degree perimeter at the crossroads. The intersection bore only a slight resemblance to what I had seen earlier on aerial photographs. The photographs did not show a cluster of buildings on the south corner or a high stone wall on the east corner about seventy-five meters from the intersection.

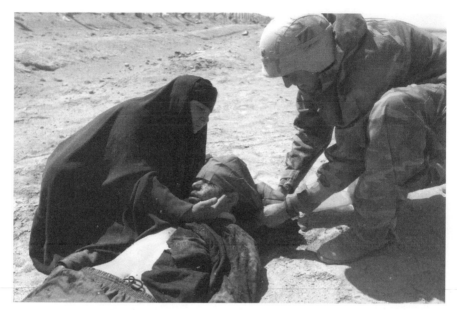

S.Sgt. Mark Strunk (right), Charlie Company's senior medic, treats an Iraqi man wounded near Checkpoint Charlie. It was unclear how the man had been wounded. (*Brant Sanderlin/Atlanta Journal-Constitution*)

The civilians from the bus, many of them women in black *abayas* wailing and keening over the dead and dying, were huddled around one another and their loved ones on the north corner. Beyond them were several dead Iraqis, some fighting positions, and mounds of dirt that stretched on for several hundred meters in the direction of two large smokestacks or towers of some sort.

On the east corner was a concrete bus stop riddled with bullet holes. A tan pickup truck carrying several fighters had crashed into it. One was hanging limply over the side, obviously dead. Another dead man was in the front seat. A third who was wounded lay in the bed of the pickup. Behind the bus stop were several bodies, some of them severely burned and still smoking, and fighting positions that stretched to the stone wall. Several shot-up cars and taxis had run off the road in that area.

The west corner contained more trenches and fighting positions and a small guardhouse. A fence line ran along the road about ten

Charlie Company soldiers Spc. Curtis Gebhard (left) and Spc. Anthony Kalis confront a wounded Iraqi fighter during the battle at Checkpoint Charlie. A dead Iraqi is slumped over the side of the truck, while another is in the front seat. (*Brant Sanderlin/Atlanta Journal-Constitution*)

meters from it and the road dipped slightly leading to the southwest. Several hundred meters beyond the fence was a large cluster of buildings that we later learned was a training camp for the local militias and Saddam *fedayeen*.

The buildings on the south corner were much closer and presented a far greater risk than I expected. As soon as I surveyed the situation, I realized there was no way two platoons would be able to effectively block the entire intersection. I called Schwartz and requested that I be allowed to keep Red at this checkpoint and not be sent out to cover Checkpoint Charlie One as well. From Checkpoint Charlie we could effectively block both intersections and not split the company, making us less vulnerable to counterattacks.

"Roger, execute," he said. He was ahead of us, driving in his tank to the bridges with Wild Bunch.

The casualties, the high winds, the blowing sand, the limited visibility, and the setting sun would have been more than enough for us to deal with on any normal day. But this was no normal day. We also were under fire, mostly from small arms and RPGs, and vehicles were still trying to drive through the intersection as we were setting up our defenses.

A Ford Bronco came racing out of Najaf and nearly clipped Mercado's PC as it pulled into the intersection.

Second platoon began setting up facing southwest and southeast near the close-in cluster of buildings. One car approached the tanks with a man leaning out the window firing an AK-47. Just as the car got close to the tanks, it went behind a van.

"Stop that car! Fire! Fire!" England ordered the crews. They shot up both vehicles. It was impossible in all the confusion to tell the difference between fighters and civilians. Often, those dressed in civilian clothes would turn out to be fighters.

Mercado's PC and the medic PC pulled into the intersection and took up positions near the wounded civilians. S.Sgt. Mark Strunk, the company's senior medic, was driving the medic PC. Riding in the back were Sanderlin, the photographer; Spc. Curtis Gebhard, our NBC expert; and Spc. Anthony Kalis, a replacement from the 11th Armored Cavalry Regiment at the NTC who had volunteered for Iraq and arrived only a few weeks earlier.

Strunk shucked his CVC, handed his 9mm pistol to Kalis, grabbed his medical kit, and dashed outside without a helmet or a weapon to start treating the wounded. Gebhard, Kalis, and Sanderlin were right behind him. Mercado sent Sullivan, the other medic, out into the maelstrom to start rounding up EPWs. Mercado stayed in the TC hatch, manning the .50-caliber machine gun to provide covering fire.

"Check the bus! Check the bus!" Mercado screamed over the wind to Gebhard. "See if there's anybody on the bus."

They checked the bus, then moved over to the pickup truck and the wounded Iraqi. Kalis pointed Strunk's 9mm at the Iraqi, who raised his arms in surrender.

"Get his weapon! Get his weapon! He's a motherfucking EPW!" Mercado shouted to the two.

I was concerned that one of the Iraqis inside our perimeter would get a weapon and start firing. That would provoke a response from Charlie Company and we could end up shooting each other. Rounding up the EPWs and taking care of the wounded were my first two priorities after our security perimeter was set.

Strunk tried to assess each victim's wounds as quickly as possible, render what aid he could, and move on. The first person he saw was a little girl who was unconscious. She apparently hit her head and was knocked out when the bus hit the Bradley. The women around her were shrieking in grief and rubbing her stomach, thinking she was dead.

"Don't rub her stomach! Hold her hand and talk to her," Strunk ordered them. Then, realizing they did not understand a word he was saying, he showed them what to do. They continued to wail, but did as he instructed.

He gave the girl some oxygen, and then treated a boy who had a broken ankle and some scrapes and bruises. Strunk told the first sergeant that the girl needed better treatment and recommended the civilians be taken back to the Forward Aid Station (FAS), a few

S.Sgt. Mark Strunk treats a wounded Iraqi fighter during the battle for Checkpoint Charlie. (*Brant Sanderlin/Atlanta Journal-Constitution*)

miles to the rear. I saw Strunk without his helmet and yelled at him to get it on before he did anything else. He went back to the medic PC, put on his helmet, and then dashed across the intersection to where the wounded Iraqi fighter lay, with Sanderlin, shooting photos, in pursuit. Strunk started an intravenous drip for the wounded man, who had a broken femur in one leg and a bullet wound in the other thigh.

"Hold this!" he ordered Sanderlin and thrust the drip bag into his hand.

Turning back to the wounded man, Strunk shouted over the din: "Tell your friends to stop firing! They're making too much noise!"

"Thank you. Thank you," the man said in heavily accented English.

Gebhard and Kalis moved into the area behind the bus stop looking for other Iraqis who might cause us problems. There was a burst of gunfire, and they dropped behind small mounds of dirt. Another burst kicked up sprays of dirt in front of them. They returned fire with their M-16s.

Mercado decided to leave Strunk and his PC at the scene so he could continue to work on the wounded. Driver Andrew Coffman would transport the first batch of wounded civilians back to the FAS while Mercado provided cover along the route with the .50 caliber.

Martz was still inside the PC, and the first sergeant leaned down from the hatch, handed him his 9mm, and said: "Ron, we've got some civilians getting in here. Get out and let them get in."

Martz grabbed the 9mm and on the way out took Coffman's loaded M-16 with an M-249 grenade launcher attached that was sitting near the rear hatch. He said later he did not think it was a good idea to leave a loaded weapon in easy reach of Iraqis, civilians or not. Just as he jumped out of the PC another volley of gunfire came ripping through the intersection. Martz ran across the road to the side of the bus stop, a weapon in each hand.

When I first saw him, I couldn't figure out who that old guy was carrying weapons in the middle of the intersection. Then I thought: "It's Ron." Now I had six people on the ground; two medics, one of whom was acting as a rifleman; two soldiers rounding up EPWs and bringing them back to a collection point near the medic PC; and two reporters.

I thought about the risks Martz and Sanderlin were taking being out there, because almost none of the tankers were on the ground. They were inside, where it was much safer, fighting the battle from there. I quickly dismissed my concerns. This is what they signed up for and had been lobbying for. Now they got it. Maybe this would stop their complaining. They told us not to make any special accommodations for them, and we did not. If this was what it took for them to do their jobs, then this is what they had to do.

I felt some comfort in the fact that they were wearing their helmets and flak jackets. And after that night, I didn't really worry about them handling themselves no matter what we got ourselves into.

The compassion of the American soldier in combat is something many people never hear about and therefore do not fully understand. But at Najaf that day, and in the days to come, I saw many instances of my soldiers risking their own safety to protect or care for a civilian who was injured or in danger.

Strunk was the first to do so. I was not happy that he got out of his vehicle without a helmet or a weapon. But his caring and concern for those he treated, civilians and Iraqi fighters alike, were the essence of what a medic should be.

That same afternoon Carlos Hernandez, one of the toughest guys in the company, showed a side of himself that I had not seen before. Hernandez, the gunner on Red One, saw a badly wounded civilian who was pulled from one of the vehicles caught in a deadly crossfire. With little regard for his own safety, Hernandez jumped off the tank, pulled the man away from the vehicle, and began administering first aid. He got an intravenous drip bag started, then helped carry the man to Mercado's PC. (Mercado and Coffman would make several trips to the FAS with wounded civilians and EPWs and had just enough time before darkness settled in for one more run. The road back was not safe in daylight. It would be worse after dark.)

The man Hernandez was tending was suffering from a gunshot wound to the left shoulder and a compound fracture of the right leg. He was in pain, but his biggest concern was never seeing his three children again.

"You'll be OK. The doctors are going to take care of you," Hernandez assured him, holding the drip bag in one hand, a 9mm pistol in another.

As the man winced in pain, Hernandez put down the pistol and began stroking his hair, assuring him he would be fine and that the doctors would get to him soon.

"Thank you," the man said weakly in broken English.

Martz was standing nearby, and Hernandez looked at him as if to say: "You can do this."

"If you've got to get back, I can do that," Martz told him.

Hernandez handed him the drip bag, grabbed his pistol, and ran back to his tank. Martz had no medical training but was told by the medics to just keep talking to the man, just keep him conscious so he did not go into shock. So he did. Finally, the wounded man was loaded onto the top of Mercado's PC for the ride back to the FAS. The top was slick with blood from previous wounded and dripped over the back. Mercado looked around for someone to accompany the man back to the FAS. No extra soldiers were available because we were still in the middle of a tough fight.

"Ron, you have to go with him and hold the drip bag. I don't have anyone else."

Martz clambered onto the top of the PC, grabbed the drip bag with his left hand, a bungee cord with his right to keep from falling off, and the PC sped off into the night; Sullivan and his M-16 on the other side of the man provided security.

The intersection looked like hell in a very small space. It was chaotic and confusing, but we were trying to stay focused on what we had to do. We had no casualties, for which I was grateful. And we were in control of the immediate area. Watching the Charlie Company soldiers perform gave me an overwhelming sense of confidence and security. At that point I didn't think there was anything my guys could not do if asked.

My confidence in them bordered on recklessness at times. At one point during the fight, I got off my tank to check on the wounded and EPWs. I did not take a weapon with me. I had taken off my

9mm because it got in the way when I was trying to get in and out of the hatch. I did not even think about taking an M-4.

When I hit the ground, with gunfire all around me, I flashed back to the movie *Apocalypse Now*, which I had watched just before the start of the war. There is the scene where Lt. Col. Bill Kilgore, played by Robert Duvall, gets off his helicopter and walks around through mortar fire with this aura of invincibility about him. That's how I felt. Nothing was going to happen because my soldiers were going to take care of me. I was finally jerked back to reality when Helgenberger came running up with an M-4 and thrust it into my hands.

"Sir," he said, "you might need this." He had his own M-4 and followed me wherever I went that afternoon.

As I looked around the intersection, I could not help but marvel at how quickly Charlie Company soldiers were responding. They

Capt. Jason Conroy (left), "Cobra Six," and loader Spc. Paul Helgenberger aboard tank "Charlie Six-Six" at Checkpoint Charlie. (*Jason Conroy*)

were doing not only what they were asked to do, but also many things they took on themselves to do. Young soldiers were taking charge of EPWs, caring for the wounded, comforting the civilian casualties, and shooting back when they were shot at. I was in awe of them and the way they responded. It was as if they had been doing this all their lives, and I was little more than an outside observer. They were taking care of each other just as they had at Objective Rams and would continue to do so throughout the war.

I talked with platoon leaders to ensure we had interlocking fields of fire around our 360-degree perimeter and began to prepare for a long night. I was expecting a counterattack from Najaf, so I focused much of my attention on that sector and Blue's defensive positions. Concertina wire was unrolled about two hundred meters in front of the tanks, along with chem lights to warn Iraqi drivers to stay away.

I told the tank drivers to flash their lights at approaching vehicles and if they did not stop to fire warning shots at the ground in front of them. If they still did not stop and got through the wire, they were fair game. I felt better once we got all the wounded and EPWs out of our perimeter because then we could focus on what was around us instead of what was in the middle of us.

My next concern was the buildings closest to where Red and White were set up facing southeast and southwest. It would have been easy for someone to sneak up behind the buildings, go inside, get to the roof, and start sniping us. We kept a close watch on the alleys and doors of the houses, looking for hot spots in the TIS all night. I called Schwartz and asked for infantry to clear the buildings but none was available.

No one slept much that night. We drifted in and out of consciousness, watching for hot spots in the TIS, startled awake at the slightest noise. We were still keyed up about the fight and tense about our tactical situation. Help was not far away, but we were out there alone and very vulnerable, an island of Americans in a sea of angry Iraqis.

Blue's sector was the busiest that first night. It was covering the south and southwest, which contained the training camp and its buildings. Throughout the night Iraqi fighters would sneak into the buildings and try to get shots off at us. David Richard on Blue Four spotted several on the way in and killed them before they had a chance to set up. One guy would come up to fire, and Richard would shoot him. Then another guy would take his place, and Richard would shoot him. The bodies just stacked up in a corner of the building, maybe a half dozen of them. It looked like he was killing guys on top of one another in the same position. They were either very dumb, or very dedicated.

Despite the intensity of the situation, Charlie Company soldiers were still being cautious about who they shot at. If they could not clearly identify someone with a weapon, they held off. Not long after midnight, Richard on Blue Four called up and said he saw three people walking about four hundred meters to his front.

"Do they have weapons?" I asked.

"I can't tell. But it looks like one of them has a weapon or a walking stick."

"Continue to monitor," I told him.

I picked them up on the TIS in my tank but I also could not tell if what the one person was carrying was a walking stick or a weapon. Richard and I continued to talk as we watched the three. We decided to let them pass and finally they walked behind some buildings, and we lost sight of them.

It was not one of the day's major events but it was significant in that it demonstrated once again how much Charlie Company soldiers wanted to avoid shooting at anyone they could not clearly identify as an enemy combatant. Making that distinction was something with which we would have to deal repeatedly over the next few days at Checkpoint Charlie and later when we got to Baghdad.

Just before dawn Malone shook me out of a fitful sleep. "Sir, I've got a hot spot," he said.

He was looking through the TIS north toward the smokestacks when he suddenly picked up a hot spot less than a hundred meters from us. The hot spot was small, but was moving back and forth, occasionally going behind a berm. We could not tell what it was and continued to watch. The hot spot was not moving any closer, but we could see some back-and-forth movement. Richard also saw it in his TIS but could not decide what it was.

As it gradually became lighter, Malone switched from his TIS to his daylight sights to get a clearer picture. Slowly, the mysterious object came into view. It was a scruffy dog, which had spent much of the night gnawing on the body of a dead Iraqi behind one of the berms. The dog apparently avoided being detected by walking behind the berm to the body. All we were able to pick up on the TIS was its head moving back and forth as it worked over the body.

It was something we would see again in the next few days. But at that point we were more concerned about the living than the dead, and what we would be facing that morning as we began our first full day at Checkpoint Charlie.

11

CHECKPOINT CHARLIE

BY dawn the nightmarish storm had passed, giving way to a cool, clear morning. What we did not realize at first was that this day, 27 March, was a Thursday, the Muslim equivalent of Saturday. Despite the carnage that had taken place at the intersection the previous day, the weekend brought out hundreds of people trying to get to market, trying to get from one town to the next, and, in many instances, trying to get away from reprisals we heard were taking place in Najaf.

A psychological operations (PSYOP) team was assigned to us and set up in the same corner of the intersection as the medic PC and the first sergeant's PC. The PSYOP team had a large loudspeaker and was able to broadcast recorded messages in Arabic that essentially told anyone within several miles to avoid the intersection because this was a military zone of operations. The team also had recordings of helicopter and tracked vehicle noises which I asked be played every so often to keep the fighters in Najaf off balance, trying to convince them there were more of us out here than there actually were.

The recordings quickly became a source of irritation for all of us. Dan Pyle was the only one in the company who understood more than a few words of Arabic, and the messages being played by the PSYOP guys had a monotone, sing-song quality about them that made our teeth hurt. And the fact that they were played twenty-four hours a day, even while we were trying to sleep, did not help our nerves. But the recordings did keep many Iraqis away from the intersection.

Morning also brought an increase in vehicle traffic. One of the first to approach us was an ambulance coming out of Najaf. It slowly maneuvered around the concertina wire, and Blue fired a warning shot. It stopped just inside the wire, and I told Richard to have it turn around and go back. We were not letting anyone through. But two guys got out and started walking toward us holding their hands over their heads. One spoke fairly good English and was quite persistent.

He told us he wanted to go through the intersection to the southeast and pick up some casualties. I told him if we let him through he also had to pick up the bodies around the intersection. There were probably a dozen dead Iraqi fighters lying around in various states of rigor mortis. Some were just outside the back hatch of Mercado's PC so that every time anyone got out of the vehicle they were greeted by several corpses frozen in death throes.

But the man said he would only take the bodies of those he knew were from Najaf. The others, he said, were from Baghdad and Karbala, and he would have nothing to do with them. He feared by doing so he would be seen as collaborating with the Saddam *fedayeen*, which were virtually controlling Najaf. The bodies were someone else's responsibility, meaning ours. In exchange for not forcing him to take the bodies, he told us about a mortar position he had seen along the road about a thousand meters to Blue's front.

The longer we talked to him, the more information he provided. He told us how the *fedayeen* were terrorizing the local residents. He told us how they killed one man with a meat hook in front of a crowd for telling other people that the Americans were there. He told us how the *fedayeen* were trying to get the soldiers to fight by threatening to kill their families. He said they were taking children from their families or staying in houses with families to force men to fight. Their plan, he said, was to fight surrounded by civilians.

If true, this would be a completely different war from the one we had trained for. Instead of fighting regular forces, we would be fighting terrorists who had no regard for themselves or the civilians around them. We would have to be wary of everyone, including the civilians.

After the ambulance attendant gave us a good deal of useful intelligence, we searched the vehicle and allowed it to pass. It was one of the few that got through over the next several days. When he returned a few hours later, he showed us eight or nine dead bodies in the back, one of them a baby. In addition, there were three or four more badly wounded, all of whom were probably dying. One man on top of the pile was in especially bad shape, with blood coming out of his mouth every time he tried to take a breath. The ambulance attendant said they were from fighting in the south, not from the intersection.

Ambulances proved to be a major headache for us. We could never tell if they were legitimate or a decoy. Late that morning we saw an ambulance go into the training school, drop off some people, and then pull back out on the road. As it got on the road, the back door opened and an RPG was fired at us.

We started taking occasional harassing RPG and mortar fire that morning, setting a pattern that was to continue over the next few days. The mortars were inaccurate but terribly irritating and kept us all on edge. The RPGs were usually way off target and became more of a nuisance than a threat. At one point we saw an RPG warhead come skittering down the street toward us, bouncing off the pavement at it rocketed along. It eventually got tangled in the concertina wire several hundred meters in front of Blue's tanks. It never exploded, and we called in the engineers to blow it up.

That morning we began to implement a number of checkpoint procedures designed to ensure our security as we found ourselves faced with a large group of civilians who were either trying to flee the city because of terrorists or simply wanted to go from one town to another. The procedures were not something we planned out, or wrote up in a formal directive. But they were procedures we built on from our checkpoint duty at Objective Rams and what other soldiers and I had picked up while doing similar duty in Bosnia. Individual soldiers, using their initiative, common sense, and wariness about the possibility of civilian suicide bombers, developed

S.Sgt. Ben Phinney pats down an Iraqi man holding a child during a weapons search at Checkpoint Charlie on 28 March. (*Brant Sanderlin/Atlanta Journal-Constitution*)

them on the fly. We discussed them, used what worked, and discarded what did not. It was an ongoing, daily experience of trial and error in a combat zone.

My time in Bosnia had given me experience dealing not only with checkpoints, but also with a local civilian population that was not necessarily happy we were there. This was somewhat of a different situation though: here we were in the middle of a shooting war. But the concept here was much the same as it was in Bosnia. We wanted the support of the civilians. We wanted to reinforce that we were here to liberate the Iraqis, to give them back their country, and make it a better place by getting rid of Saddam. Without that support we would have a difficult time stabilizing the country.

I also believed that the locals could be a great source of intelligence. Civilians would often tell us things that trained soldiers, and even poorly trained but dedicated militia, would not. One thing we learned early on was that everyone in Iraq was required to carry an

ID card. They were different colors and it was easy to tell civilian from military or Ba'ath Party member. I decided that no one would get through our checkpoints unless an ID card was produced. Much to our surprise, even the military and party militia who tried to sneak through in civilian clothes willingly whipped out their ID cards. And we happily turned them into EPWs. It was a great way to identify potential combatants and to gain additional intelligence.

We wanted to get some sense about what the civilians were thinking. We realized that initial intelligence analyses—that we would be greeted with open arms and have flowers strewn in our path, like the Americans who liberated Rome and Paris in World War II—were wrong. We had already run into tough and determined resistance, with fighters low-crawling to tanks to try to take us out. And the civilian population was anything but overjoyed to see us. So we were naturally confused about the response of the Iraqi people to our presence there and wanted to try to determine why their actions did not match up with the intelligence analyses.

Before leaving Kuwait, we had spent a lot of time talking about civilian casualties and how to avoid them. I was very mindful of the consequences of civilian casualties and did not want to have any on my conscience, or that of my soldiers. I was not sure how much impact those talks had until we got to Objective Rams. Then I had soldiers calling up in the middle of a firefight and asking: "Hey, sir, can I shoot them?"

It was not that they did not want to engage people who were shooting at them. And they certainly were not timid. They simply wanted to be reassured they were doing the right thing. They were not cowboys out there gunning people down for the fun of it. They were professional soldiers and behaved accordingly.

While I was mindful of the civilians we were starting to encounter, I was more mindful of my soldiers and their safety and well-being. Putting my soldiers at risk was not something I planned to do any more than was necessary to get us to Baghdad. When I felt it was too dangerous, or somebody called and said the number of people at a checkpoint was overwhelming them, I shut down checkpoint operations and pulled the soldiers back to a more secure area. Then we went to a very protective posture until things cooled down or the crowds thinned out. We had only about nine soldiers at any one time available to process the hundreds of civilians who wanted to get through the checkpoints. The rest of the soldiers had to stay back with the tanks to provide overwatch security for those on the ground. Checkpoint duty was even more intense than airport security checks: because the soldiers never knew who might be carrying an AK-47 or a bomb, they had to be extremely cautious with each individual. In addition, the mortars were continuing to target us, making checkpoint duty extremely stressful.

Every soldier has a right to protect himself if he feels his life is in danger. He is authorized to use deadly force if he feels it is necessary to protect his life or the lives of fellow soldiers. But if he is not threatened, even if he's dealing with an enemy soldier, the orders were to capture, not kill. The rule that we used was don't kill anyone unless you feel your life is in immediate danger and you have to return fire.

It was like being a policeman. If someone pulls something out of his or her pocket in a tense situation, that policeman has to make a snap decision about whether it's a gun or a cell phone. Charlie Company soldiers were faced with the same thing. It was a difficult psychological shift for young soldiers to make, going from a trigger-pulling combat soldier to a policeman and back again, all in the matter of a few seconds. But that's what we were expected to do, even if we were not trained to do it.

As I mentioned earlier, the American soldier has a great capacity for kindness to civilians, especially women and children. At this point in the war, our defenses went down slightly whenever we saw civilians. We had not yet seen all the terrorist tactics that the Iraqis would employ and were somewhat lucky that we got through the first checkpoint operation at Rams unscathed. We got even tougher at Checkpoint Charlie, but there we had to deal with an entirely new set of problems. Many more people were trying to flee Najaf. A number of women were among them. We did not search the women, out of deference to the Muslim sensibilities. Instead, we asked their husbands to do it, or at least in some way be able to convince us that the woman was not carrying any hidden weapons or bombs. It was not any easy task, considering our limited Arabic, and there was a great deal of impromptu sign language that went into checkpoint duty.

It also provided moments of unintended humor. Men would occasionally approach us lifting their ankle-length *dishdashas* above their head to show that they were not armed, but also showing us much more of themselves than any of us wanted to see. At Blue's checkpoint, two men approached smiling, waving, and giggling. When S.Sgt. Chhay Mao started to frisk them, they giggled more, like they enjoyed it. Either that or they were terribly ticklish. Then Mao noticed strange bulges inside one man's shirt. He motioned for the man to reveal the bulges and he pulled out two live pigeons. The other man pointed to his mouth as if to say: "That's lunch."

The identification card checks proved to be invaluable to us. Blue found one man wearing civilian clothes but carrying a uniform in a plastic bag. When his ID card was checked, he turned out to be military. We discovered another guy in civilian clothes wearing military boots and grabbed him as an EPW. The soldiers turned into good cops. They would look at people's hands, their shoes, and their feet, to determine who was privileged, which usually meant military or Ba'ath Party members, and who was not. The privileged usually had clean hands and feet, or wore shoes. The others did not.

The majority of those leaving the city were women and children. Those who spoke a little English would tell us of the *fedayeen* indiscriminately murdering people in the town, and of militia riding around in technical trucks with machine guns on top, shooting up houses and businesses.

The training camp off to Blue's left front was a continual source of enemy fire. The locals said it was a university, so we started calling it Osama bin Laden U. On the afternoon of the 27th, I decided to find out what was really down there and sent three tanks from Blue and the BFST (Cobra Three-Zero) to reconnoiter the area and see if they could take out some of the mortar positions that we believed were targeting us. They did not get far before a barrage of RPGs and machine-gun fire was unleashed on them. They fired back, shooting up bunkers and mortar pits along the road. We decided to wait until the next day to send a heavier force down the road. I could not move the entire company out of Checkpoint Charlie and leave it open. I had to wait for additional forces to come in and secure the intersection and that could not be done until the next day.

We had no intention of going into the city at that time. The division plan was to surround Najaf and cut it off to enable 2nd Brigade to move north and take some of the pressure off 3/7 Cav, which was still on the east side of the Euphrates. We were doing little more than probing. By late that afternoon, the rest of the task force had secured the bridges and 3/7 Cav was able to pull back through our lines to get refueled and rearmed. The Cav soldiers were a dusty, dirty, haggard-looking bunch when they passed us.

The night of the 27th was relatively uneventful, but the next day turned out to be one filled with events that were starting to become the hallmark of this war, a war that was part combat, part peace-keeping, and part strangeness.

This was Friday, the Muslim holy day, and by first light the crowd trying to get through the intersection was growing rapidly. More people were trying to get through than we could handle and they were stacking up by the hundreds at the various checkpoints we'd established beyond our perimeter.

Brett Waterhouse was celebrating his 36th birthday that day. He started his morning by climbing down off his tank and hopping into a nearby trench that some of the soldiers were using as a latrine. It was just outside our lines but he informed soldiers in the two closest vehicles, Randy Pinkston in White Two and the crew in Cobra Three-Zero, of where he would be and what he would be doing in the event of an emergency.

Waterhouse just finished his business and was about to pull up his pants when an Iraqi man began walking toward him, gesturing wildly, and talking in a tone that obviously was not friendly. Pinkston and Lopez were sitting on their tank nearby, shaving and brushing their teeth. Pinkston looked over at Lopez and said: "That guy's going to be trouble."

Waterhouse shouted at the man in one of the few Arabic phrases he knew, telling him to stop, but he kept coming. The man picked up a rock and threw it at Waterhouse, who ducked and shouted at him again. Still he kept coming, picking up another rock and hurling toward Waterhouse, who had his hands full of pants and was having difficulty fending off the rocks.

The man got closer and started tossing larger rocks. Waterhouse dropped his pants, picked up his M-4 and fired two warning shots at the man's feet. Another rock, bigger still, and another warning shot. Waterhouse was beginning to think the man might be a suicide bomber. Behind him, Waterhouse could hear other soldiers shouting for the man to stop.

"Shoot that guy! What the hell are you doing?" Pinkston yelled, convinced the man was determined to kill Waterhouse.

The rocks were the size of bricks by then and the man showed no intention of stopping, despite the warning shouts and shots. Waterhouse was still down in the trench, about four feet lower than the man, when the final rock came hurtling his way, directly at his head. Waterhouse, a former drummer in a marching band, blocked it with his left hand, opening a large gash. Then he fired one shot at the man's chest.

The 5.56mm round hit the man, but he kept coming. Waterhouse fired two more rounds and Lopez opened up with his M-4, firing a three-round burst, and the man went down in a heap about three feet from the trench. He died a short time later, while Strunk was trying to save him.

The whole incident took only a minute or two to unfold. And while my tank was just a short distance away, by the time I heard the commotion and was able to get there, it was over. I had requested a translator earlier that morning, and he arrived just as the shots went off. I figured he would be of some help trying to sort out what happened.

"This guy wanted to kill me, and I could tell by looking in his eyes it was either me or him," Waterhouse said. Pinkston agreed that the man was intent on trying to kill Waterhouse.

There was concern not only about Waterhouse's safety, but about whether the man was trying to get to a nearby cache of weapons that the engineers had not yet destroyed. A stash of RPGs and AK-47s was still in a small guard post just a few feet from

Waterhouse, and he said it appeared the man was headed in that direction.

The man apparently had come out of the little cluster of houses on the south corner of the intersection, and I was unsure what sort of reaction we would get from the people living there. But the skirmish had no sooner happened than the man's family rushed out. They were not angry, as I expected them to be. At least they said they were not angry. They seemed quite apologetic about what had happened. Speaking through the interpreter, one man who identified himself as the dead man's brother said they did not want any problems as a result of this.

I was apologizing that the man had been killed and said that he attacked one of our soldiers, and he was apologizing for his brother being out there. He said he didn't know why his brother had come into our area and thrown rocks at the soldiers. The family promised that if anyone came into their village who was not supposed to be there, they would let us know. They said they were happy we were there. I didn't buy it, but it made me feel better. I suspect they just wanted to be left alone at that point.

After the Waterhouse shooting and the Metheny incident a few days earlier, people started to get real particular about where they went to the bathroom. It was getting hazardous just trying to answer nature's call. Some went right next to the tanks, using MRE boxes or empty ammunition crates. Some did it in bags or boxes inside the tanks and threw the refuse off the side. There was no such thing as modesty out there when safety and survival were our primary focus.

The company was stretched pretty thin at that point because of having to run checkpoints on foot while keeping soldiers in the tanks to watch for vehicles trying to get past the barriers. Shortly after the Waterhouse incident, a white car approached Blue's checkpoint and stopped outside the wire. A man got out with his hands raised and indicated he wanted to get through the checkpoint. He was searched and allowed to come inside the wire because he spoke English. He was brought to the bus stop and I began questioning him along with several other Iraqis who said they worked at the nearby power plant.

Then James Pyle, the loader on Richard's tank, saw another white car approaching. It stopped just behind the first white car and, using it as a shield, four men with weapons got out of the second car and ran off to the left side of the road.

"I have four people. They have AKs and are carrying ammo," Pyle reported.

"Fire that car up!" Richard ordered.

The .50 caliber failed to fire. Marabello, who was scanning with the main gun sight, could see a woman in a black *abaya* inside the first car. Marabello shot the coax, walking the tracers into some bushes near the first car where the four men ran and were now firing at the tanks. But several rounds skipped off the pavement and hit the first car, flattening the front tires.

The man who had gotten out of the first car and whom I was questioning looked up when the firing began and started wailing: "My baby! My baby!" I thought there was a baby in the car.

A young man jumped out of another car and began gesturing at the first white car. Marabello stopped firing and the teen pulled an old man and the woman out of the car. The woman turned out to be a girl, no more than fourteen or fifteen. She was crying and bleeding from a small wound to her right foot where a ricochet had hit her. The old man was blind and had problems walking.

Seeing the girl's distress, Richard took his tank down to the car and got off to help her. He grabbed her by the arm and helped her negotiate the barbed wire while using the Abrams as cover as it slowly backed up to the checkpoint. As they were walking back, they began taking fire from the bushes again. Marabello raked the bushes with the coax, and I sent Pinkston around Blue's left flank to try to get a shot on the gunmen.

When the girl was brought into the intersection we learned she was the wife of the man I was talking with. She was his "baby." The old man was the grandfather of one of them. We never figured out which. At first the girl was insistent on not letting either of our medics touch her wound, which was relatively minor. She thought her husband would not want her after being touched by another man, even if it was one of medics trying to help her. Using our civilian contract interpreter, we finally convinced her to allow Sulli-

S.Sgt. (later Sgt. 1st Class) David Richard escorts a wounded Iraqi woman to safety and medical treatment after she was caught in a crossfire at Checkpoint Charlie on 28 March. (*Brant Sanderlin/Atlanta Journal-Constitution*)

van to treat the wound. We were all surprised at how young she was to be married. And we were amazed at the courage Richard displayed by walking into what essentially was a free-fire zone to help her. "I have a daughter about the same age," he said later. "I never gave it a second thought that one of them might have a bomb. My first thought was to protect the young and the old."

While the girl was being treated, Pinkston was trying to maneuver to get a shot on the gunmen in the bushes. He saw two men carrying rugs that were obviously wrapped around what he thought were weapons. One man had two young boys with him.

Pinkston sent Scott Stewart, his gunner, and Mark Gatlin, the loader on White One, down the road to check them out because the road was too narrow for his tank. The man with the two boys turned out to be an Iraqi major general, dressed in civilian clothes and trying to escape the area. The other man was believed to be a Saddam *fedayeen*. Stewart and Gatlin also found another man hiding in the bushes with an AK-47 that was still hot from being recently fired. This man wore a party ring, carried a wad of cash, and was well dressed compared with the others nearby. All were taken back to the intersection for further questioning.

We had taken some mortar rounds earlier in the day, and they were starting to get on my nerves. No one had been wounded yet, but if they were not stopped it seemed like only a matter of time before the spotters walked them in on us. In addition, they disrupted checkpoint operations and just about everything else we were doing. It was very intermittent; a few rounds every hour or so, each time getting just a bit closer to the middle of the intersection. That went on throughout the day. Every time we got hit I called the task force TOC and asked if division assets could pick up the rounds on their Q-36 and Q-37 counterbattery radar. I was told either that I was outside the coverage area or that these were controlled explosions—an explosion or controlled detonation that is set, timed, and monitored to destroy caches of weapons or equipment while avoiding human casualties—and there was nothing they could do for us. We were on our own.

The mortar issue finally hit home to the task force staff the afternoon of the 28th. Schwartz and his staff came to the intersection to interrogate the Iraqi major general and discuss the possibility of Charlie Company going into the heart of Najaf to gather intelligence, pinpoint the party headquarters building, and take out a large statue of Saddam in the city center. It would be as much a tactical blow as a psychological blow to the Iraqis. It would let them know we could go anywhere we wanted at any time.

I was not keen on the idea of going into Najaf. Neither was Schwartz. We had some aerial photographs of the center of the city but could not tell enough about how wide or narrow the streets were to get any sense of how easy or difficult it would be to maneuver in there. I was especially concerned about getting into the city, having a tank break down, and trying to tow it back out under fire. We were also getting widely varying estimates of the number of fighters who remained in there. We were hearing everything from just a few *fedayeen* to hundreds of well-armed fighters.

We were getting plenty of information from people who said

they wanted to help us, but the information was so disparate we could not get a good feel for it. I thought the Iraqi major general would have the best read on things, and his account differed significantly from what Schwartz and Perkins, the brigade commander, were hearing from other sources outside Najaf. I felt the information we were getting from people who had just been in Najaf was much more credible.

Schwartz unrolled the aerial photograph on the front slope of my tank and began asking the Iraqi major general to tell him the location of defensive positions and military strong points in the city. The Iraqi seemed to want to be helpful, pointing out the party headquarters building and several other government buildings. But he was having some problems deciphering the aerial photograph, probably because it was unlikely he had ever seen one before. We pulled out a captured Iraqi map with graphics on it and he was able to pinpoint more positions. We were trying to match the map to the aerial photo, and the task force staff was intently looking at the two.

Suddenly, two mortars hit. One was about a hundred meters to our left, the other about fifty. It was as if someone had let a dog loose in a room full of cats. I never saw so many people scramble so fast for cover. By then, Charlie Company soldiers were rather blasé about the mortars, and most of us just watched the staff hightail it back to their vehicles.

My first thought was: "Whoa! Where's everybody going? Those are just controlled explosions!"

Someone actually came on my radio and asked that question: "Sir, why is all the staff running around? I thought that was just a controlled explosion."

I was starting to personalize the mortar attacks, though. It seemed that every time I tried to eat something, get some sleep, or go to the bathroom, we would get mortared. I was eating an MRE of chicken cavatelli when those mortars hit on the 28th, and I had to abandon it.

"Those fuckers are fucking with me again," I snarled to myself.

The mortars put a quick end to the plans to go into Najaf. But we were tired of the mortars and thought with the battalion and brigade staffers around, we would be able to get some additional assets to take out the spotters.

Corp. Larry Hamilton, the gunner on Mao's Blue Two, thought he saw a spotter and another man with a weapon in one of the two tall towers to our north. Mao looked through his binoculars but thought it was nothing more than a couple of pigeons up there. But Marabello in Blue Four confirmed there were two men up in the tower, one with binoculars and the other with a weapon.

We were able to get an OH-58D Kiowa to come in with some missiles and knock out the tower. The helicopter took out *a* tower, but not *the* tower. For some reason, the Kiowa hit the wrong tower, then for some reason—maybe a lack of fuel or weapons malfunction—it could not get off another shot and left.

"Would someone please shoot that tower?" I radioed to Blue in frustration.

Marabello shot one HEAT round and knocked off the top of the tower and the two spotters with it.

"Thank you," I radioed Blue, the sarcasm evident in my voice. But that ended the mortar attacks for our duration at Checkpoint Charlie.

Perkins called Schwartz and me over to his M113 and said he wanted more intelligence on the training facility and grids to the buildings there. We were to take the company down the road while Bravo Company of Task Force 2-70 came up to hold the intersection. I pulled the company together and about 2 p.m. we began moving down the road toward Najaf. We started out in what is known as an "Israeli Box," with one platoon on line up front, a platoon on each side, my tank and the BFST in the middle, and the XO at the rear. As the road narrowed, we shifted into two columns, my tank and the BFST in the center of the formation. On the way down, we started taking small arms and RPG fire from fighters dressed all in black, the Saddam *fedayeen*. We destroyed several technical vehicles and fighters at an intersection adjacent to the training camp as we pushed toward the center of the city. We traveled about three or four kilometers, taking sporadic fire from fighters in alleys as we passed. We requested permission to advance farther, but were denied because of concern that we would push fighters out of the city into Objective Rams. We turned around at an intersection just a few hundred feet past the training camp and headed back to Checkpoint Charlie.

I kept getting radio calls from the task force TOC asking me to describe the military training facility. I gave them a brief description but told them I would bring back some video of it and give a more detailed briefing later. I had my video camera and began shooting the training camp on the return. It looked like it had been set up as a terrorist training camp rather than a standard military facility. It had obstacle courses, firing ranges, pits with mortar tubes and ammunition still in them, targets with the silhouettes of tanks on them, and a large housing complex for those who trained there. I was out of my hatch filming, thinking all the fighters were either dead or had run away, when an RPG came flying out of the camp just a few feet over my head. The whoosh it made as it went over me can be heard clearly on the video. I got down inside the tank in a hurry and that was the end of the video.

Once we returned to Checkpoint Charlie, we relieved Bravo Company of TF 2-70 and reestablished security around our perimeter. The first sergeant was insistent about burying the dead bodies. They were starting to smell and presented a health hazard. We had kept putting off the chore, thinking we were about to move north to rejoin the rest of the brigade, which by this time had moved to Objective Spartan south of Karbala. But he wanted the bus stop cleaned out so he could rig up a shower. Using ropes, we hauled the corpses into a nearby hole and buried them without any ritual or ceremony. The bus stop was cleaned up, blankets were stuffed in the windows and hung on the front, and the first sergeant enjoyed his first shower in several days.

That night, we heard wild dogs growling and snarling outside our vehicles. We thought they were getting into the trash pit and fighting over the remnants of MREs we threw in there. But when we got up in the morning, we saw that a pack of dogs had uncovered some of the dead and were gnawing at the dead flesh. We chased them off and reburied the dead, a bit deeper this time.

When we had first arrived at Checkpoint Charlie, we had been anticipating staying no more than a day. Then on the 27th, we had been told we might be there for another 48 to 72 hours. I rechecked the security we had, but there was not much more we could do at that point. We were not allowing any cars through and were careful about the Iraqis we let inside our lines. We had established buffer zones between us and whoever tried to approach. We put out signs in Arabic that informed people this was a military zone and off limits. The PSYOP broadcasts were still going. We had holding areas for EPWs before they were taken off our hands, and areas where people were staged several hundred meters from the checkpoints before they could actually start moving into them.

We were learning as we went, but we were establishing procedures that would be invaluable once we got to Baghdad. Now, it was just a matter of getting there. We still had to get out of Checkpoint Charlie and then to and through Karbala before we could even think about Baghdad. And considering the way the defenders of Najaf had fought, we knew the road to Baghdad would only get more difficult in the days to come.

12

THE ROAD TO BAGHDAD

ON the morning of 29 March, we were finally relieved of our duties at Checkpoint Charlie by Alpha Company of Task Force 2-70 and the 101st Airborne Division. Those units were now responsible for the checkpoint and Najaf. We were to move back to the intersection at Objective Rams, do maintenance, get what rest we could, and then move north on Highway 28 to rejoin the rest of the brigade south of Karbala.

We got a twenty-four-hour respite at Objective Spartan about forty miles south of Karbala before the task force moved on 30 March to within twelve miles of the city. At that point, we were once again the most northern unit in the 3rd Infantry Division. Task Force 1-64 set up a blocking position on the east side of Highway 28, while 3/7 Cav took the west side. Task Forces 3-15 and 4-64 were out to the south and southeast, making contact with the enemy in an effort to draw forces down from the north. It was a diversionary tactic to try to convince the Iraqis we were going to cross the Euphrates there.

The division plan called for a tactical pause south of Karbala for 24 to 72 hours as other operations shaped the battlefield and reduced the Iraqi military threat. Army attack aviation, MLRS, and the Air Force were used to hit enemy forces, many of them Republican Guard units, in and around Karbala and on the east side of the Euphrates. The intent was to keep the Iraqis guessing about where we would cross, at the same time drawing them into the open so our air assets could destroy them.

The shaping operations provided an incredible after-dark show. We watched in awe as the sky filled with streaks of white light from MLRS, which were followed by strings of red tracers from Iraqi air defense weapons trying to shoot them down. There were explosions and flashes of light all along the horizon to the north and northeast throughout the night. We were very much in control of the tactical situation at that point, even though the war was not going quite as quickly as anyone planned. The old adage had kicked in: "No plan ever survives the first contact."

But we were concerned about how badly the intelligence community had failed us to this point. We were running into fighters where intelligence told us there would be none. The mass capitulations had not happened and we gave up hope that they would. The fighters we were seeing were not the Iraqis we trained or wargamed to fight. We were seeing irregulars, militia, suicidal Saddam *fedayeen* and Ba'ath Party members, and civilians who did not want us there. And they were using tactics we had not expected from conventional forces: firing from behind civilians, using ambulances to carry weapons and fire at us with RPGs, hiding in mosques and schools, and using suicide bombers. These were terror tactics, and we had to learn to adjust to them quickly, on the move, before we got closer to Baghdad.

For the next three days, we were able to catch a breather. We slept on cots next to our vehicles, took our time to get something to eat, did maintenance, and even took time for church services on the 30th. It was also Schwartz's birthday that Sunday, and when we learned about it during a task force BUB (Battlefield Update Brief), sang an impromptu off-key rendition of "Happy Birthday." Martz, who sat in on the BUB, said later it was one of the worst versions he ever heard. "I'm sure glad you guys fight better than you sing," he grumbled.

On the 31st we held a promotion ceremony for four of our soldiers, including my gunner, Malone. He received a well-deserved promotion to staff sergeant. He was often the guy who fought the tank for me while I was busy fighting the company. He was always calm and in control, exactly the type soldier I needed in that position.

Michael Donohue, Richard's driver in Blue Four, was promoted to specialist; Justin Bailey, the driver for Mao's Blue Two, and Lopez were promoted to private first class.

I used the opportunity to remind the company of the significance of what we had done, and to make sure they kept their minds on what we were about to do and not get too cocky. I let the first sergeant run them over the coals a bit before I buttered them up. He did it in typical 1st Sergeant Mercado style.

"You're doing a great job," he told them. "That's why you're here and alive. But just because it's war doesn't mean you don't get up in the morning and shave and clean your ass up. When I tell you to clean your ass up, clean your ass up."

His five-minute talk to them was filled with the requisite number of profanities and I'm sure they had the proper impact. Martz was taking notes of everything and at one point Sanderlin walked up to him and asked: "How are you going to get any of that in the paper."

"Selective editing," he replied.

I told the soldiers I was proud to be their company commander for the way they handled themselves at Rams and again at Najaf. They were on a high since Najaf because they learned they could fight and do Security and Stabilization Operations (SASO) at the same time.

I also wanted to reinforce in the minds of the soldiers that to this point in the war there was nothing to be ashamed about, and that nothing should be bothering their consciences. Civilians were killed at Checkpoint Charlie, but not intentionally. They had gotten caught in crossfires. We were soldiers first and cops second.

"They are using terrorist tactics. They are using tactics we are not really used to seeing," I told them. "If you feel your life is in danger, return fire. You have every right to defend yourself and keep yourself safe."

The following morning we awoke to the sounds of the George C. Scott version of the famous speech Gen. George Patton had given to the Third Army on the eve of D-Day in 1944, in which the actor talks about "making the other dumb bastard die for his country." It was broadcast over the PSYOP loudspeakers with enough volume for all of Charlie Company to hear. Shane Williams was doing his version of Scott doing Patton. He followed that speech with his version of Mel Gibson doing William Wallace from the movie "Braveheart."

Since the V Corps commander was Lt. Gen. William Wallace, and we were under his command, every time his name was mentioned the impersonations of Gibson doing Wallace would break out in the ranks, with Williams usually in the lead.

Shortly after that, I asked the PSYOP guys to play the song "Bodies," which has the line "Let the Bodies Hit the Floor," by the heavy metal band Drowning Pool. I thought it only appropriate that the Heavy Metal element hear a little heavy metal before we headed for Baghdad.

At the task force BUB that night, Schwartz told us we would be moving the next day, past Karbala and toward Baghdad.

"They're saying the Iraqi military is on its knees," he said. "This is where we kick them in the balls and finish them off."

We knew movement in and around Karbala would be tricky. The Karbala Gap is a narrow passage through an escarpment that limits movement to a single file of vehicles. And east of the city is a series of canal roads barely wide enough to hold a tank. The task force would have to move along several different canal roads at the same time to get to our next objective south of Baghdad, a place called Objective Saints. Saints was at the crossroads of Highways 1 and 8. From there we could attack south against the Medina Division, or north to whatever waited for us there. We also knew that if we were going to get slimed, or hit with chemical or biological agents, it would be after we passed Karbala. This was where we would be most vulnerable so it was vital we were wearing all our MOPP gear and our masks were nearby.

On the morning of 2 April, we were up before dawn to get ready for the move. Then we waited, and waited, and waited as the plans changed several times before we moved out. They changed again frequently as we were on the move. The original plan was for the task force to follow Highway 28 west of Karbala through the Karbala Gap and around the city to what was known as Objective Garth, just short of the bridge across the Euphrates. But traffic was slower than expected through the gap and we were rerouted around the east side of the city on the narrow canal roads that kept us twisting and turning every which way.

Much of the route was determined by how trafficable it was and how much fire units ahead of us were taking. There were numerous stops and pauses as we moved with no discernible pattern while waiting for orders from above about which way to go. We were running into narrow canal roads, low palm trees that limited visibility, and one-story houses. It was a drastic change from the desert terrain in which we had been operating since the start of the war.

Late in the afternoon, we began moving down one canal road only to see that much of the rest of the task force ahead of us had run into a dead end. Since it was trying to get turned around, I told my crews to keep their tanks out on a main road that ran perpendicular to the canal road. Only three Charlie Company tanks had gone down the canal road but as we were attempting to get them moved back onto the highway, Larrico Alexander's Red Three went into protective mode and completely shut down. I towed him until he could get hooked up to Waterhouse's tank. In the middle of that confusion, we started taking mortar fire. A number of fuel trucks were near us and the mortars started walking in on the fuel trucks. We were in a bad spot that was threatening to get worse.

We managed to get back out on the road without taking any hits, and the task force decided to go west, back toward Karbala, because intelligence reports indicated a large concentration of enemy forces to the east. With Charlie Rock ahead of us, we started back toward Karbala. Other units trying to follow us were having a hard time, and landmarks were scarce in that area. So we used the only one available to us, a dead Iraqi lying on the west side of a berm we had to cross. Just about every vehicle that went over the berm ran over that guy. We told the other units to look for the berm with the squashed dead guy, and that's the way we were moving.

As we drove through northern Karbala, we started taking small arms and RPG fire. BMPs and antiaircraft defense positions were in the area and we began engaging those. Malone destroyed a BMP trying to hide behind a mosque. We kept moving through the night, pushing for Objective Garth. En route we passed a downed Black Hawk helicopter. We heard a report indicating that the code words authorizing the Iraqis to hit us with a chemical attack were picked up. But by that time we were so tired our feeling was: "If they hit us, they hit us." We were headed for Baghdad, more or less, and that was our ticket home.

Finally, about 3 a.m. on 3 April, we reached Garth. We were exhausted, almost out of fuel and ammunition, and dead-dog tired. I spent much of the time on the way to Garth on the radio, trying to keep crews awake, trying to keep myself awake. There was quite a bit of difficult terrain in the area, and I did not want to have one of the drivers nod off, get too close to the edge, and have the tank roll over.

We got about two hours of rest before we moved out again, this time for Objective Peach and the bridge over the Euphrates. Although we were still tired from the road march from the day before, crossing the Euphrates seemed to lift our spirits. I know it did mine. Once across the river, we were really on the road to Baghdad.

It was that afternoon on 3 April that second platoon led us through Mahmudiyah, and we destroyed seven T-72 tanks, several at point-blank range, and two BMPs in only a few minutes in a battle that took place on narrow city streets south of Baghdad. I believe that battle defined us as a company and set new standards for the use of armor in urban warfare. The more time and distance we put between ourselves and the event, the more significant it will become not only for the role we played in this war, but for the role we will play in the future of armor in combat and how tank crews train for it. We had little time to think about that then, though. We were still trying to get to Baghdad. And what we discovered was that the best way to get north was to go south.

On the morning of 4 April, we awoke to the sights and sounds of battle far to our northwest. Antiaircraft tracers and smoke trails from SAMs mingled with MLRS fire. We saw one SAM hit a plane and knock it down. The 1st BCT was attacking the main airport west of Baghdad, then known as Saddam International Airport, and moving on the city from the west.

Our mission that day was to head south again, back through Mahmudiyah. This time we were to move farther south and destroy the remnants of the Medina Division and its equipment. The intent was to isolate Baghdad from the south and prevent counterattacks. I took only two platoons, Red and White. Blue was sent out before dawn to escort 1st Battalion, 10th Field Artillery Regiment, into Task Force 4-64's area. Along the way Blue got into several fights, destroying six BMPs and several antiaircraft weapons, and I decided to leave it at the crossroads in the potato fields to get some rest.

Going back into Mahmudiyah was a strange experience. We did a considerable amount of damage to a number of buildings there and were expecting trouble from the locals. Instead, it was almost like a parade as the task force moved south. Hundreds of people

Iraqi civilians wave to soldiers of Task Force 1-64, the "Desert Rogues," as they move south of Baghdad on Highway 8 on April 4. (*Brant Sanderlin/Atlanta Journal-Constitution*)

were out in the street, smiling and waving at us. I was still concerned about people dropping grenades on us from the rooftops,
but nothing of the sort happened. It was a peaceful passage.

Once we got south of town, we started encountering artillery
pieces, trucks loaded with weapons and ammunition, and stacks
and stacks of military goods along both sides of the road. Some of
it was concealed under palm trees so it could not be seen from the
air. Wild Bunch and Rock were shooting it up as they went along,
leaving the dregs and all the secondary explosions for us. Ammunition dumps were exploding just a few meters off the road, sending
shrapnel zinging and whining in all directions.

About ninety minutes into the run, we came to an area with large
caches of artillery pieces and ammunition. Some were burning.
Some were exploding. Hunks of metal were being tossed into the
air. When a chunk landed on top of my turret, I got on the radio

1st Lt. Shane Williams, Charlie Company's executive officer, makes a radio call
during Task Force 1-64's move south of Baghdad on 4 April to destroy remnants
of the Medina Division. Smoke from destroyed Iraqi weapons billows in the background. (*Brant Sanderlin/Atlanta Journal-Constitution*)

and told everyone to button up; it was too dangerous to be standing out of the hatches.

In Jeremy England's White One, driver K. C. Brons had switched places with loader Mark Gatlin for the day. As the column moved through an area of multiple explosions on either side of the road, England was about halfway out of the hatch, Brons was scanning for enemy soldiers, his left hand on the handle of the M240, when there was a loud explosion to their left rear.

"Fuck!" Brons yelped.

He held his left hand out to England and said: "Look."

His left hand was a mangled piece of bloody meat. A piece of shrapnel split the hand, ripping off his little finger and taking a big slice out of his ring finger.

"Get the CLS bag! Get the CLS bag!" England called to Freeman, referring to the Combat Life Saver kit.

The tank stopped and Freeman began bandaging Brons's hand. Blood was splattered over the side of the tank and the top of the turret. Brons's wedding ring was sliced in half, part of it found later on top of the turret.

"How are you feeling?" Freeman asked Brons.

"Sergeant Freeman, I can't feel a thing right now," he replied matter-of-factly.

England got on the radio and told me Brons was wounded. When he told me how, I was livid. No one was supposed to be outside the hatches while we were going through that area. I called the FAS team and drove back to check on Brons. By the time I got there his hand was bandaged, and there was nothing more I could do. I waited until the FAS team arrived and tried to console him.

"You're going to be all right," I assured him.

"Roger, sir," he said, but I could tell he was going into shock and was not really sure what was going on around him. Once Brons was evacuated, I got back on my tank and caught up with the rest of the company.

We drove south for about ten miles to a place called Latifiyah before turning around and heading back. We took some AK-47 fire and a few RPGs, but nothing of any consequence. I was surprised we got that because of all the fire the task force was putting out.

Nothing that looked even remotely military was safe along that road that day. It was estimated that we destroyed ten tanks, fifty-five trucks, thirty air defense and artillery pieces, an unknown number of soldiers, and tens of thousands of rounds of artillery and antiaircraft ammunition. But there were only a few tanks. The Medina Division tanks were still out there, if they had not been destroyed by the Air Force.

We came back through Mahmudiyah and received much the same reception as when we went in earlier. But by this time my mind was elsewhere. I was thinking about what happened to Brons and getting more upset by the minute. We had our first casualty in an incident that never should have happened. I had ordered everyone inside the vehicles to protect them from the explosions but that was not done on England's tank. When I met with the platoon

A destroyed Iraqi T-72 tanks sits in the middle of the street in the Baghdad suburb of Mahmudiyah the day after Charlie Company tanks drove through town on a tank-hunting mission on 3 April. The tank battle took place at times at distances of less than fifty feet, but not a single Charlie Company soldier was injured. (*Brant Sanderlin/Atlanta Journal-Constitution*)

Captain Conroy catches a few minutes rest on a cot in the middle of a potato field south of Baghdad following Charlie Company's drive south of the capital to destroy remnants of the Medina Division on 4 April. (*Brant Sanderlin/Atlanta Journal-Constitution*)

leaders shortly after we returned, England knew I was angry with him. And it was obvious he was upset with me.

"What was Brons doing out of the hatch?" I asked England sharply.

"He was doing what a loader should be doing, *sir*. He was scanning," England shot back.

"I gave an order that everyone was supposed to button up."

"He was just doing his job, sir!"

"I told everyone to stay inside while we were going through that area!"

Heads were turning in our direction. It was not often that soldiers got to see their command group going at it. It was clear that England thought I was blaming him for what happened. And, in a sense, I was. Brons was his responsibility. When I gave an order I expected it to be carried out. In this case, it was not. I could tell he knew he was wrong but was not going to admit it. He knew my position and enough had been said.

"Well, sir," England said after we glared at one another for a few seconds, "I think I'll just walk away for a while before I say anything else."

"I think that's a good idea," I said.

By nightfall I was exhausted, emotionally and physically. I needed some rest, some time to consider all that had happened that day. But I was not to get it. About 9 p.m. I got a call to report to the task force TOC for a briefing on the next day's mission. I thought sure we would go back south again, farther this time, and find the Medina Division tanks we could not find the previous two days.

When I walked into the TOC, the first thing I saw was a map of downtown Baghdad. I knew then we were finally about to do what we came here to do. What I did not know was how few of us would do it.

13

THUNDER RUN I: SPEED, POWER, AND A SHOW OF FORCE

THE decision to send tanks into downtown Baghdad was made the night of 3 April. Maj. Gen. Buford Blount, the 3rd Infantry Division commander, was monitoring 1st Brigade's attack on the airport and getting reports from 2nd Brigade commander Perkins about our successful run through Mahmudiyah.

The Medina Division was reduced to a shambles. And while Saddam's regime had not yet collapsed as was expected following the destruction of the Republican Guard unit, the Iraqis seemed unable to mount any sort of cohesive or coordinated defense. Fighting was being done by individuals and in small groups. Command and control by the Iraqi leadership was nonexistent. Defenders seemed scattered and ill prepared. One of the telltale signs that a coordinated effort was lacking was that virtually no artillery fire was coming out of the city directed at the encircling American forces. The Iraqis were obviously reeling from our quick thrust onto their front doorstep, and Blount wanted to keep the initiative.

Traditional military doctrine calls for tanks to stay out of cities and serve as fire support systems for infantry to clear block by block and house by house. The pieces were being put in place for that to be done. The Marines were coming up the east side of the Tigris River into downtown Baghdad. The 3rd Division's 1st Brigade was in the west, at the airport. And the 3rd Brigade was in the northwest, cutting off escape routes. With the south blocked by the 2nd Brigade, the Iraqi forces had no place to run and few places to hide.

With the city virtually encircled, the next step would be to start probing the defenses of Baghdad. But it was unclear exactly what types of defenses were being deployed. The satellite photos were not showing much and there were no human intelligence reports coming out of the city. Blount decided to take a gamble. Instead of sending infantry into the city to test the defenses, he would send an armored reconnaissance force. Blount wanted to demonstrate to the Iraqis that we could move wherever and whenever we wanted in the city. On the morning of 4 April, before our second run through Mahmudiyah, Blount called Perkins and told him he wanted him to go to Baghdad the next day. He was to take a single task force, all armor, and only about seven hundred soldiers. There would be no wheeled vehicles. The task force was to drive north on Highway 8, then turn west on Highway 1 and link up with 1st Brigade at the airport. It would be a ten-mile run into the heart of Baghdad and back out again. No ground would be taken or held. It would be a quick, shoot-and-scoot mission to probe defenses and gather intelligence.

When the task force returned from Mahmudiyah, Perkins called Schwartz to the brigade TOC. Schwartz thought he was going to receive orders to head back south the next day and take out the headquarters of the Medina Division. But when he walked in the door, the place was unusually quiet. Perkins was leaning over a table intently studying a map.

"What's going on, sir?" Schwartz asked, leaning down next to him.

Perkins did not hesitate. "Tomorrow morning I want you to attack into Baghdad. It will be a seventeen-kilometer attack up along Highway 8. It will be the first strike into Baghdad."

Schwartz sucked in his breath and shook his head. "This is our nightmare," he thought to himself. "We didn't think we would ever go into the heart of Baghdad."

For the next few minutes, the two went over terrain maps and satellite imagery of the route. When Schwartz looked up he saw a lot of brigade staffers with long faces looking back at him, as if to say: "Those are the guys who are going into Baghdad tomorrow. I'm glad I'm not them."

By the time Schwartz got back to his TOC and called the task force company commanders together, he had regained his usual positive attitude. He knew he could not let his own worries about the mission get passed down the line. His briefing was quick and to the point. This was what we would do, and this was how we would do it. My focus was on intelligence. Did they have any intelligence that could tell us what kinds of forces we would be facing? Would we run into infantry or BMPs or tanks? What were the chances of suicide bombers? Would the roads be barricaded? How close to the roads are the buildings? How many stories are the buildings? All my questions were met with: "We don't know. That's why we're going in: to find out."

I knew eventually we would go to Baghdad in some form or fashion, so that did not surprise me. What did put me back on my heels a bit, though, was the news that a single task force was being asked to do it without decent intelligence. Here we were, only about seven hundred soldiers, ready to move on a city of five million people, many of whom carried weapons. In some aspects it seemed almost suicidal. I thought it more likely a brigade with its more than four thousand soldiers would be sent on a mission such as this. But it was not to be. It was just us, the Desert Rogues, taking on all of Baghdad.

It was an incredibly audacious plan, and the more I thought about it, the more excited I got. I was ready to kick Saddam's ass by this time. We had been through hell on the road marches and we were ready to go to Baghdad and get this over with. We were getting close to the end and I thought the sooner we did this, the faster we would get this done and go home. I tried to put out of my mind the fact that we were going in there blind, without a single scrap of decent intelligence on what was waiting for us.

It was approaching midnight by the time I got back to the company CP. I called the platoon leaders over to the first sergeant's PC for a briefing. When I told them the news, Jeremy England dropped his planning book and stared at me open-mouthed.

"Are you fucking serious?" he asked.

"Sir, you mean we're really going to Baghdad?" Erik Balascik chimed in.

"Of course they are going to send us to Baghdad. What else is there to do?" I responded.

Everyone seemed excited about the prospect except 1st Sergeant Mercado. He was quiet during the briefing and for about twenty minutes after. I think he knew without me saying anything that it was going to be a tough fight. Still, I told him to be ready for casualties.

I gave him some time to think about it and finally he snapped out of it and said: "Fuck it. Let's go."

And with that he went off to get the rest of the soldiers pumped up.

I tried to get a few hours' rest, but it was not a restful time for any of us that night. I kept going over in my mind what we had to do to be prepared for worst-case scenarios. My biggest concern was vehicle breakdowns. The tanks had been run hard and taken a lot of hits from small arms and RPGs. We did not have time to do the maintenance we needed to keep them all in top working order. Just about every tank had a problem or two. They were creaking and clanking and shuddering, and warning lights of all sorts were popping on and off inside many of them from time to time.

Two of first platoon's tanks, Red Three and Red Four, were out with mechanical problems and would have to be left behind. Red platoon would go into Baghdad with only two of its four tanks. But I would still lead with them. Jason Diaz's Red Two crew was one of my best. I had complete trust in Diaz and his soldiers in *Cojone, Eh?*. It was an eclectic crew: Diaz and Couvertier, two buddies of Puerto Rican descent; Trivino, the quiet Ecuadoran green-card holder; and Chris Shipley, the skinny Arizona kid who had just turned twenty but seemed unfazed by anything he encountered.

If a tank broke down en route, that tank's wingman would hook it up and drag it out of the danger zone. The rest of the platoon would provide local security while the column bypassed them and moved on. We could not afford to stop for any length of time for anything. To do so ran the risk of making us a magnet for the Iraqis. I was convinced at that point that if we lost a tank, it would be because of a mechanical malfunction, not because of enemy fire. I did not think there was a thing the Iraqis possessed in their arsenal that could take out an M1A1 Abrams.

Casualties were also a concern, but I felt confident we could deal with them. We had the medic track, and back in Kuwait the first sergeant and I decided to split the medics. Strunk would ride in the medic PC, Sullivan with the first sergeant. Neither of us wanted to risk losing both medics if they were in the same PC and it got hit. We also figured that by splitting them, they could treat more casualties in wider areas if the need arose.

The lack of intelligence created a lot of uncertainty in my mind. I did not have enough information to even begin considering all the things that might go wrong out there. As much as I tried, I could not war-game it to the degree I felt comfortable.

I encouraged the platoon leaders and platoon sergeants to be positive when they were briefing the soldiers. I wanted them to stress that this mission was something that would be good for us, and good for the Iraqi people. We would go in light and fast, hit hard, get to the airport, and then come back to the potato fields to wait for the next mission.

One thing that lifted our spirits a bit was being able to dump the MOPP suits after the mission on the 4th. We never got a full explanation, but we figured if we had not been slimed by then, we probably would not be. Either that or we were drinking too much water, so much so that we were in danger of running out. We sweated so much in those charcoal-lined MOPP suits that at times soldiers would come out of a tank, take their boots off, and pour out the sweat.

I stirred from my half-sleep about 4 a.m., just before Schwartz called to make sure we were all up and moving. It was cool and hazy and already soldiers were up prepping their tanks, getting ready to leave by 5:30. I could hear them bantering among themselves in the early morning darkness, pumping each other up.

"Let's go kick Saddam's ass," one would say.

"Let's go take Baghdad," another would say.

And on down the line it went. Their enthusiasm was almost contagious, but I could sense that some were talking to mask that sense of anxiety, to hide that knot in their stomachs that we all had and made us feel a bit lightheaded.

We moved out of the potato fields about 5:30 and were the first to the assembly area near the task force TOC. We pulled to the side of the highway while Wild Bunch and Rock moved ahead of us. Once again the line of march would be Wild Bunch, Rock, and Cobra. Schwartz wanted the Bradleys up front because they put out a higher sustained rate of fire with their 25mm chain guns than the tanks did with the main guns, which took five to six seconds to load and fire. The engineers would be interspersed throughout the column, serving at times as a QRF. Their main mission was to watch for gunmen in the upper stories of buildings and hidden in the trusses of the highway overpasses.

Maj. Rick Nussio, the task force executive officer in his M113, was just behind our medic PC. Perkins, in his M113, was behind Nussio. Shane Williams in Charlie Six-Five was rear security and the last vehicle in line. It was his job to keep the Iraqis off our butts, round up the stragglers, and make sure we all made it to the airport.

When we moved through the final barrier that Task Force 1-15 set up to mark the Line of Departure and the end of anything that remotely resembled friendly territory, there was a surreal quality to the whole scene. Women and children were walking along the road as if tanks in their midst were a normal occurrence. Some would even sprint across the road between vehicles if we left too much of a gap.

Cars were coming down the other side of the six-lane divided highway as we moved north, the drivers staring at us bug-eyed. It was obvious they did not know we were coming and believed what they were hearing on Iraqi radio, that the Americans were still more than sixty miles away. To the north, we could see large plumes of thick, black smoke rising from what we guessed correctly was the center of Baghdad.

We test-fired our weapons, and soldiers began reconning by fire, shooting into bunkers, fighting positions, and Iraqi military vehicles to draw fire. Incoming fire was light at first, but the farther north we drove the more it picked up. Ahead of us, Wild Bunch and Charlie Rock were reporting that they were starting to take heavier fire from RPGs and AK-47s. They were shooting and continuing to move, passing targets back to us that they could not get to quickly enough.

About twenty minutes into the run, we were approaching a highway overpass when I saw something streak out of some apartment buildings on the right side of the road and explode against the protective skirts of Diaz's tank. I thought at first it was an RPG, but the puff of smoke after the impact seemed considerably larger than an RPG makes.

Diaz felt the tank rock slightly and called Roger Gruneisen in Red One just behind him, to ask if he just fired a main gun round. Gruneisen said he had not and asked if everyone on the tank was OK. Diaz told him that everyone was fine and they were continuing to move.

But then Couvertier, the gunner, noticed lights starting to flash all around his station. And in the driver's hole, Shipley said warning lights were coming on there, blinking like a Christmas tree. Just then, Red Two groaned to a halt, about twenty-five meters past the overpass.

Diaz opened the turret and looked over the tank's back deck. Black smoke and yellow and red flames were belching out of the engine compartments. He pulled the fire extinguisher handles and gave the order: "Abandon tank!"

Diaz jumped onto the back deck and pulled up the engine hatch cover. More smoke and flames billowed out. He tried to pull out the V-Pacs but they were burning too, scorching his hand.

The rest of Diaz's crew emerged from inside the tank with their M-4s and began firing at a sand-bagged enemy bunker about fifty meters to their left. Heavy fire was coming from there with rounds skipping off the pavement and bouncing off the sides of the tank. We could see the muzzle flashes that looked like twinkling white lights. As Couvertier was shooting, the alarm on his watch went off.

He stopped, irritated more by it than the Iraqis shooting at him, and shut it off before resuming firing.

We were not in a good situation. The overpass was directly behind us and gunmen were up in the trusses, firing down on us. Cars and trucks were still moving along the overpass, some apparently oblivious to what was going on below. Some of the vehicles in our column that had stopped under the overpass pulled back to get a better angle on the Iraqi gunmen above them. In addition to the sandbagged bunker on the left, a metal Conex container was being used by five or six Iraqis, who would run out and shoot at us, and then run back inside.

Helgenberger spotted one of the men and asked: "Sir, he's got a weapon. Can I shoot him?"

"Hell, yes," I responded.

To our immediate right was an off-ramp from the overpass, and beyond it several sets of apartment buildings from which we were taking fire. To our left rear was another off-ramp. I pulled my tank in front of Red Two to block the closest off-ramp. But at that point the hydraulics on the tank, which had been giving me problems for some time, went out completely. We could not traverse the gun tube or the coax. Cobra Three-Zero pulled around in front of me, and Coffman angled the first sergeant's PC to the right rear corner of Red Two about ten meters from it.

I ordered White to pull around in front of the company to provide security there. My orders apparently were not clear, because White caught up with the tail end of the battalion and kept moving. They were quickly out of sight. I had good rear security with Shane Williams and several PCs so I ordered two tanks from Blue to move forward to provide security in front.

First Sergeant Mercado climbed on top of Diaz's tank and took charge of putting out the fire. He called for all the tanks to give up their fire extinguishers. When he ran out of fire extinguishers, he called for the five-gallon water cans strapped to the outsides of the vehicles.

Shipley and Don Schafer, the loader in Gruneisen's tank, were down on the road firing at the bunker on the left from behind the highway guardrail. I could hear AK-47 rounds skipping off the

Charlie Company soldiers battle a fire on Charlie One-Two after it was struck by enemy fire in the right side during the initial Thunder Run into Baghdad on 5 April. The fire could not be extinguished, and the tank had to be abandoned. It was later recovered. (*Brant Sanderlin/Atlanta Journal-Constitution*)

asphalt and pinging off the sides of tanks. An RPG went zooming over Mercado's head as he stood on top of Diaz's tank. He never noticed and seemed oblivious to all but the tank fire. Nearly a dozen soldiers were on the ground at that point, either shooting back at the Iraqis or trying to put out the fire on the tank. Nussio started collecting water cans from some of the other vehicles and ran forward with them, flinging them so they slid down the road to Diaz's tank.

When it appeared that the fire was out, I ordered Red One to hook up a tow bar so we could drag Diaz's tank back to the potato fields. But as that was being done, the fire flared back up. Mercado and Diaz kept pouring water onto it, and it would seem to go out, only to restart. What we did not realize was that whatever hit the tank ruptured the fuel cell and every time the fire died down, fuel leaked onto a hot spot and the blaze reignited.

Nobody wanted to abandon the tank, especially Diaz and his

crew. This was their home, their weapon, their transportation, and their ticket back to Fort Stewart. Without it, they would be lost and have to find rides somewhere else. A tanker without a tank is just an undergunned infantry soldier. Even if the tank could not be made combat-effective again, we could strip it for spare parts. And the idea of leaving it for the Iraqis was just out of the question. Schwartz was insistent on not abandoning tanks, for any reason. It was a matter of pride to bring back the tank, even as badly wounded as it was.

About ten minutes into the fight, while we were still focused on fighting the fire and shooting back at the Iraqis shooting at us, the first suicide bombers appeared. It was a white pickup truck with three men in the front. Two were in uniform. The third wore a white headband with Arabic writing on it. The truck was picking up speed as it came down the off-ramp directly at my tank. We could not traverse the coax or gun tube because of the hydraulic problem so Malone could not get a good shot at the truck. I fired my M-4 until it ran out of ammunition, then pulled out my 9mm and fired it until it was also out.

"Shoot it! Shoot the fucking thing!" I screamed into the radio.

Cobra Three-Zero turned its 25mm in that direction and fired, killing at least two of the men inside and shattering the windshield. The truck slowed considerably and coasted down the off-ramp. It was still coming at a pretty good rate of speed and I thought it would hit my tank.

"Brace!" I yelled to the crew as I ducked down inside.

But the truck hit a side guardrail, slowed, and then came to a stop about ten feet from us. Gruneisen called on the radio and said: "There's something in the back and it looks like explosives. It looks like one of the passengers is still moving."

Jim Hock and Shipley both fired their M-4s into the truck at the last remaining passenger. Just as they did, the truck erupted in flames. Shipley, who had run around the back of my tank before firing and not realizing the 25mm shot up the truck first, looked at his weapon as if to say: "I did that?"

I kept calling Schwartz to give him situation reports, telling him one minute the fire was out, the next that it was not. He could not figure out what was going on and was eager to keep moving. Wild Bunch, Rock, and our second platoon were in heavy contact. They were about ten minutes ahead of us on the road, although I did not realize it at the time and had paused briefly for us to catch up.

As White sat there, Phinney's White Three shot up a suicide car bomber as it came down another off-ramp, and then a police car pulled up in front of it.

"There's a police car coming," Ellis, the gunner called to Phinney. Ellis was a police officer in Jamaica before coming to the U.S. and joining the Army. At forty he was one of the oldest and most mature soldiers in the company. He also felt a special bond with other police officers. Until that moment. The Iraqi policeman got out of the car, raised an RPG, rested his elbows on the roof, and prepared to fire.

"Oh no, you're not," Ellis said to no one in particular.

"What?" Phinney demanded.

"He's got an RPG!"

"Shoot him!"

Ellis flipped the gun switch to MAIN, pressed the triggers, and a HEAT round tore through the police car. All they found of the policeman was his beret.

I knew we could not stay there much longer fighting the fire. We had been trying to put it out for about twenty minutes already and did not seem to be making any progress. Too many people were on the ground risking their lives to save a tank; the longer we stayed there, the more opportunity the Iraqis had to bring in reinforcements.

I got on the radio to Schwartz:

"Rogue Six, Cobra Six."

"Cobra Six, Rogue Six."

"Hey, sir. We can't tow this tank the way it is. We're still fighting this fire. We'll stay and fight as long as necessary to recover it. The ball's in your court. What do you want us to do? I can do either or."

There was a brief pause and the crackle of static on the line.

"Abandon the vehicle."

"Roger."

I gave the order to abandon the vehicle, and the crew started unloading everything they could. The 3/7 Cav tanks that were abandoned near Najaf had all the gear and weapons left on them, and I wanted to make sure we stripped everything off the tank before leaving. That included all weapons, all personal gear, all radios and codes, and all sensitive items including night-vision devices, maps, and pluggers. I did not want to leave anything for the Iraqis except a burnt-out shell of a tank. It was humiliating enough to leave them that.

Hernandez came over from Gruneisen's tank to help Diaz prep Red Two for destruction. Weapons and duffel bags were being stacked on Gruneisen's tank. Some were tossed into the back of Mercado's PC, along with about twenty-five empty, five-gallon plastic water jugs that were used up fighting the fire.

We were still under heavy fire, and I am amazed to this day that we did not take a single casualty. Charlie Company soldiers fought long and hard to save that tank, showing tremendous courage under fire. The first sergeant was walking around out there setting an example for all of them. He was more concerned about the tank fire than he was about the enemy fire, and was probably more upset than I that it could not be extinguished and the tank could not be saved.

I felt vindicated that our guys tried as hard as they did to save the tank. There is not a person who could have done any more than they did. They were so focused on trying to save it that I was trying to pull guys off as we were getting ready to leave. They did not want to leave it behind until they felt they had expended every resource and every bit of energy.

As Hernandez and Diaz were making their final preparations, Perkins pulled alongside in his PC and told them in no uncertain terms: "Get out of that tank!"

Hernandez pulled the pin on a thermite grenade, dropped it into the hull, and scrambled off.

I told Shane Williams to linger just long enough to shoot Red Two with a SABOT round before air assets came in and hit it again with two Maverick missiles and a Joint Direct Attack Munition, a smart bomb. We wanted to make sure it was totally inoperable before the Iraqis got their hands on it.

Red Two, the tank with the gun tube emblazoned *Cojone, Eh?*, was later seen with Iraqis swarming all over it in photographs that appeared in several national publications. Even the infamous Baghdad Bob, Iraqi Information Minister Mohammed Saeed al-Sahaf, had his picture taken on the tank before we reclaimed it several days later.

It was not yet 7 a.m., and we were having a bad day that was about to get much worse.

I checked with Mercado to make sure everyone was accounted for. The last thing I wanted to do was leave someone standing by the road without a ride. We had four tankers who needed a place to go, and I wanted to know where they went.

Trivino, the loader, jumped into Cobra Three-Zero. Diaz and Couvertier got into Red One along with Gruneisen and Hernandez. Schafer, the loader in Gruneisen's tank, and Shipley, got into Mercado's PC.

Once everyone was accounted for we tried to catch up with the rest of the task force, which had moved on and was well out of sight.

Red One was lagging behind because the extra gear it was carrying limited the view of driver Derek Peterson. The first sergeant and XO were still behind him, along with the medic PC. We were strung out over a long distance as we moved into a portion of the highway where the median was thick with trees and bushes, which helped hide bunkers and fighting positions.

Red One was hurrying to catch up with the rest of the company while firing at Iraqis on both sides of the road. As they approached an underpass, the gun tube was traversing counterclockwise after Couvertier shot the coax at some Iraqis behind them. Gruneisen saw the impending disaster at the last second but could do nothing about it. The gun tube hit a concrete bridge abutment with an ear-splitting *Boom!* and the turret began spinning out of control. It spun around, and around, and around, knocking the four soldiers inside it back against the steel walls, pinning them there.

Couvertier smashed face forward into the gunner's site and felt warm liquid cascading down his face and into his tanker's green Nomex jumpsuit. He did not know if he was shot or if the tank had exploded around him.

Duffel bags, rucksacks, weapons, MOPP suit bags, and all sorts of gear were knocked off the tank and strewn along the road.

The tank with the gun tube name *Creeping Death* crept to a halt. The makeshift crew was disoriented, out of sorts—they had no idea what had happened. They did not realize until later that the gun tube had hit the abutment. At the speed they were traveling, it had knocked loose all the hydraulics and sent the turret spinning like an out-of-control top.

By that time, Red One was running far behind the rest of the company. Gruneisen kept calling me, asking me to slow down so they could catch up. They were not sure where the turn to the airport was. I was trying to get Schwartz to slow down at the same time I expanded the company backward to help Gruneisen. Schwartz kept after me to hurry up and get my company together and link up with the rest of the task force.

It was about then that I heard over the radio that Jeremy England had been shot in the face.

England was still ahead of us with his second platoon and had just made the left turn onto Highway 1, headed for the airport. He was in open-protected mode, which means he was down inside the tank, with the hatch open about six inches. Not much space for a bullet to get through, but one did.

His head banged back against the turret. Stunned for a minute, he tried to figure out what happened. Then he realized and radioed to his crew: "I'm fucking shot!"

England put his hands over his eyes and started yelling: "I can't see! I can't see! What's wrong with me?"

Mark Gatlin, his loader, looked at England and murmured: "Oh, shit."

Freeman turned in his gunner's seat, fearing the worst, but saw England, holding his hands over his eyes.

"Sir," he said, "pull your helmet up a little bit."

England hesitated a moment, fearing his brains would fall out all over the tank.

1st Lt. Jeremy England, leader of Charlie Company's second platoon, displays the helmet he was wearing when he was hit by what was believed to be an AK-47 round during the unit's Thunder Run into Baghdad on 5 April. England suffered a few scratches to his forehead but otherwise was unhurt. (*Brant Sanderlin/Atlanta Journal-Constitution*)

When he finally got the nerve to lift his helmet, he found a small scratch on his forehead. But his CVC had a large gouge out of the left front where an AK-47 bullet hit it and bounced off. A few inches lower and it would have been through his eye.

England became enraged.

"They shot me in the face!" he screamed over the platoon net.

"Are you OK?" Phinney asked, figuring it could not be too bad if he was talking.

"I'm OK," England replied.

England had had enough. It was personal now.

"Those motherfuckers tried to kill me! Shoot everybody! Shoot 'em all! Kill 'em all!" he shouted over the net.

Meanwhile, Gruneisen's tank was wandering off into no-man's land by itself. It missed the turn to the airport and kept going straight, toward the heart of downtown Baghdad. The crew had locked down the gun tube because it was free-spinning. The tube was also bent from the collision with the bridge abutment, so it was of no use to them.

I was spending a lot of time on the radio with Gruneisen trying to reel him back to the company, with little success. He was describing what he was seeing, and I was telling him what he should be seeing and none of it matched up.

Gruneisen is not the kind of guy who gets rattled in a tough situation. But I could tell by his voice on the radio that he was anxious about this. He was stressed, but he was not overreacting. He was calm and trying to work through the difficulties he was having. I knew if he did not get turned around quickly, I would have to take a rescue party to find him. I was determined not to move any farther until he rejoined the company.

I asked what he saw ahead of him.

He said he saw an intersection, and a traffic circle. And there were soldiers blocking the intersection. Iraqi soldiers. He knew, and I knew, that he was far off track and needed to turn around. I was especially worried that if his tank got hit with whatever took out Diaz's tank, I would have more trouble on my hands than I now had.

I told him to plot a grid. When he did and relayed it to me, I was able to get some sense of where he was. He was headed directly into Baghdad with no support and very little power on his own tank. I told him to turn around immediately and retrace his path.

Gruneisen turned around before he reached the traffic circle and the Iraqi soldiers waiting there for him. The tank demolished several cars in the process before it found the correct road to the airport. I was relieved that that problem was taken care of. But no sooner was Gruneisen's tank out of trouble, than the call I was dreading came over the radio.

"Cobra Six, Cobra Seven. I've got two WIAs."

It was the first sergeant, telling me he had two wounded.

He did not say who was wounded or how bad the wounds were, but I could tell from his voice that it was not good. I had never heard him like that before. It did not sound like the first sergeant I knew.

It was not until later, when I learned the nature of the injuries, that I could understand why he reacted the way he did. Mercado came back on the radio and said Shipley and Schafer were hit. "Shipley's been hurt bad. He's been hit in the head," he said.

Shipley and Schafer were riding in the back of Mercado's PC along with Sullivan, the medic, and Martz. The three soldiers were standing up in the back of the PC with the roof hatch open, shooting at Iraqi positions as they drove along. Shipley and Schafer had M-4s, Sullivan an M-16. Armed Iraqis in cars and trucks were trying to squeeze between the first sergeant's PC and Strunk's medic PC directly behind it. Enemy rounds were clanging off both vehicles. Strunk, concerned about being fired on by Shipley, Schafer, and Sullivan, radioed the first sergeant.

"Cobra Seven, this is Cobra Band-Aid! I'm behind you! Watch where you're firing!"

Schafer took out one vehicle that appeared to be trying to ram the first sergeant's PC. Then, he looked at Martz, held up his right arm, and said: "Ow! My arm!"

Martz grabbed his arm and saw a bullet wound about halfway between the elbow and shoulder. There was another wound under the armpit, just above the lightweight tanker's vest, spurting blood.

"I'm hit!" Schafer yelled, and fell into Martz's arms. The two collapsed in a heap in the back of the PC, tangled up in the water cans and extra gear from the burning tank thrown in there.

As they fell, Martz looked up and saw Shipley, face down on the steel deck of the PC, blood streaming from wounds in his left arm and forehead. Sullivan, the assistant medic, went to work immediately. He calmly wrapped gauze around Shipley's head wound, trying to stop the bleeding. Shipley was hit in the left arm by bullet fragments and the forehead by another round. One bullet went through the lip of his Kevlar helmet, gouged out a chunk of his forehead, and ripped across the socket of his right eye, tearing out the eye. It hung loosely by shards of tissue and Sullivan gingerly bandaged over it. Shipley was moaning and begging for morphine.

Then Sullivan went to work on Schafer, who was wounded by at least three bullets. One had struck his upper left arm, shattering the bone. Another bullet went in under his right armpit. A third tore through the tanker's vest into his back just to the right of his spine. When Martz and Sullivan were finally able to get the vest off, Schafer was awash in blood. The bullet through his back had collapsed his right lung and he was having problems breathing because of the sucking chest wound.

Sullivan could not get to his medical kit because it was covered by several hundred pounds of extra gear and by Schafer and Martz. But the young medic found some green duct tape and a piece of plastic and fashioned a bandage that he had to keep pressing into place because the blood would not let it adhere to Schafer's skin.

He encouraged Martz to keep talking to the two wounded soldiers to keep them conscious, to let them know they were on their way to the airport and would soon be taken care of, and to try to keep them from going into shock.

The first sergeant continued to call on the radio, asking for grids to the medevac site. I did not have them and was becoming more concerned that he would start upsetting others in the company. We were still in a fight and had to get through this and out to the airport. I did not want everybody in the company freaking out because two of their buddies were wounded. I wanted them to focus on their jobs. Shipley and Schafer were in good hands. Sullivan was doing an incredible job for a young combat medic handling his first major casualties and would do what he could for them.

The Baghdad airport is a maze of buildings and obstructions that make it difficult to get from point A to point B. When I finally got the grids for the medevac helicopters, I sent them along to the first sergeant, who directed Coffman to the pickup point. They did an incredible job getting there in all the confusion and the unfamiliar territory. They were waiting for the birds long before they arrived.

When I finally got there, Strunk was helping Sullivan administer IVs and getting Shipley and Schafer ready for transport. I saw Schafer first. He was talking and did not look that bad. I had a good feeling he was going to recover.

Shipley was another matter. He looked bad. His head was wrapped in bandages, and blood was smeared all over his face and head. I thought it would be the last time I would see him. Here he

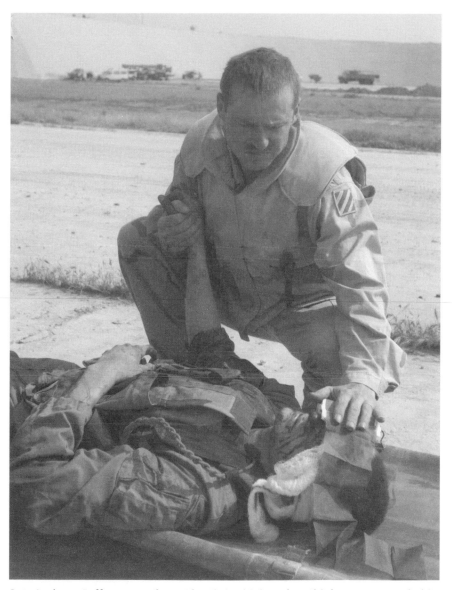

Sgt. Andrew Coffman comforts Pfc. Chris Shipley after Shipley was wounded in the head and left arm during Charlie Company's Thunder Run into Baghdad on 5 April. (*Brant Sanderlin/Atlanta Journal-Constitution*)

S.Sgt. Mark Strunk (right) shouts to a medic as he tends to a seriously wounded Private Shipley. Spc. Paul Helgenberger is holding the intravenous drip bag. (*Brant Sanderlin/Atlanta Journal-Constitution*)

was, only twenty years old, with his whole future ahead of him, lying on a stretcher, begging for morphine, his eye shot out, a huge wound in his forehead.

I felt a sense of relief, yet a sense of dread when the helicopter finally took off with the two wounded. I did not know if I would ever see either again. I was tired, angry, and frustrated.

We gathered our forces together at the airport for a few minutes' rest. The entire trip took only two hours and twenty minutes. It was not yet 10 a.m., but it seemed like we had been fighting all day.

The tops of the tanks and the PCs were covered with discarded brass from the tens of thousands of rounds we had fired. The sides were streaked with black smoke and pitted where RPGs hit them. Gear bags, duffels, and rucksacks strapped to the outside of the vehicles were riddled with bullet holes.

We had gone through a gauntlet of fire. The company suffered two seriously wounded; the task force as a whole, one killed and

Charlie Company soldiers rush the badly wounded Private Shipley to a waiting helicopter for medical evacuation. From left are S.Sgt. Strunk, Captain Conroy, 1st Lt. Roger Gruneisen, and Specialist Helgenberger. Shipley lost his right eye as a result of the wounds. (*Brant Sanderlin/Atlanta Journal-Constitution*)

three wounded. S.Sgt. Stevon Booker, a veteran of the first Gulf War and an Abrams TC in Wild Bunch, was killed when hit by machine-gun fire while standing up in the hatch. It was the first, and only, death suffered by the task force during the war.

Division officials were ecstatic over what we did, despite the casualties. They expected some casualties, but we had suffered far fewer than anyone thought we would, especially considering the volume of fire we took during the run.

We had driven into the heart of Baghdad and sent a clear message to the regime that we could go where we wanted when we wanted. We had gained invaluable information about how the Iraqis would fight us in the city and how tenacious they would be in defending the capital. In doing so we had sent them reeling.

We did exactly what the planners wanted us to do: scatter and confuse Saddam's forces and get to the gates of the city before the Iraqi military commanders could reposition their forces to mount

A weary Sgt. Carlos Hernandez, gunner on Charlie One-One, ponders the day's events following Charlie Company's Thunder Run into Baghdad on April 5, during which his tank's loader, Spc. Donald Schafer, was seriously wounded. (*Brant Sanderlin/Atlanta Journal-Constitution*)

an adequate or sustained defense. The face of Baghdad, and Iraq, was about to change forever, thanks to some bold planning, some risk taking, and the determination of the seven hundred Desert Rogue soldiers.

What we did became known as the "Thunder Run."

But at that moment, the larger, strategic issues were far from my mind. I had to make sure the company was primed and prepared in case we got into another fight on the way back to the potato fields. And I had to make sure they were prepared for the next day's mission, whatever that might be. We had been on the go and in combat for much of the last three days. We had lost three soldiers and a tank. We did not know where we would go from here. Or how quickly. We needed a break, if just for a day or so, to sort things out.

14

SORTING THINGS OUT

THE frustration and anger over the losses of Shipley, Schafer, and the tank weighed heavily on all of us throughout the following day. It was Sunday, 6 April, and we had moved out of the potato field to within a few hundred meters of the task force TOC.

We set up beside a canal that, had it not been for its murky green color, might have induced some of us to jump in and clean up. We were told to ration our water because we were running out. The logistics train could not keep us supplied with fresh bottled water. The first sergeant made sure we picked up water whenever we could up to that point, but we were still running short. There was no water to be spared for washing clothes, taking a quick sponge bath, or anything other than drinking.

The remaining crew of Red Two—Diaz, Couvertier, and Trivino—lost all their belongings in the accident when Red One hit the bridge abutment. All their military and personal gear was left scattered along the highway. They literally had only their Nomex jumpsuits, boots, and helmets. Everything else was gone. We took up a collection from the crews looking for extra clothes, socks, shaving gear, and toothbrushes for them.

Diaz's jumpsuit was streaked with oil and grime from the tank fire. Couvertier's was drenched with blood when he had banged his nose against the gunner's site in the accident and with hydraulic fluid that had gushed out when the turret went spinning.

They were tired like the rest of us. But they were also disappointed that they lost their tank, their home. They felt at loose ends without someplace to go, someplace to call their own. They spent much of the day wandering around near the first sergeant's PC, where he and they consoled one another in Spanish.

Diaz was insistent about getting back on a tank. He wanted some payback for losing Shipley and the tank. I told Gruneisen to find a place for a guy who had been one of my best and toughest soldiers throughout the war. But finding a place would be difficult. Our tanks were badly beaten up. Five of our remaining thirteen tanks were out of service. Two could be called on in an emergency, but three were down for a while.

The three that were hard down were Red One, Gruneisen's tank, with the bent gun tube; Red Three, Larrico Alexander's tank, which for no apparent reason would go into protective mode and shut down; and Red Four, Waterhouse's tank, with battery and generator problems. And with Red Two somewhere in Baghdad, being used as a photo opportunity for the Iraqis, that meant my entire first platoon—four tanks and sixteen soldiers—were out of action.

The other two tanks that I could count on only in an emergency were my Charlie Six-Six, which was still having hydraulics problems; and David Richard's Blue Four, which needed some new track.

By that time track was an issue for just about all the tanks. It was getting worn out from running on the paved roads, as were the road wheels. But as near as we could tell, none was in the supply pipeline. We could not even get water. How were they going to get us track, road wheels, and road wheel arms?

Shane Williams was given the unenviable task of trying to make sure we got the parts we needed, wherever we could get them. We begged and borrowed. We stripped parts from other tanks when we could. Just get them up and running, I told him, however you have to do it.

But it was not just Charlie Company that had problems with its armor. Wild Bunch and Rock were reporting many of the same problems. Not enough track. Not enough road wheels and road wheel arms. Not enough starters. Not enough batteries. Not enough generators. There never seemed to be enough of anything we needed, forcing the mechanics to use their imaginations to come up with new and decidedly unmilitary ways of making patches and repairs to get us through.

I spent part of that Sunday bugging the task force medics for condition reports on Shipley, Schafer, and Brons. I wanted to know their conditions so I could tell the rest of the company. We wanted to know one way or the other, good or bad, what was going on with our three wounded buddies.

Capt. Michael Dyches of the battalion medical staff spent a lot of time calling around on my behalf. He finally managed to learn that Brons was stable and doing as well as could be expected. Shipley was out of surgery and in stable condition, but Schafer was still critical. I thought at first they mixed up the two, because Shipley looked far worse than Schafer when I had seen them at the airport. But it turns out that Schafer's wounds were more serious than they appeared.

Still, the word was that both apparently would survive. We would not know until some time later that they did. But just the news that they were still alive and hanging on helped boost our morale on a day when we were all dragging a bit, physically and emotionally.

To help everyone get their minds off what had happened the day before, I requested and got permission to do a foot patrol in a palm grove about a hundred meters to our west. Some partially camouflaged BMPs were parked there, and we had been keeping a close watch on them for some time. Several crews and the first sergeant did the patrol and found about a half-dozen BMPs in relatively good shape. Also in the area were a number of fighting positions around a farmer's house and stashes of RPG warheads. It appeared that whoever had been there had left in a hurry. Clothing, food, and papers were strewn around the site, and in some places there was still tea in tin kettles.

The news about Shipley, Schafer, and Brons, and the focus on the patrol, helped relieve some of our anxiety and lift our spirits.

We got another boost when we started hearing some of the things Baghdad Bob was saying about us. Sanderlin had a small, shortwave radio on which we could occasionally pick up broadcasts from the British Broadcasting Corporation and the Voice of America if we were in the right place at the right time.

Eager for news of what we did on 5 April, we managed to lock onto a BBC news broadcast at one point in which the interviewer was treating Baghdad Bob as if he were a legitimate source of news about the war. Sure, he was the Iraqi Information Minister, but his pronouncements about the progress of the war were so outlandish that it was a surprise to us, and to Martz and Sanderlin, that anyone would put any stock in anything he said.

Yet the BBC, whose reports we found to be terribly inaccurate throughout the war, treated the man as if he had some credibility. There was no context to many of its reports, even though the network had reporters embedded with American and British troops. Yet on 6 April, we heard a repeat of one of his famous statements that was left unchallenged. "Today we slaughtered them in the airport," he told the interviewer. "They are out of Saddam International Airport. The force that was in the airport, this force was destroyed."

Those of us listening looked at one another as if to say: "What?"

"Must have been one hell of a fight last night," Sgt. 1st Class David Richard said.

Of course, it was not true. The 1st Brigade was still very much in control of the airport. I supposed most informed people were intelligent enough to know when they are being conned. Sometimes we wondered about the BBC.

But Baghdad Bob's performance explained a lot about the reaction we were getting from the Iraqi people. They were conditioned for years to believe what the government told them. So when the government told them the Americans were nowhere near Baghdad, they believed it. Right up until the moment a 70-ton M1A1 Abrams came rolling up next to them.

Later that afternoon I went to the task force TOC for a briefing about the next day's mission. There was little doubt in my mind that we would be going back to Baghdad. The only question was where.

Schwartz cleared that up in a hurry. This time instead of going north on Highway 8 and turning west to the airport, we would be going east, into what was known as the "regime district." This particular part of Baghdad on the west bank of the Tigris River housed a number of government office buildings, including Ba'ath Party headquarters, the Ministry of Information, and the Ministry of Industry and Trade. Also here were the Monument to the Unknown Soldier; the Al Rasheed Hotel, where many foreign journalists stayed during their visits to Baghdad; one of Saddam's numerous palaces; and Zawra Park, with a parade ground and reviewing stand where Saddam often reviewed his Republican Guard forces.

The big question on everyone's mind as we listened to the briefing was whether we would stay once we got there. Schwartz said that decision would be made later. The decision would depend largely on how much opposition we were getting and how defensible the place was.

This decision to return to Baghdad was made the day before, just minutes after our initial Thunder Run. Blount met Perkins at the airport and told him he wanted 2nd Brigade to do it again on 7 April. The plan was to open a route, pass a task force or more along the route into the city, and then come back out. It would once again be largely a show of force. But it would also give us the opportunity to learn more about employing multiple armor formations in the city.

This was to be a limited attack: advance and withdraw. Perkins had other ideas. He had something much more ambitious in mind.

About 3 p.m. on 6 April, Blount had just finished meeting with Lt. Gen. William Wallace, the V Corps commander, at the airport. They had discussed the limited advance and agreed on it. Lt. Col. Peter Bayer, the division operations chief, telephoned Perkins and told him the commander's intent.

"I just issued my Op (Operations) Order," Perkins replied. "I developed my plan and I told my guys to be prepared to stay. And by the way, I am attacking about one to two kilometers farther into the city than we had envisioned."

"Roger, got it," Bayer responded and went off to brief Blount, who concurred with the slight change in plans.

Perkins' plan called for Task Force 1-64 to lead 2nd Brigade up Highway 8 into the regime district. We would move into Zawra Park and take that over. Task Force 4-64 would follow us and secure the presidential palace on the banks of the Tigris. Task Force 3-15 would have the critical role of keeping open the route so we could be resupplied with fuel and ammunition if the decision was made to stay.

I think the feeling among the company commanders in Task Force 1-64 was that if we were going in, why not stay? The mission as I saw it was that we were going to Baghdad to stay. I didn't think that once we got there they would pull us out. I reinforced to my platoon leaders and platoon sergeants that it was highly probable we would stay.

The fight this time was not going to be on the road. Our fight was going to be in the city. This was going to be a quick dash in with a minimum of fighting. Our job was to lay down some suppressive fire and move as quickly as we could while 4-64 did the heavy damage and 3-15 covered our rear. Once inside the park, we would go into a defensive posture and shut down the tanks to conserve fuel because we did not know when we might be resupplied.

Morale was high, as was our confidence. Even though we had lost a tank, three soldiers had been injured in the company and one killed in the battalion, we were continuing to build on every mission we did.

We were getting better, tougher, and more cohesive as a company and as a task force. I thought once we got into the city that there was no way the Iraqis were going to bounce us back out. They just were not strong enough to coordinate their efforts.

We were getting casualty reports that we had hit the Iraqis pretty hard on 5 April. Some reports said there were more than 3,500 dead and wounded, and that hospitals were treating an average of more than 100 patients an hour for a sustained period of time. We were just not sure how much their casualties would affect their

Spc. Paul Helgenberger (left) and Spc. Curtis Gebhard congratulate one another on 6 April for making it through the gauntlet of fire the previous day during Charlie Company's Thunder Run into downtown Baghdad. (*Brant Sanderlin/ Atlanta Journal-Constitution*)

ability to come after us on 7 April. This was, after all, still a city of five million people.

I was more concerned this time than I was on 5 April about making sure everyone was protected inside their vehicles. Booker's death and the serious wounds to Shipley and Schafer nagged at me, and I did not want anyone else taking those kinds of risks. I passed the word that nobody would be outside the tanks or standing up in the back of the PC when we went in. The tanks crews would go open-protected—nobody would be outside the hatches; hatch covers would be opened just a few inches for better viewing.

"If you come out of the hatch you better have a darned good reason. Otherwise, we go in open-protected," I told them. "There's no reason for anyone to be popping out of the hatch. I don't want anyone sightseeing this time."

I knew we would be going in understrength as a company. Try as they might, the mechanics could only get eleven of our remaining thirteen tanks ready to go in. Red One and Blue One had to be left behind, and Red Two was somewhere in downtown Baghdad. The company would have thirteen vehicles on the second Thunder Run: eleven tanks, two PCs, and the BFST.

The "yes, we're staying; no, we're not staying" uncertainty of the outcome of this mission had us packing and unpacking the vehicles several times. If we were not staying, I wanted to go in light and not run the risk of losing a lot of personal gear as we did the day before. But if we got in there and it was decided that we would stay, no one would have any of their gear with them. After several unloads and reloads, we decided to keep the gear on. Not only might we need it, the extra baggage on the sides helped absorb some of the bullets and RPGs we were sure to face.

That night there were more than a few nervous stomachs and a certain amount of anxiety among the soldiers. But no one said much of anything. There seemed to be a steely resolve among them as they cleaned and recleaned their weapons, checked the ammunition feed trays, and mentally prepared themselves ready for another Thunder Run.

No one knew how bad this one would be. But we knew we were going to Baghdad again. And if we had any voice in the matter, this time we would stay.

15

THUNDER RUN II:
THE END OF SADDAM

THE initial Thunder Run was a drive-by knock on Saddam's front door to let him know we were there and that we could come into his neighborhood anytime we wanted. On Thunder Run II, we planned to break down the door and invite ourselves to stay for a while.

That morning of 7 April we made our peace with God one more time, checked our weapons and ammunition, and began the long, slow drive into downtown Baghdad. We still were unsure whether we would stay once we got there. But all indications were that Perkins wanted to stay and plant the American flag in the heart of the city.

That single act would send a message not only to the Iraqi regime, but to the world that we could do what we set out to: topple Saddam and liberate the Iraqi people from a tyranny that had controlled them for nearly three decades.

Such lofty thoughts were not exactly on my mind that morning, though. I was more concerned about getting Charlie Company's tanks into the city still in running order and have them be able to fight once we got there.

The mechanics had performed minor miracles overnight. Larrico

Alexander's Red Three and Waterhouse's Red Four were back up and running, so first platoon was now at half strength. My Charlie Six-Six was also repaired, as was Richard's Blue Four. But Balascik's Blue One broke down just before we left and he jumped into the loader's hatch of Mao's Blue Two.

That was not the only mix-and-match crew that day. First platoon bore only a slight resemblance to what it had been at the start of the war. Waterhouse had his normal crew except that Couvertier took over as his loader, replacing Spc. Brian Jasper. Gruneisen, the platoon leader, got in the loader's hatch of Red Three in place of Campos, while Diaz took the gunner's seat, replacing Sgt. Sidney Dorsey. It was only a two-tank platoon, but it had a lot of experience. I also took one of my mechanics along, Michael Williams, who rode in the BFST. Those who did not have a seat anywhere else stayed behind to work on the downed tanks to get them ready to bring forward.

Even though Blue was down to three tanks, I put it at the head of the company column that day. My Blue platoon would be the first into Zawra Park, the first to cross under the huge crossed sabers, and the first past the presidential reviewing stand and VIP box when the task force grabbed a firm foothold in downtown Baghdad.

The column moved out about 5:45 a.m. Ahead of us in the dim light we could see huge clouds of black smoke boiling out of central Baghdad. Either somebody was catching hell, or we were about to catch it.

We moved considerably faster on Thunder Run II than we did on 5 April, when the top speed probably did not get above ten miles per hour. This time we were pushing, trying to get there quickly while conserving our ammo for the fight we thought would come once we got into the city. We did not know when we would be resupplied so the order of the day was to fire only at targets that presented an imminent threat.

We paused only once, and then briefly, at a minefield the Iraqis set up across the highway. Not much thought or labor went into constructing this particular obstacle. It was about 400 meters deep, but the antitank mines were simply strewn on top of the road. A few of the mines had dirt sprinkled on top of them, but no other effort was made to hide them.

The minefield was spotted during a recon patrol prior to our movement and the engineers were called in to simply push the mines off the side of the road and clear a path for us. We passed without incident.

There was virtually no incoming fire until we got just beyond the overpass where Red Two had been shot up two days earlier. The hulk of the Abrams was still there, with a tow bar attached to the front, as if the Iraqis had tried to haul it off.

Just past the Abrams, Iraqi fighters hidden in a tree nursery on the left side of the road opened up on us with machine guns. They had given us trouble in that same spot on 5 April. But we were now moving quickly and the crews were in open-protected mode, so the rounds simply bounced off the sides and turrets of the tanks. We put out some suppressive fire with the coax and kept moving.

As my tank drew even with the nursery, however, an RPG flew out of the trees and exploded against the left side. It sounded as if someone hit us with an oversized sledgehammer. The explosion rocked the tank slightly, but we drove on. No warning lights popped on. We were in good shape.

At the maze of highways where 8 and 1 intersect, and where we had turned left two days earlier on the ride to the airport, we turned right and headed for 14 July Street, a major cross street several miles to the east.

Once again it was a somewhat surreal experience. Iraqi fighters were dug in on both sides of the road, firing at us with machine guns, AK-47s, and RPGs. But in the middle of all it we saw people driving their cars with kids in the back, or riding their bicycles down the road with AK-47s strapped to their backs. Some were in uniform, some in civilian clothes, but many acted as if this was just another Monday morning rush hour in Baghdad.

We also started encountering more suicide bombers. We were never really sure how many, if any, of the cars had bombs in them. But the Iraqis driving them seemed to think they could ram their cars into a 70-ton tank and disable it. A driver in one truck hit my tank on the right side near the rear just before I got to the park. But there was no explosion, and we barely felt it.

"We just got hit by a truck," I told Larimer, my driver, over the radio.

"We were?" he asked and continued on as if nothing had happened.

Wild Bunch was moving into the north side of the park while Charlie Rock took the intersection at the east end of the parade ground and reviewing stand, where 14 July Street and the Qadisiya Expressway intersect.

As my tank made the left turn onto the parade ground in front of the reviewing stand, I could see Blue pushing on ahead underneath the crossed sabers. Mao's Blue Two and S.Sgt. Germell Milton's Blue Three were on line, driving through the smoke and dust that made it seem as if we were looking at everything through a gray-brown filter.

David Richard's Blue Four ran over a steel guardrail on the way into the park and the long, gray piece of metal flipped up over the tank and wrapped itself around the turret and the mine plow on the front. The driver, Spc. Michael Donohue, could not see with the guardrail blocking his vision. He took his foot off the pedals and coasted to a stop against a nearby palm tree. Richard thought they had been hit.

"I think I'm hit," he called to Balascik over the platoon radio. "I can't traverse the turret."

Donohue climbed out of the driver's hole to inspect the damage, saw the guardrail, and manhandled it off the tank. Blue Four started up again and moved down the parade field to the west end of the sabers, where Blue set up a blocking position.

Even though we were in the middle of a fight, the historical significance of seeing American tanks—Charlie Company tanks—drive under those crossed sabers gave me a real shot of adrenaline. Before the war I had spent a lot of time reading about Iraq and had seen a number of photos of Saddam in the VIP box at the reviewing stand, his Republican Guard troops parading in front of him—I knew at that moment that Charlie Company was making history. We had

Charlie Company tanks roll into Baghdad's Zawra Park under the crossed-sabers monument on the morning of 7 April. The hands and arms are supposed to represent those of Saddam Hussein, who once watched his Republican Guards parade before him as he sat in the reviewing stands in the middle of the park. (*Brant Sanderlin/Atlanta Journal-Constitution*)

invaded one of the showpieces of Saddam's military might and were taking over.

To the right, about fifty meters from the VIP stand and just in front of a small, artificial pond, was a forty-foot statue of Saddam riding an Arabian stallion. I made a mental note to myself that I was going to knock Saddam off his high horse the first chance I got. But first we had to get some security inside the park. A small white car sped down the parade field from the west just as we got there. The driver wore civilian clothes but had an AK-47 in the front seat. We shot him with a machine gun, and the car rolled to a stop just short of the statue. Another car pulled up and men in uniforms with weapons got out and ran for cover among some trees between the park and a zoo just to the north.

We found bunkers and other fighting positions in the park, but no soldiers. They had run off to the north as we pulled in. White fired into bunkers with coax before some of the soldiers got on the ground to clear them with grenades and small arms.

Of all the positions Charlie Company occupied in the park, Blue's was the hottest. To the platoon's immediate front was Zaitun Street, which ran across its front roughly southeast to northwest. A few hundred meters to the left down Zaitun Street was the highway interchange with the Qadisiya Expressway. To the right, about a mile up the street was the intersection with Damascus Street and a large traffic circle.

No sooner had Blue gotten into position than it began taking a heavy volume of RPG, machine gun, and antitank fire. Apartment buildings for government workers, a school, and at least one abandoned building across the street from Blue were providing cover for Iraqi fighters. In addition, the Ba'ath Party headquarters building only a few hundred meters to the left toward the Tigris River was a source of heavy enemy activity.

On several occasions I called the task force TOC requesting that JDAMs be dropped in this area to clear out trouble spots. But I was told that some of the buildings on my target list were protected sites and could not be bombed. My soldiers were getting shot at from those buildings—there was an antiaircraft weapon on top of a school, and we could not bomb it.

As the fight went on we began taking sniper fire from the reviewing stands to our left. I requested an infantry platoon to clear the stands to give us flank security. Charlie Rock sent back a platoon and began going through the stands and the rooms in the complex that was part of it. The sniper was quickly chased out but while rooting around the rooms, our men stumbled across a treasure trove of cheap gifts Saddam had received over the years from various heads of state. Two huge rooms were filled with these gifts, many of which looked like they had been bought at a Third World flea market. The gifts were either outrageously ostentatious or shoddily made. The good stuff apparently went into the palaces, the cheap stuff stayed here.

About an hour after we entered the park, there was a slight lull in the fight. White was on the northeast side of the park tied in with Charlie Rock. The mortars and engineers set up on the west side of the Unknown Soldier Monument on the east side of the park. I sent Red's two tanks to help out Blue, giving us five tanks at that critical intersection. Our immediate area was secure. It was time to take out Saddam and the horse he rode in on.

Rick Nussio, the task force executive officer, came on the radio and asked if there were any Saddam statues in the area because the brigade commander wanted the media to witness their destruction. I told Nussio about the statue of Saddam and the horse in front of the reviewing stand that I was planning to shoot. He said to hold off until he got back to me. He relayed the information to Perkins, and word came back to me to stay put and not blow up anything until Perkins and the Fox-TV crew that was with him arrived at the park.

So we waited, and waited, and waited. Finally, about thirty minutes later, the Fox crew arrived with Perkins. At first we discussed blowing it up with C-4. I thought that a bit too pedestrian. This was a tank company, part of Task Force Heavy Metal, and I thought it a delicious irony that a tank with the name *Courtesy of the Red, White, and Blue* was already in position to take out the first statue of Saddam in downtown Baghdad. I said my crew could do it with an MPAT round.

"Make sure it takes only one shot," Perkins told me.

I gave him a "Roger, sir" and put it in the hands of my crew. I tried to impress on them how historically significant this was for us. Not only was this a clear signal that the Americans had planted the flag in downtown Baghdad, but it was a thumb in the eye of Saddam and his regime. It said their time in this town was finished.

I told Larimer he could someday tell his kids about how he put us into position to take out the statue. I told Helgenberger he was going to be the guy who loaded the round. And I told Malone: "You're going to be the guy who pulls the trigger that takes down the first statue of Saddam in Baghdad."

The Marines were still two days away from their much more photographed statue destruction on the east banks of the Tigris. We could rightfully claim we were the first military unit to knock Saddam off his pedestal, literally and figuratively.

"Just make sure you hit the damned thing," I told Malone.

"Sir, you don't have to tell me," Malone replied, the sarcasm evident in his voice.

I told Malone to lase the target and get the sights laid on. We were less than fifty meters from it. Perkins was going to give the thumbs up when the TV crew was ready. When he gave me the signal, I called "Fire!" and the round toppled the statue perfectly.

I could not have asked for a better shot. There was enough left of the statue for many of the soldiers to grab a piece for a souvenir. Several used an axe to cut off the head of Saddam. I put it on my tank and it rode with my crew and me the rest of the war. It was a moment of great exultation for the company, the task force, and the brigade. But I was quickly yanked back to reality by a radio call from Erik Balascik.

"Sir, Sergeant Mao's been wounded," Balascik said.

Balascik was so calm and matter-of-fact that he sounded like this was a training exercise.

"How bad is it?" I asked.

"Looks like it's a flesh wound. It took a chunk out of his arm."

I escorted Mark Strunk in the PC to the area to pick up Mao. That sector was still taking a lot of fire, and I wanted the medics to have some cover. It was not until later that I found out what had happened.

During the lull in the fighting, and while I was shooting the statue, Third platoon soldiers started cleaning some of the spent brass off the tops of their tanks. Within minutes an RPG flew out of the buildings across the street, hit one of the crossed sabers, and exploded. It was quiet for a few minutes before David Richard heard another loud explosion and saw a cloud of dust erupting around Mao's tank about thirty meters from him. Richard got on the radio to Balascik and asked what was going on.

"I can't see! I can't see!" Balascik yelled. The dust momentarily blinded him.

Mao, standing in the TC hatch, was rocked by the explosion of the RPG, which hit the left side of the tank just a few feet from him, shredding his rucksack. The impact was so hard he thought he'd lost his right hand. It was numb, and he was still trying to regain

Charlie Company soldiers remove the head of Saddam Hussein that was part of a statue in Zawra Park. S.Sgt. Nathan Malone, gunner on Captain Conroy's tank, blasted apart the statue on the morning of 7 April when the 2nd Brigade Combat Team went into Baghdad to stay. It was the first statue of Saddam in Baghdad to fall to American troops, two full days before the Marines toppled a larger statue on the east side of the Tigris River. Clockwise from left top are Spc. Randall Murrell, Spc. Josh Metheny, S.Sgt. James Kosters, and Spc. Tony Lyman. (*Brant Sanderlin/Atlanta Journal-Constitution*)

The crew of Cobra Six-Six and the head of Saddam taken from a statue in Zawra Park on 7 April. From left, Spc. Matt Larimer (driver), S.Sgt. Nathan Malone (gunner), Captain Conroy, and Spc. Paul Helgenberger (loader). (*Jason Conroy*)

his senses. "Oh, Lord," he prayed to himself, "don't tell me I lost my right hand."

When he finally looked down, the right hand was still there. By then the dust was clearing.

"Sergeant Mao," Balascik said, "I think you got hit on the left side. Look at your arm."

Mao looked at the back side of his left arm and saw blood seeping through his uniform. A piece of shrapnel from the RPG had gouged out a quarter-sized chunk of his left arm above the elbow. A few meters away, Germell Milton in Blue Three got on the radio to Mao's driver, Pfc. Justin Bailey.

"Blue Two driver, back up. Back up!" Milton ordered.

Bailey did as ordered, and Milton and his crew began pouring .50 caliber and 7.62mm machine-gun fire and 120mm main gun rounds into the abandoned building where the RPG appeared to come from.

Lt. Col. Rick Schwartz (left), commander of Task Force 1-64, and Maj. Rick Nussio, executive officer, display pieces of Saddam's destroyed statue. (*Jeff Molfino*)

Waterhouse in Red Four came up and shot a main gun round into a fuel tank at the edge of the park where he thought he had seen another RPG team. The fuel tank exploded in a mushroom ball of fire and smoke and burned throughout the day, that night, and long into the next day.

Mao, a stocky, tough, native of Cambodia, got into the back of Strunk's PC. Sgt. Robert Taylor, one of the task force medics, had been assigned to Charlie Company for a brief period to help with casualties and he began examining Mao.

"Fix me up, doc, so I can get back out there," Mao insisted.

He was angry that he had been shot, and angrier still that he had lost his rucksack. He wanted some payback.

Taylor cleaned the wound and bandaged it, and Mao was back on his tank in about twenty minutes.

As we consolidated our positions throughout the day, mortar

S.Sgt. Chhay Mao has an arm wound tended by medic Sgt. Robert Taylor on 7 April. Sergeant Mao's tank had been hit by a rocket-propelled grenade. The native of Cambodia told the medic to patch him up so he could get back into the fight. He returned to duty within minutes. (*Brant Sanderlin/Atlanta Journal-Constitution*)

and sniper fire continually harassed us. Multistory buildings ringed the park, so it was easy for someone with a decent sniper scope to shoot down on us or spot for the mortars.

The snipers were a nuisance, especially one who had climbed into a tall construction crane overlooking the park and took shots at us. But I could deal with the sniper fire. If snipers stay in the same spot and continue to fire, as this guy did, they can be targeted. A Bradley with its 25mm chain gun fired up the construction crane and dispatched that sniper in short order.

The mortars were another matter. Mortars, like artillery, are very impersonal and cause a lot of anxiety for everyone. And there is nothing you can do about mortars unless you have access to counterbattery fire. I never had the luxury of that the entire war. Our mortar platoon tried to fire back when it had the opportunity, and was usually quite accurate in knocking out whatever was harassing us. But the mortars kept coming and were even more irritating than the frequent RPG attacks.

What we did not know that day was that just a few hundred meters to our north, opposite the Zawra Park Zoo, were dozens of mortars, artillery pieces, and antiaircraft weapons that were the source of the intermittent rounds that had caused a few minor wounds among task force soldiers, though none in Charlie Company.

The company had been given responsibility for securing the zoo area, but we could not get to it that first day. We could see the zoo off to the north from where we were, and the gunners could even pick out individual animals with their sights on the tanks. At one point Richard called on the radio and said: "Hey, sir, I've got bars and animals and cages."

"Are you joking me?"

"No, sir. I've got a bear in a cage down here."

That afternoon we caught another one of Baghdad Bob's performances over the BBC. He was better this time than the previous day. Here we sat in Zawra Park, less than a mile from the Ministry of Information, within sight of the Al Rasheed Hotel and the Ba'ath Party headquarters building, and Baghdad Bob was still trying to convince people that there were no Americans in Baghdad. He stood on the roof of the Palestine Hotel, just across the river from us, surrounded by foreign media. They could hear the rumble of tank guns and see the smoke and fire from the attack. And still he insisted: "The Americans are not there. They're not in Baghdad. There are no troops there. Never. They're not at all. . . . There is no presence of American infidels in the city of Baghdad."

We had a good laugh at his expense.

Despite Baghdad Bob's claims to the contrary, the task force had a solid foothold inside the park. We had a 360-degree security perimeter and good fields of fire in all but one area. That area was the back side of the reviewing stand. There was no way we could cover it from where we were. Charlie Rock infantry cleared it out during the day but we were concerned that someone could easily sneak back in under cover of darkness. It was our blind side but there was little we could do about it. Task Force 3-15 was supposed to block the intersection at Zaitun Street and the Qadisiya Expressway denying movement into the area on the back of the reviewing stand.

But Task Force 3-15 did not get there that night. It was involved in a major fight trying to keep open the supply route along Highway 8. TF 3-15 had three key intersections to secure, code-named Objectives Larry, Curley, and Moe, before it got to the area of the park. It was vital to keep these open because without our control of them the unarmored ammunition and fuel trucks would not be able to make it through to us in the park. At each of the objectives the task force was involved in hours-long battles with Iraqi fighters. Fuel trucks and ammo trucks were shot up and burning along the route but 3-15 was keeping the lines open. The brigade had more than eighty tanks inside the city, and without fuel and ammo they would be relatively useless hunks of steel.

Perkins suggested to division that 1st Brigade might be able to spare one of its task forces to assist 3-15. Higher command concurred, and a mechanized infantry task force, 2-7, began moving out of the airport, south along Highway 1 to Objective Saints, then north on Highway 8 to give 3-15 some added muscle.

Perkins' other two task forces, 1-64 and 4-64, were faring relatively well. TF 4-64 was in control of the presidential palace on the riverbank, and 1-64 had a lock on the southern side of the park. Opposition in both those sectors was lighter than expected. The counterattacks we were getting did not appear to be coordinated. Individuals and small groups were instigating them, nothing that either of the task forces could not handle.

The opposition coming into Baghdad that morning was not anywhere near as difficult as two days earlier. And now two of the 2nd Brigade's task forces were sitting in relatively secure positions, and the Iraqis seemed unable to mount any organized effort against us. He decided we would stay for the night.

"I want to stay," Perkins told Blount.

"OK, you stay," Blount answered.

Blount then got on the secure tactical phone to Wallace, the corps commander.

"I think we can stay," he said.

"Are you sure?" Wallace asked.

"Roger," Blount responded. "We've got all the intersections secured. We can run fuel tankers in. We can run ammunition resupply in. We've got good lines of communication. I recommend we stay."

"OK," Wallace responded. "Have a good fight."

Blount called Perkins back and told him it was a go. What was to have been a limited advance was now an advance to seize and hold ground. We were in Baghdad to stay. The flag was planted, and from all appearances the regime was crumbling around us. There was no effective control of the military and no concentrated effort to kick us out of Baghdad.

Still, Blount had one more piece of advice for Perkins: "Don't lose your whole brigade in one night."

16

ROOTING OUT THE REMNANTS
OF SADDAM

THAT night we sat inside our tanks and waited for something to happen. It never did. The night of 7 April and early morning of 8 April in the center of Baghdad turned out to be much quieter than our first night at Checkpoint Charlie in Najaf.

As I drifted in and out of sleep, I once again felt good about what we had accomplished. We were in a strong defensive position and it did not matter what the Iraqis threw at us because we knew we could kill them far more easily than they could kill us. What else could they do? Drive tanks at us? If they did, we would kill them like we did at Mahmudiyah. Shoot RPGs at us? They had tried that, and it had proven to be a miserable failure. Fire artillery at us? They no longer seemed to have that capability. My only concern was WMD. But even that was not a major issue any longer. If they were going to do that, they probably would have done it before we got to Baghdad.

My worries were more mundane and revolved largely around making sure my own soldiers did not get too cocky or overconfident. We still were taking occasional sniper rounds but soldiers were starting to move around without helmets or flak jackets while doing maintenance on their vehicles. At the time, only a few of us had the Interceptor body armor, so many of the tankers were wearing their lightweight chicken vests, which might stop some shrapnel but would not stop an AK-47 round. But the more protected they were when they stepped out of their vehicles, the better I felt about their safety. I insisted that helmets and vests be worn whenever soldiers were outside their vehicles.

It was difficult keeping young soldiers cooped inside the tanks, where they had more protection than anywhere else. The inside of a tank is a tough place for anyone to live. It's cramped. There are dials and knobs and sharp edges everywhere. It smells of hydraulic fluid and sweat. You get restless. You get itchy. You have to get out and get your feet on the ground. You want to do something other than sit there and look through the GPS or TIS for hours. It was especially difficult for us because we had been living inside these tanks for twenty-two straight days, sleeping there and eating there when we were not fighting from in there.

We were all stiff and sore by morning from another night spent sitting up or leaning back against a cold steel turret. But we were safe. We awoke to the sound of an Air Force A-10 Warthog plowing up nearby enemy positions with its 30mm cannon. When the A-10 fires, it makes a distinctive sound, like long, drawn-out burp, or someone passing gas. When you're a tanker or an infantry soldier, the sound of an A-10 working over the enemy is wonderful to hear. That sound meant we finally had some close air support, which we had not had throughout the war. We could not see the plane because of the smoke and low cloud cover hanging over the city. But it was working only about two blocks from us and the soldiers cheered it on.

Shortly after wakeup, I received orders from Schwartz to take the company and expand the task force's perimeter by sealing off another key intersection. We were to move up Zaitun Street to the Mansoor Square traffic circle and turn right there onto Damascus Street. We were to continue east on Damascus Street to the intersection with 14 July Street and block the two roads there. The intent was to prevent any vehicles from moving east on Damascus Street to 14 July Street, both of which bordered the park.

On the north corner of the intersection was the Baghdad Central

Railway Station. Beyond that were the Ibn Bounnieh Mosque and the Iraq National Museum. The parliament building and a bus stop were on the east corner. On the south was the park. As we got closer, we could now see that area of the park and zoo was brimming with mortars, artillery, and antiaircraft pieces.

On the west corner of the intersection was what once was known as Al Muthana Airport. Now it was the site of the under-construction Saddam Grand Mosque, which was to be the world's largest mosque, a tribute to the Iraqi leader that would last long after his death and be a monument to his reign. It was still in the early stages of construction and the site contained a number of unfinished buildings.

This was big Ba'ath Party country, and our reception was sure to be anything but pleasant. Blue was getting fired on from that area even before we took off from the park. Charlie Company soldiers could see Iraqis with weapons congregating around trucks and cars at the traffic circle as if massing for a counterattack.

We knew we would eventually have to fight our way through that area so I figured we might as well do it now, while they were still disorganized and reeling from our attacks of the past three days. It was fairly clear to us by then that nobody was in charge of the Baghdad defenses, and those who fought were doing so out of fear or a misguided belief that they could somehow stop our tanks with rifles and RPGs.

Just about everyone I have talked to who was in Iraq during the war has a personal story about some stretch of road they refer to as "RPG Alley." For some it might be the road through Nasiriyah. For others it might be Samawah. For still others it might be Highway 8 leading into Baghdad.

Our "RPG Alley" started on Zaitun Street and continued along Damascus Street into the intersection. The rockets were hitting the sides of tanks with a boom and a metallic clang. They were zooming overhead, skittering down the road, and flying in all directions as we moved deeper into Baghdad. Mao's Blue Two took three direct hits that day but suffered no major damage.

Bunkers lined both sides of the roads, and many Iraqis fought and died in them as we passed. Others preferred not to fight as soldiers. The closer we got to the intersection, the more uniforms we saw scattered on the sidewalks. In some places it was possible to walk for considerable distances stepping only on uniforms and never touching the sidewalk. We could have outfitted the entire task force with the Iraqi uniforms we saw discarded along that route.

We saw this tactic before, at Objective Rams. But the closer we got to the heart of Baghdad, the more of it we saw. The soldiers would strip off their uniforms, often revealing civilian clothes underneath, throw them to the ground, then run off into the crowds with their weapons.

Blue led again as we pushed out from the park. It found antiaircraft weapons on top of the train station and knocked them out. It was fired on by fighters hiding in and around the mosque. A volley of RPGs sailed toward the platoon as it got closer to the National Museum. Bunkers and trenches were built up around the museum, and soldiers were firing at us from the roof of the Children's Museum.

White moved into the northwest side of the intersection and set up on 14 July Street, securing it under heavy fire. Iraqis in civilian clothes were running out of side streets firing weapons as soldiers got off the tanks and began unrolling concertina wire across the road to stop traffic.

Second platoon soldiers were struggling to get the wire out on the ground far enough in front of the tanks to serve as a deterrent to vehicles attempting to get through the intersection. But the wire seemed to have little effect. People kept trying to drive around or through the coils. If they did that and ignored the warning shots, soldiers shot into the vehicles. Once the vehicles got inside the wire and started speeding up and driving directly at the tanks, the soldiers could only assume they were being driven by suicide bombers. Some were; some were not. We had no way of telling one from the other.

When Red relieved White so it could return to the park for fuel and ammo, it was more of the same. Seven or eight cars were already shot up and burning just a few hundred meters from the

An Iraqi man begs for help after he and three companions failed to heed warnings to stop and ran their car at Charlie Company tanks in downtown Baghdad on 8 April. The man in the background was shot in the jaw and seriously wounded. Two other men in the car were killed. Soldiers found weapons in the trunk. (*Brant Sanderlin/Atlanta Journal-Constitution*)

tanks. But within minutes of Red taking over, two more vehicles came at its tanks at high rates of speed.

The first was a white pickup truck. It blew through the first set of wire about 200 meters in front of the tanks. Diaz, serving as Waterhouse's gunner, fired warning shots from the coax in front of the truck. It did not stop.

About 100 meters from the tanks, Gruneisen gave the order: "Take him out."

The truck was hit multiple times but slowed only slightly. Waterhouse estimated it was still going about forty miles per hour when it hit Red Three. Everyone ducked, expecting a bomb to explode. There was only the sound of glass breaking and metal on metal as the car hit the tank. Less than a minute later, another car raced around the concertina wire. It came at the tanks doing close to fifty miles per hour. Its driver also ignored warning shots and a second row of concertina wire about fifty meters out. That car also was shot to pieces.

That day we ended up transporting close to a dozen civilians, and several soldiers masquerading as civilians, to the battalion aid station to have their wounds treated. Some were severe. One man had his lower jaw shot off. Another took a .50 caliber round in his right foot and it was just hanging on by shreds of skin. The aid station was set up in the park and by late morning the medics were scrambling to treat all those being brought in. Mercado and Coffman made several runs in the PC back and forth on RPG alley that day, carrying the wounded for treatment.

We needed something more substantial than the concertina wire to stop the cars and trucks. Mercado found some wrought-iron barricades in the park and brought them out to each checkpoint so the soldiers could place them across the road. The barricades were

Sgt. Robert Taylor treats a baby that was wounded in downtown Baghdad by Iraqi mortar fire on 8 April. She and her father, who was also wounded, had been transported to safety by Sgt. Andrew Coffman under heavy enemy fire to a forward aid station. (*Brant Sanderlin/Atlanta Journal-Constitution*)

curved, with long, sharp points, and would serve as the first line of defense.

We did not know it then, but even while we were engaged in tough, street-by-street fighting, on 8 April we were beginning to transition from combat operations to Security and Stabilization Operations. It was a difficult transition for all of us. We were concerned about civilian casualties and wanted to prevent them at all costs. But we were having problems once again figuring out just who the legitimate civilians were. So many people carried weapons that it was impossible to make the distinction with any certainty before it was too late. Charlie Company soldiers were angry and upset with themselves whenever they learned civilians were in a car they had shot up after it had sped through the barricades and came at the tanks. But how could they tell the difference between an innocent civilian and an Iraqi trying to kill them with a car bomb or truck bomb?

That day at the White checkpoint a minivan with four men in civilian clothes approached the concertina wire, went around it, then got up on the sidewalk and started racing for the tanks. The soldiers fired on it, and the van blew up as soon as it was hit. Only one man made it out of the van, and he died on the sidewalk. The other three were crowded into the driver's seat, fused in death by fire as they tried in vain to escape the flames.

Charlie Company soldiers who had been in combat for nearly three straight weeks now were being asked to make split-second decisions based on very little information. If they hesitated, they ran the risk of dying in a fiery car bomb explosion. If they did not hesitate, they ran the risk of killing innocents along with the fighters. Those were not easy decisions to make because they had to be made even while we were still taking sniper fire and occasional mortar rounds at the checkpoints.

Later that afternoon, Schwartz came to our sector along with two platoons of infantry from Charlie Rock to clear the site where the mosque was being built. We found some Iraqi fighters in there, along with two tracked vehicles, one of which appeared to be a command-and-control vehicle. We wanted to have those buildings cleared by dark to prevent snipers from getting in there and shooting at the tankers while they were manning the checkpoints.

The amount of incoming fire and the number of suicide vehicles decreased later in the afternoon at three of the approaches to the intersection. But the north approach, where Blue was set up, kept getting probed by what we later learned were Special Republican Guard forces that had a headquarters building in the area.

Just before dark, we began putting chem lights out with the barricades to serve as warning lights for drivers who might approach. We had tried red and orange lights at Checkpoint Charlie, but those did not seem to deter drivers. Blue eventually came up with what proved to be a novel approach to crowd and vehicle control. When a dismounted squad was sent out to set up the chem lights, Germell Milton, who carried a box of green lights, accompanied it. He wore gloves and made such a production out of setting up the lights he apparently was able to convince many Iraqis that they were radioactive.

He would gingerly take each light out of the wrapping, carefully set it on the ground, and slowly back away. In the morning, he reversed the process. Once Blue started putting out the green lights, their problems with crowds at night diminished. It seems no Iraqi wanted to get near those lights. But they had to be green. Red or orange lights did not deter them.

"They've been watching too many American movies," Mao snorted in derision.

But the Iraqis had their own way of doing things and of testing us. They would often send out the neighborhood crazy man to see if our soldiers would shoot him. He pranced around, waving his arms, shouting things at us. Sometimes, the crazies would lift their *dishdashas* for us to see they were not carrying any weapons, and often not wearing underwear. If the crazies were not killed, the rest of the locals would venture out.

The night of 8 April we had tanks widely scattered around the intersection, with several hundred meters separating the platoons. I put the two PCs on top of the overpass in the middle of the intersection and instructed the crews to keep watch for possible snipers moving into buildings around us. From the overpass they could see down on the roof of the train station and several other buildings. While the tanks controlled the road access, the PCs were responsible for making sure no one got inside our loose perimeter.

Every tank had at least one soldier awake at all times scanning with night-vision goggles, while one vehicle in each platoon had TIS watch. We anticipated a certain amount of probing that night, but there was little. We could hear explosions and gunfire rattling off to our east, across the Tigris, which was little more than a mile

Sgt. 1st Class Ray White, riding in the loader's hatch of Charlie Two-Three, moves along Baghdad's Damascus Street on 9 April. To his right is S.Sgt. Ben Phinney, tank commander. Behind them is the blue dome of the Ibn Bounnieh Mosque near the Baghdad Central Railway Station in the Mansoor District. (*Brant Sanderlin/ Atlanta Journal-Constitution*)

away. But our sector was relatively quiet until morning, when Blue had an RPG fired at it as a breakfast wakeup call.

On 9 April we began clearing the government buildings in our sector and a bunker complex in a soccer field to our immediate west. With the assistance of Charlie Rock's infantry, we made a slow, methodical search of the buildings, looking for documents or photographs or anything that might provide information about weapons of mass destruction or defenses the Iraqis had constructed in the area. We cleared the train station first, where we found a stash of Ba'ath Party literature, some AK-47s and spare parts, and about thirty empty satellite telephone boxes.

We moved on to the parliament building and the bus station. Everywhere we went were photographs of Saddam. Every room had at least one picture of the man. We were later told by some of the local residents that the law required a picture of Saddam be displayed in every house.

We looked at the Ibn Bounnieh Mosque, but did not go inside, mindful of Muslim sensibilities. We saw Iraqi military uniforms all around the building and a motorcycle with a machine gun at the front door. The Iraqi soldiers obviously were not as mindful of the Muslim sensibilities as we were.

From there we moved down to the Ministry of Housing and Construction, a ten-story office building in Blue's sector. The infantry went in first, clearing room by room, floor by floor. It was hot, sweaty, demanding work. But neither they, nor I, wanted to run the risk of being ambushed by some fanatical Iraqis hiding out in the building. The building turned out to be deserted except for a cleaning crew.

In the tenth floor corner office of the Minister of Housing and Construction, we found papers strewn all over, as if someone had grabbed a few vital documents and taken off before we got there. Some were in English, most in Arabic. But we did find a few interesting pieces, including U.S. Federal Emergency Management Agency information on the effects of nuclear bombs and Government Printing Office documents on the State Defense Building in Topeka, Kansas. There were drawings of the bunker system in the

Captain Conroy kicks in a door during a search of an Iraqi government building in downtown Baghdad on 9 April. Soldiers from Task Force 1-64 spent most of the day clearing buildings, looking for weapons and documents. (*Brant Sanderlin/ Atlanta Journal-Constitution*)

Mansoor district and blueprints of many of the buildings in Baghdad.

We quickly realized we needed some help and called Schwartz, who came up to advise us. He spent a short time looking at some of the documents before telling us: "I think we've gotten in a little over our heads here. We can only seize territory and then we turn it over to someone else. The interim government is going to have to come in and use this. Let's leave it for them."

The minister's office was actually a suite of offices, with a bedroom and a Western-style bathroom. The minister either spent a

Captain Conroy examines documents in a government office building in downtown Iraq. Soldiers were told to look for evidence of weapons of mass destruction but were unable to find anything of value. (*Brant Sanderlin/Atlanta Journal-Constitution*)

lot of time here, or liked to be pampered. He had the first porcelain commode many of us had seen for more than seven months and several soldiers stopped by just to take a look at it.

That afternoon we cleared one more building, this one on the site of Saddam's Grand Mosque. It served as the planning building not only for the mosque, but for the numerous projects Saddam was having built throughout the country to honor himself and his legacy. Most incorporated a large statue or bust of Saddam in some form or fashion. We found detailed drawings of many of the projects and elaborately constructed dioramas of what they were eventually to look like. It was amazing to see the amount of work that went into them. It was also amazing to see the high regard in which Saddam seemed to hold himself. It was obvious he wanted to be remembered for hundreds of years. He was a modern Nebuchadnezzar building shrines to himself.

But seeing the plans for the projects made me realize that while the Iraqis had been subjugated and brutalized for many years, they had some marvelous architects who could have been doing wonderful things for their people. Instead, they were forced to massage the ego of one man.

Once the planning building was cleared, we decided to use it as our CP, at least temporarily. We did not know what type of missions we would be given over the next few days. But for the moment, this was to be our home. It was not much of a home. The infantry had done a great job smashing glass and breaking furniture, so the place was a mess and needed some cleaning up. But there were a few rooms where soldiers could stretch out for a while under decent cover and shuck their helmets and flak jackets for a while.

That day we started to see evidence of widespread looting in our sector. We would clear a building, leave the area, and the civilians would come in right behind us, carrying, rolling, and hauling away anything that was not anchored in steel or cement. The looting started at a hospital. People were carting off everything from bedpans to a heart-lung machine. They took what they could get, for what reasons I'll never know, although I suspect some of it was revenge for what the regime had done to them. Much of what they took was useless to the average citizen. But given the opportunity, people will loot.

While in Bosnia I had seen much the same thing. In some places everything imaginable was stripped out of houses, from the electrical wiring to the copper tubing to the door hinges. It was as if human locusts had swept through, devouring everything but the shells of the houses. Now it was happening in Baghdad. But how do you stop looting once it starts? Shoot the very people we came to liberate? That did not seem the best way to win hearts and minds and stabilize a country that no longer had a government or police force.

Iraqi citizens on the west side of the Tigris River begin looting government buildings on 10 April as American forces moved into the area and Iraqi officials abandoned it. (*Brant Sanderlin/Atlanta Journal-Constitution*)

That afternoon Blue called in reports about the looting at the hospital and in the area of the Iraq National Museum. They also reported taking occasional AK-47 and RPG fire from that area and that the museum grounds were being used as a cut-through for fighters changing positions. I called the report up to Schwartz.

"I need you to tell me if you see people carrying stuff outside the museum," Schwartz said.

I told him I could not tell without moving Blue closer to the museum to get a better view of what was going on inside. Schwartz told me to move Blue up to the edge of the museum grounds. But as the platoon began to move, a barrage of RPGs and AK-47 fire was unleashed from the side streets and the museum grounds. I reported that to Schwartz and he said the platoon should pull back to its original positions and hold there.

Schwartz saw looting earlier in the day while with us but it seemed largely confined to government buildings. He called Perkins and described what he called "extensive looting" and told the brigade commander he did not have the manpower to stop all of it. Perkins told him it was part of the natural process and was likely to go on only for a few more days. Our soldiers were to neither condone it nor try to stop it, because if we tried to intervene we might be associated with Saddam's regime.

At the task force BUB on the morning of 10 April, Schwartz made it official: Do not interfere with civilian looting. "We don't get involved in that," he told the company commanders, first sergeants, and task force staff. "It's a natural process. There are some very, very angry people out there. We are not into stabilizing the civilian community. This is still a combat operation and we need to maintain that focus."

Schwartz reiterated that we had taken over what he referred to as "the heart and soul of Iraq, the Washington Mall of Iraq" and that we were to preserve as much as we could from here on out because "we are slowly going to return this thing back to the people of Iraq."

He wanted us to maintain our focus on combat operations because it was unclear just how much of a threat remained. No one knew if the Ba'ath Party still existed, or whether its leaders had fled the area. But it was clear that many of the fighters we were now facing were either die-hard Republican Guards, who were in a minority, or Syrians imported especially for the job of killing Americans, a job for which the Iraqi leadership apparently did not have the stomach.

"The only ones fighting now are the Syrians. They are saying the Iraqis are cowards. They are saying the Republican Guards have fled the city," Schwartz went on. It was estimated that as many as three thousand to five thousand hard-core Syrian fighters were in the city, many in our area. So we needed to be alert and not start losing our focus even as combat operations started dying out around us.

Then he offered a note of hope: the 1st Armored Division was on its way from Germany with thirty-eight ships loaded with equipment. This was to be our replacement, we thought. We would get our tickets home once they arrived. We could feel the end drawing near.

It was good news, but also troubling news. Once that got back to the soldiers they would start to think more about going home than on finishing the fight. This was one of the most dangerous times for a soldier who has been in combat. He's ready to go home, hears he might soon be going home, and starts to relax, making him vulnerable to mistakes, accidents, ambushes, or any manner of things that could wind up with him being shipped back in a body bag. I feared that was going to happen to Charlie Company soldiers. The first sergeant and I had to come up with missions to keep them busy, and keep them focused, while we waited for the call to go home. Baghdad was starting to settle down, but we could not afford to do that.

What I did not realize was that within a few days my wish would be granted. We would get a mission that would keep us focused. But this mission would test not so much our combat skills as our diplomatic skills, as well as our patience. The National Museum was about to become the source of international controversy, and we were about to be dumped right into the middle of it, whether we wanted to be there or not.

17

BAGHDAD BEDLAM AND OTHER NATIONAL TREASURES

BY 11 April, the war was beginning to wind down around us. We could hear the occasional rattle of gunfire in other parts of the city, along with bombs and artillery exploding with hollow thuds. And soldiers at the checkpoints were still being targeted by snipers. But the frequency of the shots decreased considerably and the number of suicide bombers declined dramatically. Baghdad residents from nearby neighborhoods were starting to cautiously venture out of their homes and approach the checkpoints, trying to get from one side of the city to the other. Civilians began offering food, gifts, and information if we would let them through. I put out the word that the soldiers were not to accept any food or gifts, but needed to be aware of information that could help us identify fighters still in the area. Blue captured a Special Republican Guard first sergeant in its sector, and he talked like he had just been granted immunity. We got out of him what we could about nearby weapons caches and safe houses then sent him back to the task force TOC for additional questioning.

We were trying to ease out of the combat mindset and into the SASO/peacekeeping mindset. But we had to be able to toggle back and forth in an instant. It was much the same thing as we had done at Najaf, but we did not have the open spaces to work in now that we did then. And the nature of the war was changing. We still had occasional firefights with Syrians operating in our area, and they would usually slink off shortly after engaging us. We could tell the war was drawing to a close; these occasional engagements were more likely to be the exception, not the rule. Sustained combat was about over for us.

Anyone we saw with a weapon was still fair game, but we were seeing fewer people overtly carrying AK-47s or RPGs. They were either leaving them at home or stashing them in a cache somewhere. As we moved around, we uncovered hundreds of weapons caches that the locals must have known about. In one cache behind the Ministry of Housing and Construction, we found about a hundred AK-47s with ammunition and a sign in Arabic that read: "Use in case of emergency." We consolidated the weapons and brought in the engineers to destroy them. We found tons of weapons, but knew there were many more still hidden out there.

It was on this day that we completed the task of burying the Baghdad dead in our sector. Schwartz told us on 10 April he wanted the dead buried and all the disabled and abandoned vehicles removed by 3 p.m. that day. But there was no way we could do that. There were just too many dead, dozens of them scattered on both sides of the streets in bunkers and fighting positions, in buildings, in cars, and, in one instance, a dump truck. A blue dump truck with about a dozen bodies in the back, all uniformed soldiers, sat in the right lane of 14 July Street. It had been there for days, and the bodies were beginning to bloat and ooze fluids as the days got warmer. The stench permeated everything within several hundred meters.

Schwartz called it "Operation Bury the Dead." He wanted the sector cleaned up and cleared out as quickly as possible so we could get the Iraqis back to some sense of normalcy, at least within the task force sector. We had to determine which of the dead were Muslim and which were not. The non-Muslims, we were told, had a cross tattooed on their right hands. The Muslims were to be buried according to custom, on their right sides, facing Mecca, which was southwest of us.

An Iraqi man lies dead on the sidewalk in downtown Baghdad after he and three companions sped through a roadblock to try to ram Charlie Company tanks. The soldiers fired on the van and it exploded almost immediately, killing all four and destroying a stash of AK-47s. (*Brant Sanderlin/Atlanta Journal-Constitution*)

"I know that's a tough one, but we've got to do it," Schwartz ordered.

I ordinarily would have given the job to a senior noncommissioned officer, but I did not have one to spare. So the job fell to my XO, Shane Williams. I knew he and any of the headquarters people he could round up would do the job as well as circumstances permitted. The circumstances were not particularly good.

Some of the bodies were starting to decompose and fall apart. Others were so frozen from rigor mortis that they were almost impossible to get out of their vehicles. Still others were nothing more than piles of charred bone. It was not a pleasant job, but one that had to be done. We had done it at Najaf. This was the same thing, only on a larger scale. Williams opted to do much of the job himself. "I already have nightmares about this. I don't want you guys to have them, too," he told the soldiers.

1st Lt. Shane Williams, Charlie Company's executive officer, removes an AK-47 from a vehicle as he goes about the grim task of burying the dead on 10 April. (*Brant Sanderlin/Atlanta Journal-Constitution*)

It took him a while to round up the assets he needed, especially engineers with a backhoe to dig a common grave for those not claimed by the Red Crescent. He took heavy drapes from the planning building in which we were staying and wrapped the corpses in them, trying to maintain some integrity and keep body parts from falling off. We also found a tow truck that we used to haul off the abandoned and destroyed vehicles, including the dump truck with the bodies in the back.

When Williams climbed into the back of the truck to remove the bodies, he nearly fell when he slipped on the body fluids that were pooling on the steel floor. In another instance, he had to use two hands to pry the fingers of a dead man off the steering wheel of his car. On other cars he had to remove seats to extricate the bloated bodies. In a few instances he had to use a shovel to scrape up the remains of those burned to ashes in fires started when their vehicles exploded. Often the stench got so bad he donned his gas mask so he could continue working.

Sgt. 1st Class Solomon Ball mans a .50-caliber machine gun under a portrait of Saddam Hussein as Charlie Company soldiers patrol the streets of Baghdad on 12 April. (*Brant Sanderlin/Atlanta Journal-Constitution*)

On 12 April we moved out of the planning building. We were glad to leave there, because with the warmer weather it had become a haven for mosquitoes. All of us who spent any time in the building at night emerged in the morning with our faces dotted with red spots. We looked as if we had measles. We had started taking antimalarial medication on 1 April before we moved into Objective Saints, but I reinforced to the soldiers that they needed to take it every day to keep from getting sick.

Our new home was the Ministry of Industry and Trade. It was just down 14 July Street from the Al Rasheed Hotel and across the street from the Unknown Soldier Monument. It looked more like a high-rise hotel than a government building, with its spacious lobby, high ceilings, and chandeliers. It had been shot up pretty well, and few of the windows had emerged intact. But what it offered were small office suites where groups of soldiers could set up their cots, stow their gear, and get a good night's sleep outside their tanks and out of the elements.

We discovered a number of computers and a pile of audiovisual equipment in the building, along with a refrigerator that we could hook up to the generator and finally chill some of our bottled water. We had been drinking nothing but hot and lukewarm water for weeks and the mere thought of a chilled drink was exciting.

With the computers and audiovisual equipment, we were able to set up an entertainment center in the lobby where soldiers with downtime could come to relax, play computer games, or watch vid eos. Many of the soldiers brought movies on DVDs with them and there was usually a video on around the clock.

It was about this time we were also occasionally required to show up on the parade ground in front of the reviewing stand to display the battle damage to our tanks to senior officers who were starting to come through the area. Lt. Gen. David McKiernan, the commander of all ground forces during the war as head of Coalition Forces Land Component Command, was on one such inspection tour along with Blount. I would have preferred they come down to see where the soldiers were living and talk to them there. But we dutifully lined up some of our tanks along with Wild Bunch and Rock vehicles.

The soldiers would show the battle damage, explain how it happened, and McKiernan would say something like: "I guess you would say that's a pretty survivable piece of equipment, soldier."

The soldier would respond: "Roger sir," and the general would move on.

What struck me as odd about all this was that it seemed like something more appropriate for a much later time. Many of the soldiers did not want to start telling war stories to outsiders yet. They were still in the game. They were still getting shot at on a regular basis and had little time to reflect on the war. They were intent on getting out of there alive. When we told war stories, we told them to each other. Anybody who was not there when we went through our fights was an outsider. Only those who were there understood it.

Our primary mission was reduced to two checkpoints. We had responsibility for the intersection on the west end of the parade ground at Zaitun Street, as well as the area near the museum. We did not have responsibility for the museum itself. Neither the task force nor the company had orders to take control of it. Blue kept reporting that it saw people getting into the museum grounds through a back entrance but could not confirm if anything was being looted. I continued to send the reports to higher command but our orders were to continue to observe and report.

By 13 and 14 April, soldiers at our checkpoints reported they were getting a lot of smiles and thumbs-up from local residents. We were seeing more acceptance from the residents of Baghdad than we had from those at Najaf. Many seemed genuinely happy to see us. But I made it clear we were not to trust anyone. I knew that some who did not want us there would use any trick they could to kill us the first chance they got. They might use women or kids to get to us, so I was particularly upset with the tank crews whenever they allowed children to get up on the tanks. That meant the crews were probably watching the kids enjoy themselves and not monitoring the crowd at the barricade.

On 16 April, Martz and Sanderlin left the company and headed back to Atlanta. They were sore, tired, and dirty and figured there was not much more they could do here. The major shooting part of the war was about over, and that was what they had come to report on. The day and night before they left, they opened up their two satellite phones to the company and let everyone who wanted have some time to call home. Just a few minutes on the phone did a great deal for the morale of everyone in the company.

Charlie Company was greeted with open arms by many residents of Baghdad grateful that Saddam Hussein was finally gone. (*Jason Conroy*)

About the time Martz and Sanderlin left for Baghdad airport, we received a new mission from the task force TOC: move to the Iraq National Museum and secure the buildings and the grounds. With combat nearly at an end, the international media were in the market for stories about what in their view the Americans did wrong, or at least did not do right. The museum was the first issue on their agenda to criticize our efforts.

It was being reported that more than 170,000 items, many of them priceless antiquities, had been looted from the museum following our arrival in the area on 8 April. It was claimed that we were responsible for failing to secure the museum and thus protect the national heritage of Iraq. The media often mistakenly put responsibility for this on the Marines, even though it was an Army sector, but we were all the same to them: Americans in uniform who had no sense of culture or history and were more interested in protecting Iraq's oil reserves than its antiquities.

The reporting almost universally condemned us as the stories breathlessly reported claims from experts in the field that this was an international disaster.

Zinab Bahrani of Columbia University said, "By April 12 the entire museum had been looted. Blame must be placed with the Bush administration for a catastrophic destruction of culture unparalleled in modern history."

Trevor Watkins of Edinburgh University in Scotland equated it to other great tragedies in history, "like the burning of the Library at Alexandria, and Britain and the U.S. will be to blame."

Some even suggested that American forces should have risked their lives to save these national treasures. Of course, those who suggested it were far from the fighting, making those judgments from the comfort of their living rooms. They did not have to run a gauntlet of RPG or AK-47 fire. They did not have to put their lives on the line to protect the museum.

By 16 April the museum had become something of a focal point for international media coverage in Baghdad because of the reports of looting. We received orders to secure the museum complex and stop the looting. A platoon of infantry from Charlie Rock was dispatched to assist us. We expected to get shot at along the way and were prepared to fire back. We were not looking for a fight, but were ready for one.

What we were not ready for was the traffic. When we got close to the museum, we found ourselves in the middle of a major traffic jam. No traffic lights were working in the area and since Iraqi police were not available to direct traffic, drivers did whatever they pleased, whenever they pleased. We had five huge tanks trying to squeeze through a tangle of small cars, taxis, and buses. The infantry soldiers had to get out of their vehicles and create a buffer between the civilian vehicles and us. We were very mindful of the possibility that someone in one of the cars might pull out an AK-47 and open up on us, or that a spur-of-the-moment suicide bomber might hit us.

For the most part, the Iraqis were accommodating, slowly clearing a path for us. It was almost like parting the Red Sea. As we inched forward, a path would open. We saw a number of smiling faces, but we also had the occasional stare of death. Despite the cooperation, it took about an hour to move just a few blocks.

As we approached the museum, we saw a crowd of people and about two dozen cars on the street outside. Balascik thought a demonstration was in progress. I was not sure what was going on. About fifty people were outside, trying to get in. Another twenty or so were inside, behind locked gates, trying to keep the others out. I got off my tank and approached the locked gates with some of the infantry.

My first concern was security. Before I did anything else, I wanted to ensure that the museum grounds and buildings were clear, that Blue was set up in positions with good fields of fire, and that all the entrances to the museum grounds were covered. I ordered the street closed to all traffic and positioned Blue tanks so they could provide covering fire if necessary. Because of the amount of fire we had taken from the area in recent days, I was taking no chances

It was clear that Iraqi fighters had used positions inside and outside the museum grounds. Sandbagged bunkers with live RPGs were on the sidewalk in front and discarded Iraqi uniforms littered the street. A Special Republican Guard headquarters was directly across the street. The Special Republican Guard, the elite of Saddam's elite forces, were expected to protect the palace gates and lay down their lives for their leader.

I ordered everyone who was inside the museum grounds behind locked gates to move outside so they could be searched and asked who was in charge. Dr. Jabir Khali, director of the National Organization of Iraqi Antiquities, and Dr. Donny George, the museum's research director, identified themselves as museum staff. Both spoke relatively good English.

"Why were you not here providing security all along?" George huffed.

The question did not go over well. I had been there less than five minutes and already my patience was being tried. I took a deep breath and tried to explain that we were just given the mission to secure the museum and were here now to do just that.

Suddenly, a microphone was thrust into my face and people

began closing in on me, firing questions about why it had taken us so long to get there and how did I feel about allowing looters to steal so much of Iraq's priceless heritage.

I realized the group outside the gates was media, most of them international journalists. I brushed past the reporters, telling them I would try to answer their questions later, hoping I could find some way to avoid it. I was told this would be a delicate situation, and I was not keen on the idea of being the sole American spokesman for what we did, or did not do, at the museum.

Jabir and George were reluctant to unlock the gates. I told them that we were going to clear the museum and grounds with or without their cooperation. They could either unlock the gates and let us in, or we could break them down. They were concerned about the artifacts in the museum. I was concerned about possible fighters in the museum

They finally agreed to open the gates and come outside. I put Blue's tanks at each of the four corners inside the grounds and took some of the infantry and a few soldiers from Blue to inspect the complex. All my questions to Jabir and George were about security. Where are the weapons? Who's in the museum? Are there any soldiers in the museum?

They replied that all the soldiers were gone. But there was plenty of evidence that they had been here and apparently in large numbers. Balascik and the infantry went behind the main building and found bunkers, a large cache of weapons, and a number of uniforms. They saw several RPG firing positions inside the walls, including on top of the children's museum. Blood trails in the area indicated we had hit someone during the heavy exchange of gunfire in recent days. A building in the back had a door that opened up to another street. It was not locked and apparently had been the route used by fighters and looters in an effort to avoid being seen by Blue during earlier fighting.

We found military maps and other military gear in the administrative offices. A military trailer was parked next to the mosque just behind the museum. Targets were painted on the back of the museum wall for RPG teams, the same sorts of targets we had seen earlier in Najaf.

In the administrative portion we found more weapons and uniforms and indications the Special Republican Guards had used it as a command-and-control node. They had also ransacked the place before they left, tipping over file cabinets and tearing out air conditioners. By the time we were ready to move into the display areas, Blount, the division commander, and Schwartz showed up to assess the situation.

With the infantry leading the way, we slowly began moving through the galleries. Jabir went with Blount and Schwartz, Donny George with me. Based on what I was hearing second-hand about the widespread looting and destruction, I was expecting a catastrophe. It was anything but. Most of the glass cases, although empty, were still intact. Just over a dozen of the hundreds of cases were damaged. When we got to the area of the coin collection, the cases were intact but there was only a picture of coins. I asked where the coins were, and George replied they had been removed before the war and taken to a secure location.

Some of the larger pieces on display were damaged, but Jabir and George told us they could not provide a list of what was missing and what was damaged until they did a complete inventory. I kept asking what was looted, what was taken. Neither could provide specific answers, but George said much had been taken to a secure room in the basement.

When we got there, he acknowledged that it had not been penetrated or disturbed. "Is that where the artifacts are now?" I asked.

"Yes," he replied.

During the ninety-minute inspection tour, Jabir and George repeatedly told us many of the items had been moved to secure locations. They would not say where and whenever we tried to pin them down on what had been taken, they were evasive, refusing to answer.

In one area that contained old scrolls, there was no evidence the door had been forced. Either it was entered with a key, or it was left unlocked. But someone went through and took only specific scrolls. It looked as if whoever did it knew exactly what they were looking for and had methodically gone through the scrolls picking out the most valuable.

By the time we finished the tour, I had a good feeling. Jabir and George seemed happy that we were there to secure the museum and prevent further looting. We felt that the looting had not been as serious as we were led to believe and that much of what was thought to be missing was actually locked in secure vaults. Jabir, George, and the staff seemed to have done a good job getting the museum ready for the war and protecting the artifacts. I felt badly that the Iraqis had lost even a small portion of their heritage. But I did not feel that we, as Americans, were to blame for it. It was one of those tragedies of war, and there was little anyone could do about it at that point.

Although George had indicated to me during the tour that he could think of no more than eight to ten pieces that were actually missing or damaged within the museum, he nevertheless went outside to the media and repeated the claim that more than 170,000 artifacts were missing and probably lost forever.

I did not hear his claims at the time. I was off finishing with Blue's deployment around the grounds. Our guard was still up, but it seemed most of the fighting forces were gone from this area. When I returned to the front, I gave a few brief interviews to the media, saying I had seen just a few file cabinets overturned, and some minor damage to the artifacts, but that the bulk of the items were safe.

It was not until the next day that I found out from Schwartz that George was continuing to tell the media that the number of items missing was astronomical. When I confronted George about his statements, he said the media had misquoted him, that he actually had said the reports of so many items missing were incorrect. For the next week to ten days, I talked to George virtually every day. And every day he would tell me one thing, and then tell the media another. I am not sure if he was pursuing his own agenda, looking for international sympathy, being pressured by Ba'ath Party sympathizers, or just upset that we had not arrived sooner. But from then on I watched what I said around him and had a healthy skepticism about what he told me.

At the time, we did not realize it had become a big story, and I am not sure how big it was to most Americans. It was big in the art world, but probably bigger than it should have been considering the circumstances. It was big in the international community, however, and as a result we found ourselves dealing with a media contingent at the museum that was far different from the embedded media we had had during the war. Many of those we encountered at the museum were seasoned, professional journalists and were as interested in getting the story straight as we were of making sure they had the opportunity to get the story. Balascik helped organize daily press briefings with museum officials who could spare only so much time from their inventory of missing pieces. We had good relations with many of the media, and some would allow us to use their satellite phones and occasionally put soldiers' names in their stories. But there were others who seemed intent on casting Americans in a bad light and questioning our motives in Iraq. And although they tried our patience at times, we tried to be as fair with them as we were with the others.

Even the mild-mannered, soft-spoken Balascik was sometimes pushed to the limit. On one occasion a reporter was trying to muscle his way into the museum compound and was pushing on the gates, attempting to get past Balascik. "The next person who pushes on this gate or touches one of my soldiers is going to be zip-stripped!" Balascik barked, referring to the plastic handcuffs we carried with us. He may have seemed like just another tough American soldier trying to throw his weight around, but in my eyes he was just trying to do his job to protect his soldiers and the museum staff.

While the sole focus of some of the reporters was on the missing artifacts, others took the time to walk the museum grounds to get an understanding of what a tough fight we had been in. They looked at the fighting positions, the blood, and the evidence of the gun battle that included the hole one of our HEAT rounds made in children's museum.

As the story of the missing artifacts played out over the next week, more information came to us through local residents that helped us get a clearer picture of the situation. Without being asked, some Iraqis returned artifacts they said were given to them or that had been sold in local markets. Corruption among the museum staff apparently was an ongoing problem. In addition, regime leaders would go into the museum, take a piece they fancied, and walk out with it. Many of those will probably never be unearthed.

We were accused of being insensitive to the Iraqi cultural heritage by failing to get to the museum faster than we did. But at what point do you commit a force to save some historical artifacts in a part of the city that is still heavily defended? And how large a force would it have taken in this case? Certainly larger than a tank company. We were stretched thin as a task force and a company on 8 April and for the week after that. We would have needed a much larger force to take the building that early in the fighting and had we tried to do it then, the museum undoubtedly would have been much more heavily damaged than it was. Instead, we moved up to the museum in incremental advances and minimized the damage to it and the danger to Charlie Company soldiers. We did exactly as we were instructed. We got to the museum when we were told to get to it, secured it when we were told to secure it, protected it day and night, and saved much of the heritage of Iraq.

About a week into our mission at the museum, we got word that a Marine Reserve colonel out of New York City would be arriving with a thirteen-man team to assist museum staffers and begin an investigation into the missing pieces. Col. Matthew Bogdanos was a Manhattan district attorney who was in the news back home for his prosecution of rap star Puff Daddy Combs. Bogdanos came in and quickly took over the job of dealing with the press, which was fine with us. We were content going back to handling the security end of the mission. He was there to find out what had happened; we were there to keep the museum and the team of agents from Customs, the Federal Bureau of Investigation, the Bureau of Alcohol, Tobacco and Firearms, and the Immigration and Naturalization Service safe. Blue lived side-by-side with the team in the museum library and assisted it when it went on artifact raids.

Some months later, when Bogdanos issued a report on his investigation, he concurred with our original assessment that the damage had been not nearly as bad as the international media and

George had claimed. "It is clear," he said, "that the originally reported number of 170,000 (missing pieces) was simply wrong."

But finding those still missing, he admitted, "will likely take years."

By the third week of April, many of the Baghdad markets in our sector had reopened, restaurants were starting to offer services, the hospital staffs were returning, and the Iraqis were making an effort to try to regain some sense of a normal life, although the transition from dictatorship to free society would be anything but easy for them.

The difficulty I was having as a commander was convincing the soldiers each day that there was still a threat out there and they needed to treat everything with a high concern for their security and safety. I relied on the platoon leaders and platoon sergeants to keep the soldiers aware of proper procedures at the checkpoints and to ensure they maintained proper uniform standards, which included vests and helmets. It was a constant battle keeping soldiers in the proper uniform because the weather was getting hotter and checkpoint duty was tedious and often boring. But the first sergeant and I went out every day trying to make sure they adhered to the standards we established.

To help maintain some of the edge, we kept changing how the checkpoints looked, adding barricades and extending the standoff distance. Blue changed the security procedures at the museum on a regular basis. We ran security at the museum almost like an airport, where we checked people before they got into the museum to prevent someone from bringing in an explosive device. We prohibited anyone from parking cars along the walls or fences that surrounded the compound. We were going into more of a defensive posture, but it was for our benefit. By establishing these procedures, I wanted our soldiers to realize that we were no longer taking the fight to the Iraqis. If there was still fight in them, they were going to have to bring it to us and we had to be prepared for it.

The museum became a focal point for our operations. We were the only Americans in the area and anyone with a problem or information to offer would come to the museum. They would come to the gate and want to talk about artifacts or Saddam or someone with a gun or someone who had done them wrong. They didn't look at us as providing security for the museum; they saw us as their police force.

Many of the people in the neighborhood wanted to give us gifts or food or cold drinks to show us how appreciative they were for what we did. I thought back to what I had read about Vietnam and how the Viet Cong would poison food or drinks. I put out an order not to accept anything from the locals, but it was hard for a young soldier to turn down a Pepsi or Coke, something none of them had had for three months. The soldiers felt that they would insult the Iraqis by turning down the offers.

I briefed the soldiers that this would be a different type of operation for the rest of our stay in Baghdad. Our checkpoint operations were not going to be anything like those at Najaf. This was the time to build relationships with the locals. The angry, tough-guy American approach would not work. Although they had to keep in the backs of their minds that some Iraqi talking to them might want to kill them, they could not be sure of anyone's motives and so had to try to convince the people we encountered that we were there to liberate them and empower them to build a better country.

But problems were few. Everywhere we went in Baghdad people accepted us and we became part of the community. Baghdad was not then, and would not be while we were there, the troubled city that it later became. The people were as curious about us as we were about them. In Blue's area the soldiers helped reopen a girls' school behind the museum. It had been used only days earlier as a fighting position. But once the neighborhood was secure, the headmistress, a woman the soldiers called Miss Osama, returned to get the school open again. She was educated in England and welcomed our help. She said the young girls needed to have their minds opened to what was going on in the world around them and should not be sequestered behind doors and veils. The soldiers taught the girls to throw an American football and gave them what supplies they could.

Staff Sgt. Germell Milton, who had two young kids of his own back home, was a big hit with the youngsters in the area. He passed out bright yellow band-aids that he brought with him and taught

Sgt. 1st Class David Richard reaches across a makeshift barrier on 12 April to shake the hand of a young Iraqi boy at one of Charlie Company's checkpoints in Baghdad. Shortly after this photo was taken, Richard and other third platoon soldiers began taking sniper fire. (*Brant Sanderlin/Atlanta Journal-Constitution*)

the kids to brush their teeth. Every day they returned to him to show off their teeth and ask for more toothpaste.

In other areas the soldiers received regular intelligence reports from local neighborhood leaders. They would tell us if anyone who should not be there had come into the neighborhood the previous night. The soldiers helped track down thieves, Ali Babas as the locals referred to them, setting up stings to nab them with the stolen goods. Wherever we went, Charlie Company soldiers showed kindness and compassion to the Iraqis, and for the most part it was returned. I think part of the reason we were successful was that we did not act as if we were occupiers or conquerors. I tried to impress on the soldiers that that was not our intent, and they got the message. We were simply there to help the Iraqis help themselves.

When we had been in Kuwait prior to the war, we had heard frequently that once we got to Baghdad and secured it, we would be going home. There was never anything official, though, so it was more hope than reality for many of the soldiers. But now it was May, President Bush had declared major combat finished in Iraq, and Baghdad was becoming more peaceful by the day—people started to think about going home. And thinking about going home, without any firm commitment or orders to do it, can work on soldiers' nerves. It did on ours.

It was a daily effort to keep the soldiers busy. If they were not on one of the checkpoints, we had them doing vehicle maintenance or laundry. We also had the entertainment center in the lobby of the Ministry of Industry and Trade building. It was good to have that building because soldiers were scattered around a few to a room. That gave them the opportunity to go off by themselves and have some personal time, alone with their thoughts.

What we had been through had taken its toll on us emotionally. People had been doing something very violent and very foreign to most of us: killing other humans. We had been very aggressive but were now putting the brakes on. There was a great deal of pent-up anger and aggression and no place to get rid of it. As a result, it started to manifest itself in loud arguments, yelling, and throwing things. Some of it was accepted as merely blowing off steam and some of it we shut down quickly by making sure the soldiers received counseling. I did not want to take any of that home with us.

But the question all of us were asking was, just when would we be going home? And the answer kept coming back: "Maybe June, maybe July." There was no certainty to when, or even if, we would leave.

Then came the Sunni Triangle, and Fallujah.

18

BEYOND BAGHDAD

FALLUJAH is a city of about 230,000 that sits on a flat, dusty plain about forty miles west of Baghdad. Known as the "city of mosques" for the large number of mosques there, it sits astride the Euphrates River and is the last major population center along the waterway before it turns south to form what once was known as the Fertile Crescent southeast of Baghdad. Before the war, Fallujah was a hotbed of Saddam supporters. It was even more of a bastion after and became home to regime loyalists and Ba'ath Party members escaping Baghdad after Saddam was deposed. Sunni Muslims were the predominant religious faction here, and the city quickly became known as the heart of the resistance within what was referred to as the Sunni Triangle. The base of the triangle went west from Baghdad through Fallujah to Ramadi, where the triangle turned north to Tikrit, Saddam's hometown, and south again to Baghdad. Within this triangle lived some of the most hardcore Ba'athist and Saddam supporters in Iraq.

Although Charlie Company had experienced few problems in our sector of Baghdad through April and May, other areas of the city were starting to see the emergence of a resistance that relied on many of the terror tactics that the Viet Cong had used in the early stages of the Vietnam War. There were random assassinations of soldiers and political leaders, car and truck bombings, attacks on convoys with RPGs and AK-47s, and roadside bombs that were dubbed IED, for Improvised Explosive Devices. An IED could be just about anything that would blow up—mortar shells, artillery rounds, dynamite, C-4 plastic explosives or the Eastern European version of that, Semtex. Wired with either a timer or an electrical switch with a garage door opener or keyless entry device for a car, the bomb could be detonated by virtually anyone without arousing the slightest suspicion.

Third Infantry Division soldiers were starting to become targets for these attacks. On 8 May, Pfc. Marlin Rockhold of 3rd Battalion, 7th Infantry Regiment, was directing traffic at a Baghdad intersection when a man walked up behind him and killed him with a single shot. On 26 May, Pfc. Jeremiah Smith of Task Force 2-7 was killed when an IED exploded under his Humvee as he was escorting new troops to the airport. He was two days away from going home.

But the number of random attacks in Baghdad had not yet reached the level they would in the months to come, and with the 1st Armored Division moving in to replace us, coalition officials believed the 2nd Brigade Combat Team could better be used in other hotspots. Specifically, we were picked to go to Fallujah to show some American muscle and try to keep a lid on the unrest there.

We learned of the Fallujah mission the last week of May. All of us had been anticipating going home as soon as the 1st Armored Division arrived. But then we got the news that not only were we going to Fallujah, we were going to stay in Iraq "indefinitely." The news hit us hard. It was a big letdown for everyone, not only those of us in Iraq, but our families back home, who had already started planning "Welcome Home" parties and were painting banners to celebrate our arrival.

As company commander, it was my job was to ensure that we were combat-ready after a relatively quiet six weeks. I could not let my own disappointment be passed on to the soldiers. So I gathered them together and told them to feel bad for themselves for a day and then get over it because we had to go out and perform another mission where there were a lot of bad guys waiting for us.

"Do what you need to do, feel bad for yourself, then get over it because there is nothing you can do about it," I told them. "Get geared back up to do some more missions."

The soldiers did not mask their disappointment. Most wanted to know: "Why us?"

"Very simple," I responded. "We were chosen for this because of what we have done. They believe we are the best unit for this job."

That was the spin Perkins put on it when he called us together to break the news. Whether that was true or not, I do not know. But it sounded good. And it helped us get through our initial disappointment and get ready to make the move west.

There was the expected complaining, but that is only natural among soldiers. Charlie Company quickly bit the bullet and started doing necessary preparation on the vehicles, especially the machine guns. We did not know what to expect when we got to Fallujah. And we did not know how much fighting we might face. But based on what we were hearing about what was going on in the rest of Iraq, it would probably be individuals or small teams we would be facing, and machine guns would be the best way to deal with them.

But we wanted to be ready for anything. There had been some casualties in the firefights in Fallujah, and we were determined that since we made it this far without anyone getting killed, we were not going to lose someone now to stupidity or lack of focus because they were thinking about going home. Those thoughts of home and complaining about getting the short end of the stick were useless exercises and did us no good. The word "indefinitely" kept ringing in our heads whenever the subject of our stay in Iraq came. We had to focus on the mission at hand. If we did not, we were likely to regret it.

We were then virtually the same company that arrived in Baghdad nearly two months earlier, with a few exceptions. Curtis Gebhard, our NBC specialist, had returned to the U.S. to get out of the Army and go to college. He had dragged a Clemson University T-shirt with him through the war and made sure he got a photo of himself with the T-shirt at the reviewing stand before he left. Chris Freeman, the gunner on Jeremy England's White One also went home to get out of the Army and become a librarian. England moved to the battalion staff where he became the assistance maintenance officer. Second Lt. Perry White, a newcomer to the unit, replaced him.

Our specific mission in Fallujah was to protect and provide security for a bridge and dam south of the city that controlled the flow of Euphrates River water in that region. Our home would be some distance from the dam, inside a large military compound that had once served as the base and training ground for an Iraqi armored brigade. On 2 June, I sent an advance party to begin preparations for our arrival and on 3 June began moving the bulk of the company west along the main highway. The last few vehicles arrived on 4 June, and by 5 June, I had been briefed by and done a recon of the dam with soldiers of the 3rd Armored Cavalry Regiment's Fox Troop, which had taken temporary responsibility for the area from the 82nd Airborne a few weeks earlier.

My predecessor had not taken the time to talk to the dam workers to find out the situation there so I felt it was imperative that we get some sense from the Iraqis at the site about who they were and whether they would work with us. We did not know if they were Saddam loyalists, Ba'ath Party members, or simply members of the community who might harbor a grudge against the Americans. Whoever they were, I wanted to start a foundation for a working relationship with them. That was something Schwartz encouraged us to do and which he did well in his own low-key way. He had a way of making people feel comfortable around him, especially the Iraqis. He was not the larger-than-life, macho American guy coming in to tell people how to run their lives and their community. He was a tough soldier but he treated the Iraqis as human beings and spoke to them on their level, not down to them. He was respected because he gave respect to those around him, and was as good a diplomat as he was a warrior. As we watched how he handled himself and dealt with difficult and sensitive political situations, we all learned a great deal.

When we first met with the dam workers, we explained who we were and what we were going to provide for them. We wanted to empower them and reassure them that this facility was their responsibility, not ours; we were simply helping them do their jobs. We came up with the idea of giving each a photo ID badge and some rudimentary training to deal with certain situations. (Having one's photograph on a badge was to become a sign of status in the area.) A few would be given AK-47s so they could eventually take charge of security there.

I felt that if we went in and did everything for them, we would be seen as the ones in charge and would become the target for the insurgents. But if we shared the responsibility with the people who lived in the community—who knew what was going on in the community—they would have a vested interest in what they were doing. It was not our dam; it was theirs. If we treated them accordingly, they would be more inclined to do a better job. It was also important to do this because eventually we would leave and this would once again be their city and their dam. The sooner they took responsibility, the faster they would become comfortable with it and the more the people of Fallujah would come to accept it.

In order to facilitate this handover, one of the first things we had to do was identify the workers and determine the chain of command. After that, we could issue them ID badges and train a small number in security. Since we wanted to make sure the security force was a structured thing and not just a bunch of hooligans running around with weapons, once we determined who was in charge, we did a cursory background check on him. We decided he was relatively neutral. (In Fallujah it was difficult finding anyone who was particularly outspoken about their fondness for Americans, so "neutral" was about as good as it got.) We then allowed the leader to select his staff, most of which turned out to be sons and brothers and cousins, but that was the way business was done there. Still, with that sort of nepotism, it was in the family's best interests to keep the dam secure. It was job security for all of them.

We also did as much as we could to determine who the other workers were, but it was not as if we could run their names through a database or grill them intensely. Some admitted they had been Ba'ath Party members, but seemed ashamed to tell us. We realized that in that dirt-poor town, if you were not a member of the party you did not get much.

The Iraqis liked the idea of us being there for a while until they got comfortable in their new roles. Their biggest problem seemed to be fishermen using hand grenades near the dam. It was a simple and easy process: just toss a grenade into the water, let it explode, and dozens of dead or stunned fish would float to the surface. It was much easier than dangling a hook a line in the water for hours at a time. But neither we nor the Iraqis liked the idea of people throwing grenades around the dam. There was too much danger of an errant throw, or an intentional throw, that could damage the dam or target the workers. Some of the legitimate fishermen took huge carp out of the spillway below the dam and sold them on the local market. But I told the staff at the dam that hand-grenade fishing was going to cease immediately. Once they had the weapons, I told them, they had the power to stop it.

"If they get too close to the dam, shoot them," I instructed. They never did while we were there, but the numbers of grenade-tossing fishermen seemed to decrease once the Iraqis got their AK-47s for security.

For the first few weeks in Fallujah, we sent a platoon out to the dam each night to block the road leading across it and to provide security for the workers. We also sent patrols in the morning that would take different routes through the city, just in case someone decided to target us with an IED. But no matter what route we took, we were always greeted by mobs of kids who came out to wave at us and ask for food, gesturing with their hands and pointing at their mouths because we could not hear them over the roar of the engine and the clanking and groaning of the track treads.

"Some days I feel like I'm running for president," David Richard said one day from the turret of his tank as he watched the parade of armor and kids through the city.

The older residents of Fallujah were much more reserved. They might give us an occasional wave, but seldom did we see a smile. They were almost as unhappy as we that we were there.

Despite Fallujah's reputation as a tough and lawless anti-American bastion, we had very few incidents directed at us in the two months we were there. The first was 5 July, when three or four men in a boat came up a canal that ran perpendicular to the west end of the dam. They climbed a steep, slippery bank and fired one RPG at one of our tanks. The RPG flew high and exploded harmlessly against a concrete piling. But it caught us a bit off guard because things had been so quiet around there. We became more alert after that and were ready two nights later when another group, or maybe the same group, fired three RPGs and some AK-47s at us. Charlie Company unleashed holy hell on them with machine guns and main guns. Two of the attackers ran north toward a marshy area, while two fled south into a residential area.

Soldiers told me they believe they killed the two that ran north because where there had been hot spots in the tank's TIS, there were no longer hot spots. And we could clearly smell decaying flesh down in the marsh whenever we drove past there over the next few weeks. We just never went to investigate. The other two escaped because the soldiers were trained to stop firing as soon as attackers went into residential areas.

The growing Iraqi insurgency in Fallujah was not as big a problem for us at that time as the heat. The rather comfortable spring in Baghdad had given way to a terribly uncomfortable summer. The wind blew hot and hard virtually around the clock. By noon each day, the temperature readings were in triple digits and climbing. In July and early August, we averaged 115–120 degree temperatures each day. Night brought little respite as the temperature often never got below ninety degrees. Going on patrol in the middle of the day in those conditions was difficult even for those soldiers in the best of shape. The heat just sucked the energy right out of us and made us wonder how anyone could live in a place like this. It was not unbearable, but it was close. It was definitely inhospitable.

The company occupied two one-story buildings at the southwest end of a high-walled compound that contained the task force and brigade headquarters and a number of the brigade's other assets. Wild Bunch was next door to us. We were responsible for security in that area and kept some of the tanks in a ready position to be able to fire back in the event of an attack.

The problem with our mission in Fallujah was not the amount of enemy activity. It was relatively calm while we were there. It may have been the fact that our tanks presented a far more daunting and dangerous target for them to take on than unarmored Humvees and large trucks that seemed to be favorite targets.

Our daily problem was finding enough to do to keep from going crazy. We did some platoon and company training, and occasional maintenance. But there was plenty of downtime. Some soldiers played dominoes. Some played cards. Some listened to music. A few read. Others whiled away their time playing computer games in the common area. We also had a TV in there that we rigged to pick up a station in Saudi Arabia. It ran a number of old American sitcoms and music videos, but we would watch just about anything it offered. The highlight of many days was 7:30 p.m. when the latest episode of "Friends" came on. The room would fill with soldiers looking for a seat to watch what the six friends were up to. The episodes were all several years old, but we did not care. It was a little slice of home and their strange world provided a little sense of normalcy in our stranger world.

Except for my fascination with "Friends," I spent time designing my dream house. By mid-July it had three floors and more than 7,000 square feet and was still growing.

We were getting two hot meals a day, and some local vendors would come in at lunch to make sandwiches for us in the mess hall. But we could not stay cool, and could not stay clean, and many of the soldiers seemed to be constantly battling some nagging malady or another. Frequent bouts of diarrhea from questionable food and water and sinus infections from the blowing dust were common complaints and were rampant not only in Charlie Company, but throughout the task force.

In addition to our security work at the dam, we helped rebuild schools, built soccer fields and handed out soccer balls, provided fresh and canned food for the local residents, made sure gasoline for their cars and propane and butane for cooking got into the city, and tried to do what we could to help the people of Fallujah. Schwartz was out and about in the community virtually every day, talking to people, dealing with the mayor and police chief, trying to get people comfortable with our presence there. But our resources were limited. Our engineers could do only so much. We did not have the assets or the expertise to repair or modernize their power grid. The same went for their water supply. We did what we could with what we had available, but often it was not enough.

We were tired, restless, worn out, and ready to go home. But in mid-July we again got word that our stay was being extended, this time for as much as two months. Units in theater were supposed to stay twelve months. We had only been here ten so we were expecting the worst. Many of the soldiers did not take this news well. They were angry with the leadership, all the way from President Bush and Defense Secretary Donald Rumsfeld on down through division officials for not shooting straight with them. All they asked was that they be told the truth—don't keep leading them on, promising them something, only to yank it back a few weeks later. I sympathized with them, but as their commander there was not much I could do but console and counsel. This was a professional, all-volunteer Army. We knew when we signed up that our lives were in the hands of others. They made the decisions and we followed them. It was not up to us to decide when we went home. That would be decided for us. They grumbled and griped and took out their frustrations as best they could, considering the circumstances. And despite their obvious unhappiness with the situation, they continued to do their jobs because they were professional soldiers.

Back home at Fort Stewart, many wives were in a frenzy over the on-again, off-again redeployment. It was probably more difficult for them than it was for us. We still had a job to do. They had been promised several times we were coming home, only to be later told we were not. The sense of frustration was building there just as it was among the soldiers in Iraq. Some began to complain publicly. Blount's wife told them that complaints that she was hearing aided the enemy. "When the Iraqis see media coverage of disgruntled Americans publicly campaigning for the return of our soldiers from Iraq, they are encouraged and believe their strategy is working," she wrote in an open letter to the wives of 3rd Infantry Division soldiers.

My wife, Susan, was head of the company Family Readiness Group and often had to field late-night telephone calls from angry and frustrated wives, some blaming her for the decisions others were making. As the company commander's wife, she was an easy target. But she was just as frustrated as the rest of the wives over the delay and, like me, had to put on a good front and deal with it and our two daughters as best she could.

As I looked back later on our time in Fallujah, I believe the time we spent there actually had a positive side to it. While there, we were able to vent our anger and frustrations with one another, far from home and our families. The extra time we had as a company, and as individual soldiers, gave us a chance to deal with many of the issues we had stemming from the war. Those who wanted to talk about their feelings were able to talk to other soldiers or to counselors brought in specifically for that purpose. Those who wanted to be alone with their thoughts to deal with them that way had that opportunity. We were required to attend classes on anger management and decompression from the combat zone. But I believe that the long period of time away from Baghdad, and away from the danger of continual combat, before we got on the plane to go home helped most of us find peace with ourselves for what we had done during the war.

The war was still around us, although on a much lesser scale. Every so often someone would lob a few mortars inside our compound. But the compound was so large they never hit anything but sand. Then on 18 July, a Task Force 4-64 soldier was killed in Fallujah when an IED exploded next to his Humvee just after it crossed to the west side of the Euphrates a few miles north of the dam. It was a wakeup call that told all of us that we were not out of this yet, and that any minute any of us on patrol could become a statistic and another name on the Pentagon's casualty list. Those who went on patrol in tanks felt considerably safer than those in Humvees, and rumors that we were to swap the tanks for Humvees did not go over well at all among tankers. It never happened, and I am not sure what would have happened had they tried to do it. I am confident Charlie Company soldiers would have saluted and gone about their duties whether they were in tanks or Humvees, because they were soldiers first.

On 22 July, when our spirits were dragging from all the uncertainty, we finally got the news for which we had been waiting for weeks: We were getting out of Iraq. Schwartz called it a "change of mission." We would be relieved in place over the next four days by the 3rd Armored Cavalry Regiment, which was returning to Fallujah. Our orders were to return to Kuwait and wait there for another mission as what was being referred to as the "strategic reserve" for Central Command. No matter what they called it, many of the soldiers saw it as a long-deserved reprieve from four weeks of tough combat and four months of dangerous peacekeeping duty. We hated Kuwait while we were there, but the place sounded like heaven to us now after what we had been through. It was time to pack up and head back down the road that all of us knew would eventually take us home.

Before we left Fallujah, we had one last piece of business to attend to. For soldiers, a medal or a ribbon is an acknowledgment of a job well done or a tribute to courage under fire. On 25 July, Charlie Company had an awards ceremony. Jason Diaz was

Lt. Col. Rick Schwartz , commander of Task Force 1-64, pins a Silver Star on S.Sgt. Jason Diaz during a medals ceremony in Fallujah on 25 July. (*Brant Sanderlin/ Atlanta Journal-Constitution*)

awarded a well-deserved Silver Star for leading the company into combat for much of the war. Ten of my soldiers received Bronze Stars with "V" devices, indicating they were for valor earned in combat against the enemy. Couvertier, Gruneisen, Hernandez, Mao, Mercado, Richard, Shipley, Strunk, Sullivan, and Ray White stood at attention while Schwartz pinned on their medals. Many more Charlie Company soldiers were nominated for awards, but many of them were downgraded, others lost in the shuffle of the bureaucracies that decide these things. Still, it was a tribute to them that so many were honored for their wartime efforts.

"The rest of the world doesn't know what you've been through," Schwartz told them. "The guys who will know are sitting right here next to you. It's the brotherhood."

The next day, 26 July, we finished packing our gear, loaded the tanks on HETS, and began the long, slow, and exhaustingly hot road march back to Kuwait on the first step to home. We were leaving Fallujah behind, which no one minded. After nearly two months living in that sand-scoured inferno, we had had enough of the place. Once again, we had done exactly what we had been asked to do. We had come into a dangerous place, calmed it down, and left it better than we had found it. Although the situation in Fallujah would deteriorate over the next few months and American soldiers would die by the dozens, we felt we had done a good job: we had few problems while there and no Task Force 1-64 soldiers were killed or seriously wounded.

Our movement back to Kuwait was without incident, but was not easy. We had 120 vehicles in the convoy and went into it as a combat mission. We were alert the whole time in case we were targeted by IEDs en route. Red zones, or danger areas, were just west and south of Baghdad. We went fully armed, ready to fire back if fired on. Tank crews rode in their tanks on the HETs. It was not comfortable there or in the Humvees, where temperatures at times reached 140 degrees. The convoy got split up soon after leaving Fallujah and portions of it had to find their own way back to Kuwait.

Shortly before 6 p.m. on 28 July, my Humvee was the last in the task force to cross back into Kuwait. When we arrived, some sol-

S.Sgt. Larrico Alexander (left) and S.Sgt. Jason Diaz joke with one another as they wait at a holding facility in Kuwait for their flight home on 7 August. (*Brant Sanderlin/Atlanta Journal-Constitution*)

diers got out of their vehicles and kissed the sand they had once despised. Others lit up victory cigars. And others rolled in the sand, giggling like schoolboys given a reprieve from after-school detention. All of us thankfully climbed out of our body armor and let the wind blow through our sweat-stained and grimy uniforms. It had taken us more than thirty-six hours to make the trip, which had been interrupted frequently by blown and shredded tires on the HETs, victims of the heat and too much wear-and-tear.

It would be another eleven days before we got home to Fort Stewart. Much of that time was spent outprocessing in Kuwait, turning in gear and equipment, making sure all our records were in order, cleaning up as best we could, and trying to endure the blistering heat of the Kuwaiti summer. We never were used as Central Command's strategic reserve, but that was fine with us. We were ready to go home. We had battled to Baghdad and beyond. Charlie Company's war was over.

Sgt. 1st Class Ray White (right) and S.Sgt. Germell Milton share a hug after arriving at Hunter Army Airfield in Savannah near Fort Stewart on 8 August. (*Brant Sanderlin/Atlanta Journal-Constitution*)

19

EPILOGUE

CHARLIE Company soldiers had two questions foremost in their minds before they went to war in March 2003: "Do the people back home support us?" And, "Are we doing the right thing?"

The first question was asked of any new arrival from the States or anyone who had been outside our little circle of soldiers for even the briefest of moments and might have been able to cull some information from the Internet, a newspaper, or a telephone call home. It was clear to me the soldiers were well aware of what happened during Vietnam and wanted to believe it would not happen to them when they returned home.

The second question was not asked as openly or as often, but I know it was something many of us thought about in the months leading up to the war. I think we all wanted to believe that we were doing the right thing, that there was a moral certainty about our cause and our mission, just as there had been for our grandfathers in World War II. Whether it was to find weapons of mass destruction, rid the world of a megalomaniacal dictator, or stop the spread of international terrorism, we wanted to be sure that we were doing the right thing when we went across the border and lined up Iraqi soldiers in our gun sights.

In my briefings to the soldiers before the war, I repeatedly stressed that the reasons we were going to war were noble and just.

Saddam Hussein was known to have had weapons of mass destruction and use them against his own people. He encouraged and sponsored international terrorism by paying the families of Palestinian suicide bombers. He murdered his own people by the thousands. I believed then and still believe that to rid the world of Saddam was in and of itself a noble cause. I also believe that in the years to come, what we did will be viewed more favorably by historians than it has been by those with particular political or religious agendas who questioned our motives and methods in the months following the war. The twenty-four-hour instant news analyses picked apart every detail of what we did. There has been no consensus about the rightness of our cause, except among those of us who fought it. In later years I believe historians will put into proper perspective the reasons we went to war in Iraq and why the soldiers and Marines who fought there did a great service for the rest of the world, especially for those living in the Middle East.

As soldiers, we naturally want to believe that what we do is right and decent. And I feel that in our minds we believe that. But as soldiers, we are also required to do what our country asks of us and in this case it was to rid the world of Saddam Hussein and his henchmen. It was not a simple chore or easy, and we had friends who died doing it. The loftier goals and ideals for which this war was fought will become clearer in the future.

There is no doubt some Charlie Company soldiers were disappointed that we did not find any weapons of mass destruction or evidence that would lead to their discovery. That would have been a great coup for us. We did some perfunctory searches for WMD, especially for paperwork in some of the government office buildings we cleared once we got to Baghdad. But as line soldiers we quickly realized we were in over our heads on that issue. We did not have the expertise in the weapons or the language to know what we were looking at when we found documents. Finding the weapons was not our job. We were soldiers with a mission to rid Iraq of Saddam Hussein and then to provide for the security and stabilization of Iraq.

But the fact that we found no WMD did not in any way negate in our minds what we did. It was more important for us to be able to say at the end of the day, at the end of our tours, at the end of our careers, that we gave the Iraqi people a chance at freedom, a chance to take control of their own lives and to govern themselves. We could only do so much to help them help themselves. It was up to them to take advantage of that opportunity. At the same time we were doing that, we had to be cognizant of our own force protection. We were especially mindful after we got to Baghdad of making sure we did nothing stupid that would get one of us killed after major combat operations had ended. We wanted to make sure we all came home alive, and we did, which I attribute in large part to the professionalism of our young soldiers.

The larger policy implications, and in-depth analyses of why we fought the war, were not things we spent too much time pondering in the immediate aftermath of Operation Iraqi Freedom. The Iraqi people with whom we dealt in Baghdad and later in Fallujah made us feel by their kind words that what we had done was the right thing for them. And for us that made it worthwhile. Although that apparently changed significantly in the months after we left, we went home with the belief that what we had done was honorable and right in the broader sense. Once assured of that, we as soldiers began looking more at the details of what we did and how we did them. We looked at what we did right and congratulated ourselves. More important, we looked at our weaknesses and what we did wrong and began to explore ways to improve so future generations of soldiers could benefit from our mistakes.

The war we set out to fight in Iraq was not the war we fought. The enemy we war-gamed to fight was not the enemy we fought. The tactics, techniques, and procedures we trained on as tankers to a great degree were not those we used during Operation Iraqi Freedom. The very nature of the war forced us to be adaptive and innovative about how we used our tanks and ourselves. We were forced to learn on the fly, in the middle of combat, as we were faced with multiple unique situations that ran the spectrum from combat in urban environment, traffic checkpoints, peacekeeping, and how to deal with small unit actions utilizing armor. The grand schemes of tacticians and planners often gave way to snap judgments on the battlefield by young soldiers and young commanders facing enemy fire for the first time. They did what they thought was right at the time, and in most instances, it was.

Even as we adapted to what the enemy was doing, they adapted to what we were doing. And if the weaknesses in our system and faults in our training are not addressed soon, it is likely that those who were watching and taking notes for the time when they come up against American forces will have adapted to take advantage of them. As the commander of a tank company during Operation Iraqi Freedom, I am naturally prejudiced about the effectiveness of the M1A1 Abrams tanks in this campaign. It has its faults, but by and large it was the one piece of equipment that enabled this war to be fought with such intensity and be concluded so quickly. It was the singular difference in the war. The 2nd Brigade Combat Team of the 3rd Infantry Division (Mechanized) moved farther and faster than any tank unit in the history of warfare in our dash through the deserts of southern Iraq and into the Euphrates River Valley south of Baghdad. The speed with which we moved and the combat power we brought to every fight enabled us to keep the Iraqis off-balance and confused throughout the war.

The significant role that tanks played in this war cannot be understated. The Air Force can make all the claims it wants about precision bombing and the impact that had on the demise of the Iraqi regime. But were it not for tank treads hitting the road and grinding through desert sand, the Air Force might have been bombing for months before Baghdad fell. It took our tanks to get it done quickly and more efficiently than anyone thought possible. And using light infantry to try to do the job the tankers did would have resulted in far more casualties than would be acceptable by any standard. Tanks did not win the war by themselves, but the M1A1 Abrams was the key factor in why the war was won so quickly.

There were numerous instances when the vital role tanks played in the war were clearly demonstrated. Checkpoint Charlie in Najaf is one. A light infantry unit might have been able to dig in there and hold the intersection from waves of assaults by attackers in technical trucks using RPGs and small arms. But it would have been difficult without indirect fire support and costly in terms of dead and wounded. We set up our fourteen tanks at the intersection and were not moved unless we wanted to move. We provided our own fire support systems and performed our mission without a single Charlie Company casualty.

The two Thunder Runs are also prime examples of the importance of tanks in this war. Had we not taken tanks in on those days and instead relied on PCs or Strykers, we would have had a number of vehicles destroyed and more than one soldier killed in the task force. With one exception, our Red Two tank, the superior armor on the Abrams defeated everything the Iraqis could throw at us.

It was much the same at the battle for Mahmudiyah. I believe the true significance of that fight on 3 April has been eclipsed by the larger successes of the two Thunder Runs. But Mahmudiyah demonstrated two things that proved to be valuable lessons that directly resulted in the success of the Thunder Runs. The first was that we could take armor into urban environments, even tightly constricted areas. The second was that we could defeat enemy armor in battles fought at point-blank range. With the confidence bred from Charlie Company's fight at Mahmudiyah, Task Force 1-64 was able to make the initial Thunder Run a victory and the brigade was later to move into Baghdad on 7 April and begin to secure it, routing the Iraqis and ensuring the downfall of the regime.

The battle at Mahmudiyah also demonstrated how quickly soldiers can adapt to difficult and dangerous situations. In armor training, you train to kill at the farthest distance possible. But Charlie Company tankers had no training in how to fight at the closest possible distance. In gunnery training, you usually know the scenarios that are coming up and are able to ease into them. In Mahmudiyah we learned that real life does not follow the training script. The reality of it was that we did not know what was coming up next. We did not know if we would be fighting troops, a BMP at two thousand meters, or a T-72 just around the corner at twenty-five meters or less. Jeremy England's Second platoon soldiers reacted quickly to this changing scenario, but in another battle or another war, soldiers might not be able to do the same without sufficient training in dealing with the unexpected.

Changes should be considered in how tankers train. The 2,000-

meter and 3,000-meter kills out in the desert or in open terrain are likely to be the exception rather than the rule in future combat, especially in the war on terrorism. The Iraqis learned from the first Gulf War that digging in out in the desert did no good against the Abrams. It merely meant they were easy to bury once we killed them because the hole had already been dug. Future wars are not likely to be fought like that. They are more likely to be fought in towns and cities, with tanks going against bunkers or troop concentrations or technical trucks or light armored vehicles.

Our tanks proved to be a major asset even after we got into the SASO part of our mission in Baghdad. A tank makes a big statement and has a huge footprint that a PC or Humvee does not. People are less likely to mess with a tank than they are with any of the other vehicles in the American arsenal. A case in point was during our mission at the Iraq National Museum. A gas station blew up near the museum and several hundred people started gathering. Some medics and other soldiers went to investigate and help with the injured. They were on the ground and suddenly found themselves in the midst of what was rapidly becoming an angry mob.

Erik Blascik, the Third platoon leader, called me and asked if he could take some tanks down there to try to restore order. I was not sure what was going on at the time but did not want other Americans to be put in jeopardy. We sent the tanks over, and the crowd quieted down and parted almost immediately to let them through. The medics, who were in PCS and Humvees and were in danger of being overwhelmed, were able to start treating the injured. The angry crowd retreated and was not a problem again as long as the tanks were there.

There is a big difference between soldiers on the ground and soldiers in tanks. When you're riding in that tank, you feel indestructible. There is a cocoon of virtually impenetrable armor around you and at times there is a tendency to get too cocky inside that mobile bunker. Small arms can't penetrate, RPGs can't stop it, suicide car and truck bombers have little impact. It was no wonder that Charlie Company soldiers got the impression they could do almost anything and go anywhere while they were inside that tank and not have to worry about their safety.

As mentioned earlier in the book, tankers have an adage that is only half in jest: "Death Before Dismount." Tankers are usually very reluctant to get off their tanks at any time for anything, especially in a combat situation. But in Operation Iraqi Freedom, we got off our tanks more than we had planned or anticipated. We cleared buildings, normally a job for the infantry. We ran checkpoints, normally a job for the military police. We dealt with angry mobs and injured civilians, usually a job for the military police and medics. Charlie Company soldiers were a combination of tanker and infantryman throughout the war. Those are skills every soldier should have, but the specialized Army has gotten away from that. Our soldiers adapted well to these new roles, but had to learn on the job. Future tankers should be given the opportunity to train for a variety of missions that have them frequently getting off the tanks to perform tasks that have little to do with the tanks.

Among those tasks is checkpoint and roadblock duty that involves dealing with people face-to-face on the ground. We had had some training in this in Kuwait prior to the war. But most of our training in Kuwait was high intensity, intended to prepare us for combat. Security and Stabilization Operations, including checkpoint duty, are considered low-intensity missions and the training is usually not stressed for those units about to go to war. What is needed is a hybrid training program to teach a soldier how to make the transition from a combat operation to a peacekeeping mission and then back over the space of a few hours. That is what we had to do in the middle of a combat zone under sniper and mortar fire. We were expected to be both combat soldier and peacekeeper at the same time, a difficult transition for a young soldier to make, but one that we had to make in a split second and make without any mistakes.

What hindered many of our soldiers, including myself, was the lack of Arabic language skills. We were given some handouts with phrases in Arabic phonetically spelled out, but we were far worse with our Arabic than the Iraqis were with their English. Having an interpreter assigned to each task force would have been a great help, but it is doubtful that that will happen because of the shortage of Arabic language speakers in the Army. And the contract civilian interpreters that were brought forward to help us on occasion were not keen on being so close to the front.

Soldiers also have to be better prepared for close-quarter combat using their tanks, the kind of fighting we faced regularly throughout the war. We ended up firing far more M-4 and 9mm rounds than I ever thought we would because in many instances the Iraqis were within just a few feet of the tanks. These were like gunfights at the O.K. Corral, and tankers are not trained to do that. So how does the Army train for those situations?

First and foremost, it has to rethink the gunnery table. Our loaders carried much of the fight in close-quarters combat with their M240s. But TCs must also be better trained in using their M-4s and .50 calibers. Quick reaction was often the key to whether we could take out a gunman or RPG team or whether they were able to escape into the crowd. You only have so much time to engage somebody once they engage you. When we spotted an Iraqi with an RPG, we usually would have no more than five to ten seconds to engage him before he fired at us and took off.

The M1A1 Abrams was a multipurpose piece of equipment during the war and was able to handle multiple tasks. We took out technicals. We took out armor. We took out bunkers and troop concentrations. We blocked intersections and traffic. We identified targets with the night-vision systemstwo thousand meters out and more. It provided protection yet was mobile enough to take into the cities and fight there. For us, it was the perfect piece of equipment.

But that is not to say a tank does not have some chinks in its armor. Its fuel-guzzling nature makes it a slave to the fuel truck. In rough terrain it has a propensity to lose road wheel arms. And because of the speed with which it can move, it is able to easily outdistance the logistics lines, meaning spare parts and vital fluids to keep the thing working were frequently in short supply during the war.

And at a few places in the armor, there are some soft spots, especially in the rear, as we learned on the initial Thunder Run on 5 April. The official Army report on Red Two's demise said that an RPG penetrated the ballistic skirts on the right side and started an engine fire. I am still not convinced of that theory because after being hit repeatedly by RPGs and after seeing many of Charlie Company tanks get hit by RPGs, I know that what I saw hit Red Two was different. The explosion was different from the normal RPG, as was the smoke. I do not know what it was, but I suspect some sort of antiarmor weapon killed Red Two rather than a standard RPG-7.

Red Two was one of the first M1A1 Abrams ever disabled in battle by enemy fire. Nearly five months later, a second Abrams was crippled when a pencil-thin projectile that puzzled the experts penetrated its hull armor. They did not know if it was a new weapon or simply a million-to-one shot.

Although virtually all the hits to the tanks were on the sides or front, the Iraqis late in the war began to target us from above and the rear, where we as tankers are most susceptible. They began to adapt to fight us even as we adapted to fight them. They were coming up with new techniques to compensate for their inferior and outmoded equipment. The Abrams was designed as an offensive, frontal attack weapon. Going into cities where attackers can more easily hit from 360 degrees makes it more vulnerable. The first Gulf War demonstrated the superiority of the Abrams, and this war only enhanced its reputation. But there is no doubt in my mind that our enemies have learned from the Iraqis' mistakes during Operation Iraqi Freedom and will not make the same mistakes. They will come up with new ways to use old weapons to try to defeat us. Preventing that will be the job of soldiers who will be expected to adapt more quickly to what the enemy is doing than the enemy is able to adapt to what we are doing.

I will leave it to the diplomats and politicians to sort out the issues and the arguments over whether we were prepared enough for what happened in Baghdad after the war. I do know that my soldiers had very few problems with the residents of Baghdad with whom we dealt during our six-week, postwar stay there. The people in the neighborhoods around us were, for the most part, kind and thoughtful, and enjoyed us as much as we enjoyed them. Many were well educated and spoke English far better than any of us spoke Arabic. They wanted us to stay and be a part of their community. When we left for Fallujah, many pressed gifts on us. Many wanted their pictures taken with us so they could remember us once we were gone. Many cried.

I do not know how things deteriorated so quickly after our departure and will not speculate as to the reasons why. All I know is that we treated them with respect, and they returned that respect.

We did not have the same sort of reception in Fallujah. But we also did not have the same troubles that our predecessors or successors had with the residents there. Within a few weeks of our departure, the 82nd Airborne had returned and again were involved in an incident that inflamed the locals. In what was termed a "friendly fire" incident, soldiers from the 82nd killed eight Iraqi policemen and a Jordanian guard in the midst of a handover from one unit to another

The Marines had their own problems when they went into Iraq in early 2004. They went in light, with little armor, and found themselves confronted by several thousand determined fighters. The Fallujah in which we operated so freely became the focal point of Iraqi resistance in the war's aftermath. The developments left those of us who had been there scratching our heads in bewilderment, wondering how and why things had deteriorated so quickly.

I am not sure if we did something different from what other units were doing, with one exception: we were operating tanks and for the most part they were not. Tanks provided the heavy metal fist of this war, setting new standards in the use of armor in modern warfare that are not likely to be duplicated anytime soon. Tanks made a statement that individual Iraqi gunmen found impossible to argue with. And tanks provided the necessary protection and firepower to overcome the most determined resistance. Tanks may not be the best tool for winning hearts and minds, but they set the stage for making that possible. The M1A1 Abrams tank played a vital role in this war and what we did will likely be studied and dissected by armor officers for years to come. The soldiers of Charlie Company may not yet fully understand the significance of what they did, either politically and economically, for the people of Iraq, or militarily with their innovative and courageous use of tanks in modern warfare. But as they age and look back on what they did, they can rest assured that Charlie Company will have a special place in the history of armor warfare.

Appendix: Charlie Company Vehicle Assignments and Roster

Authors' note: The following does not reflect permanent crew assignments throughout the war. Loaders and drivers swapped tanks frequently depending on mechanical problems or needs at any particular time. The number of soldiers here, seventy-nine, includes several who joined Charlie Company during and shortly after the war.

M1A1 Abrams
First Platoon (Red)

Charlie One-One (Red One)
Creeping Death/Cruel Intentions

1st Lt. Roger Gruneisen (tank commander, platoon leader)
Sgt. Carlos Hernandez (gunner)
Spc. Donald Schafer (loader)
Spc. Derek Peterson (driver)

Charlie One-Two (Red Two)
Cojone, Eh?

S.Sgt. Jason Diaz (tank commander)
Sgt. Jose Couvertier (gunner)
Pfc. Fausto Trivino (loader)
Pfc. Chris Shipley (driver)

Charlie One-Three (Red Three)
Call Yo' Chaplain

S.Sgt. Larrico Alexander (tank commander)
Sgt. Sidney Dorsey (gunner)
Psc. Jose Campos (loader)
Spc. Tony Lyman (driver)

Charlie One-Four (Red Four)
Crazy Horse

Sgt. 1st Class Brett Waterhouse (tank commander)
Sgt. Phillip Riley (gunner)
Spc. Brian Jasper (loader)
Pfc. Travis Jones (driver)

Second Platoon (White)

Charlie Two-One (White One)
California Dreamin'

1st Lt. Jeremy England (tank commander, platoon leader)
Sgt. Chris Freeman (gunner)
Spc. Mark Gatlin (loader)
Pfc. K.C. Brons (driver)

Charlie Two-Two (White Two)
Columbia 2

S.Sgt. Randy Pinkston (tank commander)
Sgt. Scott Stewart (gunner)
Pfc. Artemio Lopez-Martinez (loader)
Pfc. Justin Mayes (driver)

Charlie Two-Three (White Three)
Carnivore

S.Sgt. Ben Phinney (tank commander)
Sgt. Steve Ellis (gunner)
Psc. Derrick Hemphill (loader)
Pfc. Jeremy Menerey (driver)

Charlie Two-Four (White Four)
Combat Tested

Sgt. 1st Class Ray White (tank commander)
Sgt. Cullie Alexander (gunner)
Pfc. Abraham Zambrano (loader)
Spc. Joshua West (driver)

Third Platoon (Blue)

Charlie Three-One (Blue One)
Compliments of the USA

2nd Lt. Erik Balascik (tank commander, platoon leader)
S.Sgt. Danny Justice (gunner)
Spc. Peter Liedman (loader)
Pfc. Christopher Rarick (driver)

Charlie Three-Two (Blue Two)
Catch 22

S.Sgt. Chhay Mao (tank commander)
Cpl. Lawrence Hamilton (gunner)
Pfc. Justin Bailey (loader)
Pfc. Daniel Drumm (driver)

Charlie Three-Three (Blue Three)
Call to Arms

S.Sgt. Germell Milton (tank commander)
Sgt. Eric Leon (gunner)
Pfc. Maximiliano Guerra (loader)
Spc. Michael Harris (driver)

Charlie Three-Four (Blue Four)
Crash Tested

S.Sgt. David Richard (tank commander)
Sgt. Anthony Marabello (gunner)

Pfc. James Pyle (loader)
Spc. Michael Donohue (driver)

Headquarters Element

Charlie Six-Six (Cobra Six)
Courtesy of the Red, White, and Blue

Capt. Jason Conroy (tank commander, company CO)
S.Sgt. Nathan Malone (gunner)
Spc. Paul Helgenberger (loader)
Spc. Matt Larimer (driver)

Charlie Six-Five (Cobra Five)
Case Closed

1st Lt. Shane Williams (tank commander, company XO)
Sgt. Casey Bruton (gunner)
S.Sgt. Jabari Williams (loader, company master gunner)
Sgt. Chad Walker (driver)

M2 Bradley Fighting Vehicle

Cobra Three-Zero (BFST)

1st Lt. James Hock (vehicle commander)
S.Sgt. James Kosters
Spc. Joshua Metheny
Pfc. Randall Murrell

M113 Armored Personnel Carriers

Cobra Seven-Seven

1st Sgt. Jose Mercado (vehicle commander)
Sgt. Andrew Coffman (driver, company armorer)
Spc. Shawn Sullivan (medic)
Sgt. Daniel Pyle (driver, admin)

Cobra Band-Aid

S.Sgt. Mark Strunk (driver, senior medic)
Spc. Curtis Gebhard (NBC specialist, rifleman)
Spc. Anthony Kalis (replacement driver, rifleman)

Cobra Wrench (mechanics)

Sgt. 1st Class Solomon Ball (team chief)
S.Sgt. Michael Williams (maintenance NCO)
Sgt. Steven Glasco
Sgt. Joseph Pruitt
Sgt. Robert McCollum
Cpl. Stephen Reynolds
Spc. Stephen Korol-Locke
Pfc. Jason McDowell
Psc. Kyle Kennedy

Cobra Supply

Sgt. Edison Santiago (supply sergeant)
Spc. Steven Hawkins (driver)

Cobra Communications

Spc. Markelle Tucker

Glossary of Terms and Abbreviations

Military Titles (if full name used)

1st Lt.	First Lieutenant
1st Sgt.	First Sergeant
BMO	Battalion Maintenance Office
Capt.	Captain
Lt. Col.	Lieutenant Colonel
Pfc.	Private First Class
Pvt.	Private
Psc.	Private Second Class
Sgt.	Sergeant
Sgt. 1st Class	Sergeant First Class
Spc.	Specialist
S.Sgt.	Staff Sergeant

General Military Terms

3/7 Cav	3rd Squadron, 7th Cavalry Regiment, 3rd Infantry Division (Mechanized)
AA	Alpha Alpha, or Assembly Area
AAA	Anti-Aircraft Artillery, also referred to as "Triple A"
ADA	Air Defense Artillery
Afcap or aft cap	Metallic base of 120mm main gun round that is ejected from the breech inside the tank after the round is fired
BCT	Brigade Combat Team, usually 2,500–5,000 soldiers, the main combat maneuver element of a division
BDA	Battle Damage Assessment

BFST	Bradley Fire Support Vehicle; a Bradley fighting vehicle rigged to transport fire support specialists who accompany front-line units and call in artillery and mortar fire.
BMP	Soviet armored amphibious infantry combat vehicle with a 73mm main gun
BRT	Brigade Reconnaissance Team
BUB	Battlefield Update Brief; a meeting of commanders to discuss events of the day and get orders for the next day
Charlie Rock	Charlie Company, 3rd Battalion, 15th Infantry Regiment, 3rd Infantry Division (Mechanized); also referred to as Rock
Chem lights	Chemically activated light sticks in six different colors; used as markers and warning signals
Chicken Vest	Small, lightweight flak vest worn by tankers; also referred to as a spall vest
CO	Commanding officer
Coax	Coaxial 7.62mm machine gun fired by the tank gunner along the same line of sight as the main gun tube
Cobra	Call sign for Charlie Company, Task Force 1-64, 2nd Brigade Combat Team, 3rd Infantry Division (Mechanized)
CLS	Combat Life Saver kit
CP	Command Post
CVC	Combat Vehicle Crewman helmet; lightweight Kevlar helmet for armor crews containing communications headset and microphone
DU	depleted uranium; a SABOT tank round carries a depleted uranium penetrator rod for killing tanks and is sometimes referred to as a DU round
EPW	Enemy Prisoner of War; sometimes referred to as POW, for prisoner of war
FAS	Forward Aid Station
FBCB2	Force XXI Battle Command, Brigade and Below, a small, satellite-based computer monitor

GPS	Global Positioning System; hand-held navigational device; when referring to a GPS in a tank, means Gunner's Primary Site (to differentiate between it and Global Positioning System, tankers referred to the navigational device as a "plugger")
HEAT	High Explosive Anti-Tank
HET	Heavy Equipment Transporter, a 40-wheel lowboy trailer designed to carry heavy vehicles, including the Abrams, up to 70 tons
Indirect fire	Mortar or artillery fire
JDAM	Joint Direct Attack Munition; a smart bomb
JSLST suit	Joint Service Lightweight Integrated Suit
LNO	Liaison officer
LD	Line of Departure; usually the starting point for a movement or attack; "to LD" is to cross the line of departure
MILES	Multiple Integrated Laser Engagement System
MLRS	Multiple Launch Rocket System
MOPP	Mission Oriented Protective Posture; five levels, ranging from 0 to IV, with each higher level indicating how much chemical-biological protective gear should be worn, e.g., MOPP-IV
MOUT	Military Operations in Urban Terrain
MRE	Meals Ready to Eat; pre-packaged meals carried by members of the military when they do not have access to food service facilities
MPAT	Multi-Purpose Anti-Tank
NBC	nuclear, biological, and chemical
NTC	National Training Center
OPFOR	Opposing Force, usually referring to a friendly unit serving as the enemy, or opposing, force during a training exercise
PC	Armored Personnel Carrier, usually an M113 configured to carry soldiers, medical evacuees or to serve as a command and control vehicle
PSYOP	Psychological operations

QRF	Quick Reaction Force
RPG	Rocket-propelled grenade, a shoulder-launched weapon that was a favorite of Iraqi and Saddam Fedayeen forces against American troops
REDCON	Ready Condition; REDCON ONE means be ready to move at a moment's notice; REDCON 1.5 means tank crews are aboard and ready but engine is not running
Rock	Sometimes referred to as Charlie Rock; call sign for Charlie Company Task Force 3-15; the infantry company assigned during the war to Task Force 1-64
RUBA	Rotational Units Bivouac Area
SABOT	120mm tank main gun round with a depleted uranium penetrator rod designed to destroy armored vehicles
SAM	Surface to Air Missile
SASO	Security and Stabilization Operations
Section	When referring to a tank platoon, a section is two tanks, either the Alpha section, tanks one and two, or the Bravo section, tanks three and four
Spall Vest	Same as a chicken vest
TAA	Tactical Assembly Area
TC	Tank commander or track commander; can also be used to refer to a vehicle commander
TIS	Thermal Imaging System; sight on a tank that identifies heat sources
TOC	Tactical Operations Center
TRP	Target Reference Point
UCMJ	Uniform Code of Military Justice
Wild Bunch	Call sign for Alpha Company, Task Force 1-64, 2nd Brigade Combat Team, 3rd Infantry Division (Mechanized)
WMD	weapons of mass destruction
XO	Executive officer, second in command
ZOS	Zone of Separation

Index

281

About the Authors

Born in 1972, *Jason P. Conroy* is from Apalachin, New York. He enlisted in the Army in September 1991 and attended basic training at Fort Dix, New Jersey. Upon completion of the AH-64 Attack Helicopter Repairer Course at Fort Eustis, Virginia, he was assigned to the 2nd Battalion of the 101st Aviation Regiment at Fort Campbell, Kentucky. After graduation from Officer Candidate School in September 1995, he was commissioned as a second lieutenant of armor. In March 1996, Conroy was assigned to the 4th Battalion of the 67th Armor Regiment in Friedberg, Germany, as part of the Ready First Combat Team and deployed to Bosnia, where he participated in Operation Joint Endeavor as the Implementation Force (IFOR).

In 2001, Captain Conroy earned a B.S. in education from Austin Peay State before reporting to 1st Battalion of the 64th Armor Regiment at Fort Stewart, Georgia, in July. He took command of Charlie Company in February 2002 and led it throughout Operation Desert Spring and Operation Iraqi Freedom. He is currently assigned to the Army Space and Missile Defense Command at Redstone Arsenal, Huntsville, Alabama. His military awards and decorations include the Presidential Unit Citation, the Army Superior Unit Award, the Silver Star, the Bronze Star, the Army Commendation Medal, the Army Achievement Medal (three Oak Leaf Clusters), the Good Conduct Medal, the Expeditionary Medal, the Global War on Terrorism Expeditionary Medal, the NCO Professional Development Ribbon, the NATO Medal, the Air Assault Badge, and the Aircraft Crewmen's Badge. Captain Conroy is married to the former Susan Morrow of Clarksville, Tennessee. They have two daughters, Ashlie and Amanda.

Ron Martz is the military affairs correspondent for the *Atlanta*

Journal-Constitution. He is a veteran of the U.S. Marine Corps (1965–68), a 1979 graduate in mass communications from the University of South Florida, and the coauthor of three books, including *Solitary Survivor: The First American POW in Southeast Asia* (with Col. Lawrence R. Bailey, Jr., USA [Ret.]) *and White Tigers: My Secret War in North Korea* (with Col. Ben Malcom, USA [Ret.]). Both were published by Brassey's, Inc. Martz and his wife, Mary, live in Cumming, Georgia.